CONTEST FOR
CONSTITUTIONAL
AUTHORITY

CONTEST FOR CONSTITUTIONAL AUTHORITY

The Abortion and War Powers Debates

SUSAN R. BURGESS

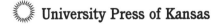 University Press of Kansas

Published by the University Press of Kansas (Lawrence, Kansas 66049), which was organized by the Kansas Board of Regents and is operated and funded by Emporia State University, Fort Hays State University, Kansas State University, Pittsburg State University, the University of Kansas, and Wichita State University

Library of Congress Cataloging-in-Publication Data

Burgess, Susan R.
    Contest for constitutional authority : the abortion and war powers debates / Susan R. Burgess.
       p.   cm.
    Includes bibliographical references and index.
    ISBN 0-7006-0522-3 (cloth)   ISBN 0-7006-0629-7 (pbk.)
    1. Political questions and judicial power—United States.
2. United States. Supreme Court. 3. United States. Congress—
Powers and duties. 4. United States—Constitutional law—
Interpretation and construction. 5. Abortion—Law and
legislation—United States. 6. War and emergency powers—
United States.
I. Title.
KF8700.B87 1991
342.73—dc20
[347.302]   91-34979

British Library Cataloguing in Publication Data is available.

Printed in the United States of America
10 9 8 7 6 5 4 3 2

The paper used in this publication meets the minimum requirements of the American National Standard for Permanence of Paper for Printed Library Materials Z39.48-1984.

For the Little One . . .
who showed me that fierce protectiveness
and compassionate sensitivity are,
after all, two sides of the same coin.

Posterity may know that we have not, through silence,
permitted things to pass away, as in a dream.

—Richard Hooker

Thought speaks with authority about who we are and how we should live only when it puts our ideals and self-understandings through the skeptic's flame, risking nihilism for the sake of insight.

—*Roberto Unger*

CONTENTS

Preface   ix

Acknowledgments   xiii

1 Who Shall Interpret the Constitution? Judicial Supremacy
   or Departmentalism   1

2 Departmentalism and Judicial Activism:
   The Abortion Debate   28

3 Departmentalism and Judicial Self-Restraint:
   The War Powers Debate   65

4 Departmentalism, Constitutional Consciousness,
   and the Rule of Law   109

Appendix 1   Proposed Abortion Legislation   127

Appendix 2   Selected Congressional Resolutions Relating
             to the War Powers   129

Notes   135

Selected Bibliography   163

Index   169

PREFACE

Judicial supremacy is a political practice that gives the federal judiciary final and indisputable say in constitutional interpretation. Under judicial supremacy, when the Supreme Court interprets it forecloses any further discussion. The other branches (and the states) must accept the Court's interpretation in the case at hand and follow it in all similar cases that arise subsequently. Departmentalism is a political practice that challenges judicial supremacy. Under departmentalism, each branch of government (or "department"–hence the term "departmentalism"[1]) has a right or perhaps a duty to interpret the Constitution, even if that interpretation challenges the judiciary's constitutional interpretation. Thus, if the other branches (or the states) find the Court's interpretation to be errant, they are not obligated to follow it in subsequent cases. Advocates of departmentalism point out that, in principle, judicial supremacy gives the Supreme Court absolute authority over constitutional matters and that such a grant of authority counters the principle of limited, constitutional democracy. They contend that a dialogue among the several branches of the federal government (and perhaps the states) fosters the practices or civic culture necessary to maintain limited and decent government. Accordingly, they reject the judicial monologue.

Without exploring the empirical consequences of congressional constitutional interpretation, some scholars and public officials have pessimistically asserted that constitutional authority would be damaged if Congress practiced departmentalism.[2] They say that skepticism about constitutional authority and the rule of law would deepen considerably. Others, however, have contended that constitutional authority would be deepened and the rule of law would be strengthened by a congressional-judicial dialogue that focuses on constitutional meaning. They hope that when Congress interprets the Constitution independently, all the "departments" will be compelled to define and redefine their positions on constitutional issues, thereby creating a dialogue about constitutional meaning that will improve the constitutional discourse and broaden constitutional authority. Thus the question I explore in this book is this: Is constitutional authority broadened and the rule of law strengthened when Congress practices departmentalism?

I address this question through a detailed examination of two extremely intense constitutional debates: the congressional-judicial debate about the constitutional status of the right to abortion and the congressional-executive debate about the constitutional allocation of the war powers. The abortion debate takes place in the context of judicial activism. Congress practiced departmentalism by challenging *Roe v. Wade* and judicial supremacy in the 1981 human life bill debates as well as in the 1985 debates on the proposed Abortion Funding Restriction Act. The Court continued to actively interpret the Constitution in the abortion debate, issuing major rulings in *Akron v. Akron Center for Reproductive Health*, 462 U.S. 421 (1983), and *Thornburgh v. American College of Gynecologists and Obstetricians*, 476 U.S. 747 (1986). The war powers debate takes place in the context of judicial self-restraint and involves the executive and Congress in conflict about the constitutional allocation of the war powers. Although the Court has traditionally deferred to the wisdom of the "political" branches in cases that have raised questions concerning military issues and foreign affairs, this deference has not undercut the Court's self-asserted supremacy over "legal" matters. However, the Court's deference has made it possible for the executive to assert its supremacy in military and foreign policy matters. The legislature frequently has automatically deferred to executive authority and thus abdicated responsibility for participating in military and foreign policy decisions. However, following the initial challenge by Congress to executive supremacy in the 1974 War Powers Act, Congress again practiced departmentalism by challenging executive supremacy in the 1987 Persian Gulf debates.

The abortion and war powers cases have parallel as well as contrasting aspects. Both cases explore the same fundamental question: Does constitutional authority broaden when Congress practices departmentalism? Both cases take place in a political and legal culture that largely embraces a fundamental assumption: Once the Court speaks, its word is final. However, the extent of judicial finality appears to be more narrowly construed in the war powers case because the Court has chosen not to address the constitutional allocation of the war powers. Thus, in that case Congress practices departmentalism most obviously by challenging the supremacy of the executive. Yet Congress is challenging executive supremacy in a broader political and legal context that remains characterized and shaped by judicial supremacy—even if the assertion of judicial supremacy is much narrower in extent in the war powers case.

Many scholars and public officials say that constitutional conflicts of the kind discussed in this book do not, or at least should not, occur, mainly because they believe the Court's constitutional interpretation is not, or should not be, contestable. However, I will show that Congress, in fact, does from time to time challenge judicial decisions on the grounds that the Court's decisions are based on errant interpretations of the Constitution. On the basis of this congressional practice, I articulate an alternative model of constitutional authority called the levels of constitutional consciousness.

In Chapter One, I set the debate about judicial authority and departmentalism in its scholarly and political context. I show that widespread acceptance of judicial supremacy dominates and constricts the contemporary constitutional debate. I discuss departmentalism (an alternative form of constitutional interpretation that challenges judicial supremacy), review the theoretical claims that scholars have made for and against it, and then critique the rigidity as well as the panhistoricity of the "benefit-cost" framework of analysis that flows from these claims. Finally, I introduce the framework of analysis I will use to evaluate whether departmentalism is a viable alternative to judicial supremacy, namely the levels of constitutional consciousness.

In Chapters Two and Three, I compare the theoretical claims that scholars and public officials have made about departmentalism with Congress' practice of departmentalism in the abortion and war powers debates. I explore whether departmentalism strengthens or weakens constitutional authority through a detailed reconstruction and interpretive analysis of those two debates. Some scholars and public officials claim that constitutional authority will deepen only if Congress challenges judicial supremacy in the context of judicial activism. Thus, in Chapter Two, I explore departmental practice in the context of judicial activism in the abortion debate. I examine Congress' consideration of the constitutional status of a woman's right to choose to terminate pregnancy in the human life bill debates and the Abortion

Funding Restriction Act debates, as well as subsequent judicial and public discussion of these matters.

Other scholars and public officials claim that constitutional authority will deepen only if Congress challenges judicial supremacy in the context of judicial self-restraint. Thus, in Chapter Three, I explore departmental practice in the context of judicial self-restraint in the war powers debate. I examine Congress' consideration of the Constitution's allocation of the war powers with respect to committing troops to hostilities. I compare the 1964 Tonkin Gulf debates, which occurred before Congress passed the War Powers Act, with the Persian Gulf debates, which occurred after Congress passed the War Powers Act.

In Chapter Four, I discuss my findings and evaluate departmentalism as an alternative to judicial supremacy. I find that constitutional authority did significantly broaden when Congress practiced departmentalism in both the abortion and the war powers cases, but not as much as some scholars may have hoped. Thus, I address concerns and resistances that were raised in those debates which may have obstructed broadening constitutional authority. I also consider the import that alternative perceptions of intense conflict may have for constitutional authority and discuss the kind of constitutional consciousness that the polity must foster in order to continue to broaden constitutional authority.

ACKNOWLEDGMENTS

Although I spent only a few years researching and writing this book, I've been working through the problems that it addresses—in one form or another—for at least ten years. I'm pleased to be able to acknowledge publicly several friends and colleagues who shared the joys and struggles that I felt in creating the book, and who helped to sustain my effort throughout those years.

I start at the beginning, by thanking James Christner for believing from the start. Jim shared his understanding of pace and balance with me and had the wherewithal to see the project finally end. I also thank Christie Smit for sticking with me through thick and thin. Her staying power was important to me, especially near the final stages of this project. I also give special thanks to Daniel Reagan and Catherine Little for their support and understanding. At several important junctures, Dan and Cath were struggling with me to turn confusion into understanding and resistance into acceptance. My golf partner, Frank Guilluizza, also deserves special mention. He and I discussed legal, spiritual, and political matters seriously, without forgetting to laugh frequently. Thanks also to Stephen Percy and Thomas Holbrook for their support and for providing new insights on the importance of discourse and shared understanding in the context of disagreement.

Professors Gerald Berk, John Brigham, Donald A. Downs, Edward A. Goerner, Frank Guilluizza, Gary J. Jacobsohn, Donald P. Kommers, Robert Morgan, Daniel Reagan, and Phyllis Farley Rippey read earlier drafts and offered criticisms and insights that helped me to clarify many of my arguments and examples. Professors Robert Clinton and Edward Keynes also carefully read the manuscript and made several important suggestions that served to strengthen the work. Kim Glapion and Helena Fischer patiently proofread various versions of the manuscript. I deeply appreciate their time, assistance, and encouragement.

I also want to acknowledge the people with whom I played soccer while I was working on this book—especially my friends on the "Tin Foil Line" of the South Bend Rockets, as well as my current teammates on the "Dynasty" and "Élan" teams in the Milwaukee Women's Soccer Association. They were as important to me in working out the problems this book explores as any intellectual source I cite in the pages that follow. In that regard, I also thank Rita Donley and Dorothy Dow. And finally, I thank my family—Sas and Lucy, and Casmira and Ralph Tiogoly—for standing by me.

CHAPTER ONE

Who Shall Interpret the Constitution? Judicial Supremacy or Departmentalism

JUDICIAL SUPREMACY, SCHOLARLY RESEARCH,
AND THE LIMITATIONS OF CONTEMPORARY
CONSTITUTIONAL INTERPRETATION

Judicial supremacy is an institutional arrangement that gives the federal judiciary final and indisputable say in constitutional interpretation. As Walter Murphy has noted, while judicial review grants the Court the authority to strike down legislative and executive acts, judicial finality (or judicial supremacy) further obliges the elected branches "not only to obey that ruling [in the specific case at hand], but to follow its reasoning in future deliberations."[1] Under judicial supremacy, once the Court has interpreted the Constitution, its word is final and cannot be questioned by the other branches.

Perhaps not surprisingly, the judiciary itself has propagated the notion that the Court is the "ultimate interpreter" of the Constitution. However, it is often overlooked that the Court did not explicitly declare itself the ultimate interpreter until 1958 in *Cooper v. Aaron.*[2] *Cooper* addressed the state of Arkansas' noncompliance with *Brown v. Board of Education,*[3] the famous school desegregation decision of 1954. In *Cooper*, the Court asserted that the principle that "[t]he federal judiciary is *supreme* in the exposition of the law of the Constitution" is a *"permanent and indispensable* feature of our constitutional system."[4]

In *Baker v. Carr*, the 1962 case that declared that issues of legislative apportionment and districting were justiciable rather than political questions,[5] the Court once again asserted finality: "Deciding whether a matter has in any measure been committed by the Constitution to another branch of government, or whether the action of that branch exceeds whatever authority has been committed, is itself a delicate exercise in constitutional interpretation, and is a responsibility of this court as *ultimate interpreter* of the Constitution."[6] In 1969, the court reaffirmed its adherence to judicial finality in *Powell v. McCormack*,[7] a case that declared that the Court, not Congress, would have the final say about qualifications for membership into the House. In *Powell*, the Court once again asserted that "it is the responsibility of this Court to act as the *ultimate interpreter* of the Constitution."[8] In *U.S. v. Nixon*,[9] the Court declared itself supreme over the executive branch, citing both *Powell* and *Baker* to support the claim that the Court is the ultimate constitutional interpreter. Taken together, in *Cooper, Baker, Powell,* and *Nixon* the Court explicitly declared supremacy over the states, Congress, and the executive.

Many scholars and public officials assume that *Marbury v. Madison*,[10] the famous case in which the Court first exercised judicial review in 1803,[11] established the same sort of judicial supremacy that is evident in *Cooper, Baker, Powell,* and *Nixon*.[12] However, *Marbury* itself did not claim finality. Furthermore, finality was certainly not an accepted practice at that time. The *Marbury* Court did assert that it had the authority to interpret the law when it claimed that "it is emphatically the province and the duty of the judicial department to say what the law is."[13] Coupling that assertion with the establishment of judicial review may very well have made it possible for the Court to claim at a later date that judicial constitutional interpretation is final and unchallengeable. Indeed, the Court cited *Marbury* as precedent each time it claimed to be the ultimate constitutional interpreter in *Cooper, Baker, Powell,* and *Nixon*.[14] This may explain why scholars and public officials assume that *Marbury* established not only judicial review but also judicial supremacy. However, creating the opportunity for judicial review to become inextricably linked with judicial supremacy is not the same as establishing a widely accepted practice.[15]

Furthermore, although *Marbury* and other cases that strongly support judicial power, such as *Dred Scott v. Sandford*[16] and *U.S. v. Butler*,[17] may have paved the way for the Court to claim ultimate interpreter status at a later date, they do not expressly support the idea that the Court's word is final. For example, although the ultimate interpreter assertion collapses constitutional and judicial authority, *Dred Scott* seems to maintain the possibility of distinguishing constitutional from judicial authority. There, the Court stated that "if the authority [to enact the Missouri Compromise] is not given [to Congress] by that instrument [the Constitution], it is the duty of the Court to declare it void and inoperative, and incapable of conferring freedom upon any one who is held as a slave under the laws of any one of the States."[18] Similarly, *U.S. v. Butler* recognized broad judicial power, yet clearly fell short of declaring finality. Thus, *Butler*, which signified the beginning of the Court's acceptance of the New Deal, declared that "the *only* check on our own exercise of power is our own sense of self-restraint."[19] Although *Scott* and *Butler* indicate the growing power of the Court and thus perhaps a movement toward judicial finality, the fact remains that the Court simply did not declare itself to be the ultimate interpreter of the Constitution before *Cooper v. Aaron* in 1958.[20]

When this historical examination is extended beyond judicial materials, support for judicial supremacy in American political development decreases further. Several presidents, including Thomas Jefferson, Andrew Jackson, Abraham Lincoln, and Ronald Reagan, rejected the ultimate interpreter reading by challenging the constitutionality of particular judicial decisions. On several occasions Congress also offered constitutional interpretations that rivaled the Court's. Contending that the Court could interpret the Constitution incorrectly, both Congress and the executive have argued that *constitutional* supremacy requires each branch to remain faithful to its best understanding of the Constitution rather than to accept automatically the Court's interpretation. Arguing that the Court rather than the Constitution would rule if other branches followed errant judicial decisions, various executives and members of Congress have claimed that fidelity to the Constitution obliged them to oppose such errant rulings.

Even though the federal judiciary upheld the Sedition Act of 1798,[21] as president, Thomas Jefferson announced that he thought that the act was unconstitutional. Jefferson argued that fidelity to the Constitution obliged him to use executive power to pardon those who had been punished and prosecuted under the act. Explaining the reasoning behind his position, he distinguished constitutional authority from judicial authority. He argued that each branch had the right and duty to determine the constitutionality of laws and actions in the course of performing its own functions.

The Judges, believing the Sedition Law constitutional, had a right to pass a sentence of fine and imprisonment; because that power was placed in their hands by the Constitution. But the Executive, believing the law to be unconstitutional, was bound to remit the execution of it because the power has been confided to him by the Constitution. The instrument meant that its co-ordinate branches should be checks on each other. But the opinion which gives to the Judges the right to decide what laws are constitutional, and what not, not only for themselves in their own sphere of action, but for the Legislative and Executive also in their spheres, would make the Judiciary a despotic branch.[22]

In 1840, Congress also distinguished constitutional from judicial authority, arguing that the Sedition Act was "unconstitutional, null, and void, passed under a mistaken exercise of undelegated power, and that the mistake ought to be corrected" by returning all fines that the government had previously collected as punishment for the act.[23] In 1964, the Court itself admitted that the act had been struck down by "the court of history."[24]

As president, Andrew Jackson also rejected judicial supremacy by distinguishing constitutional from judicial authority, contrary to the ultimate interpreter approach. His "Veto Message," written in 1832, explained why he thought Congress' attempt to recharter the Bank of the United States was unconstitutional, despite the Court's proclamation in *McCulloch v. Maryland* that Congress' establishment of the Bank was constitutional.[25] Jackson maintained that his adherence to constitutional rather than judicial supremacy prompted him to challenge *McCulloch*, which he regarded as an errant, or unconstitutional, decision. Opposed to the supremacy of any one branch, Jackson argued for the coequality of Congress, the executive, and the judiciary in constitutional interpretation.

It is as much the duty of the House of Representatives, of the Senate, and of the President to decide upon the constitutionality of any bill or resolution which may be presented to them for passage or approval as it is of the supreme judges when it may be brought before them for judicial decision. The opinion of the judges has no more authority over Congress than the opinion of Congress has over the judges, and on that point the President is independent of both.[26]

He argued that the conflict that would inevitably arise under departmentalism would be resolved in part by distinguishing stronger from weaker arguments. "The authority of the Supreme Court must not, therefore, be permitted to control the Congress or the Executive when acting in their legislative capacities, but to have only such influence as the force of their reasoning may deserve."

Emphasizing the important role that the people would play under departmentalism, Jackson stated that "mere judicial precedent . . . should not be regarded as deciding questions of constitutional power except where the acquiescence of the people and the States can be considered as well settled."[27] And, he concluded, the question of the constitutionality of the Bank was far from being settled. Senate debate on the Bank bill subsequent to Jackson's veto reveals that several senators also distinguished constitutional from judicial authority and thus found Jackson's action appropriate. For example, Senator Hugh Lawson White claimed that Supreme Court finality extended only to the parties involved in the particular case before the Court. According to White, the Constitution does not oblige the other branches of government to follow the Supreme Court's interpretation in subsequent, similar cases. He argued that

> whenever a suit is commenced and prosecuted in the courts of the United States, of which they have jurisdiction, and such suit is decided by the Supreme Court, as that is the court of the last resort, its decision is final and conclusive between the parties. But as an authority, it does not bind either the Congress or the President of the United States. If either of these co-ordinate departments is afterwards called upon to perform an official act, and conscientiously believe the performance of that act will be a violation of the constitution, they are not bound to perform it, but on the contrary are as much at liberty to decline acting, as if no such decision had been made.[28]

Abraham Lincoln also challenged judicial supremacy and distinguished constitutional from judicial authority. Arguing that the *Dred Scott* case was an unconstitutional ruling, he conceded that the particular parties to a case (for example, Dred Scott and John F. A. Sanford) were obliged to accept the Court's decision as final. However, Lincoln also maintained that the other branches of government were not duty bound to follow the Supreme Court's reasoning in subsequent actions if they thought that the Court's constitutional interpretation was errant. In his first inaugural address, he stated:

> I do not forget the position, assumed by some, that constitutional questions are to be decided by the Supreme Court; nor do I deny

that such decisions must be binding, in any case, upon the parties to a suit, as to the object of that suit, while they are also entitled to very high respect and consideration in all parallel cases by all other departments of the government. And while it is obviously possible that such decisions may be erroneous in any given case, still the evil effect of following it, being limited to that particular case, with the chance that it may be overruled and never become a precedent for other cases, can better be borne than could the evils of a different practice.[29]

Earlier, in his famous debates with Stephen Douglas, Lincoln cited Jefferson to support the distinction between constitutional and judicial authority.

[Judicial supremacy] would place us under the despotism of an oligarchy. Our judges are as honest as other men, and not more so. They have, with others, the same passions for party, for power, and the privilege of their corps. . . . The Constitution has erected no such single tribunal [for interpretation], knowing that to whatever hands confided, with the corruptions of time and party, its members would become despots. It has more wisely made all the departments co-equal and co-sovereign within themselves.[30]

More recently, Ronald Reagan distinguished constitutional from judicial authority by encouraging Congress to pass a statute challenging the constitutionality of *Roe v. Wade*.[31] He argued that "the issue of abortion must be resolved by our democratic process. Once again I call on Congress to make its voice heard against abortion on demand and to restore legal protection for the unborn *whether by statute* or constitutional amendment."[32]

On October 21, 1987, in a well-publicized speech given at Tulane University, Ronald Reagan's attorney general, Edwin Meese, also distinguished constitutional from judicial authority. He argued that there was a "necessary distinction between the Constitution and constitutional law [that is, judicial interpretation of the Constitution]."[33] Citing Lincoln, Jackson, and Jefferson, Meese contended that judicial decisions were binding only on the particular litigants in question. Further, he encouraged citizens to respond to unconstitutional judicial decisions "through the presidents, the senators, and the representatives we elect at the national level . . . [as well as at] the state and local levels."[34] In short, he concluded, "constitutional interpretation is not the business of the Court only, but also properly the business of all branches of government."[35]

Clearly, judicial supremacy rests on extremely tenuous grounds, logically and historically. Yet scholars of both the political right and left widely support the ultimate interpreter reading at the levels of theory and practice. Robert Nagel states that "heavy reliance on the judiciary—in various ideological directions—is fast becoming an integral part of the American system; already it is difficult for many, whether in or out of the academy, even to imagine any alternative."[36] Major scholars in the contemporary interpretive debate as disparate as Raoul Berger, Ronald Dworkin, Robert Bork, John Hart Ely, and Michael Perry disagree about what the Court should say when it speaks but agree that once it has spoken, its words are final.

Perhaps surprisingly, several leading advocates of judicial self-restraint support judicial finality. Although they may support a narrower range of judicial power than the judicial activists, these restraintists nevertheless accept that judicial power is absolute and unchallengeable within that carefully circumscribed range. For example, despite his ardent support of judicial self-restraint, Raoul Berger argues that judicial constitutional interpretation can only be challenged by changing the Constitution itself. He contends that "decisions of constitutional question cannot . . . be overruled by the legislature; resort must be had to the 'cumbersome' amendment process."[37] Berger does not see the contradiction between his adherence to judicial finality and his alleged fidelity to constitutional supremacy. Even though he asserts that "we must . . . reject . . . Charles Evans Hughes' dictum that 'the Constitution is what the Supreme Court says it is,' " he nevertheless maintains that the other branches and the states cannot challenge judicial constitutional interpretation.[38] He would like to separate judicial from constitutional authority, but he embraces the very position that logically prevents him from effectively doing so. Thus, despite Berger's protestations to the contrary, it seems that for him the Constitution is what the Supreme Court says it is. In his attempts to distinguish constitutional meaning from constitutional law, Robert Bork, another leading opponent of judicial activism, seemingly allows for the possibility of errant judicial constitutional interpretation. But in the end he too embraces judicial supremacy: "The judges decide what the Constitution means. When the Supreme Court invokes the Constitution, *whether legitimately or not*, as to that issue *the democratic process is at an end*."[39]

Perhaps less surprisingly, several leading activists also support judicial supremacy. John Hart Ely, who attempts to ground a moderately active use of judicial review on the basis of democratic proceduralism, accepts judicial finality. He argues: "When a court invalidates an act of the political branches on constitutional grounds, . . . it is overruling [their] judgment, and normally doing so in a way that is not subject to 'correction' by the ordinary lawmaking process."[40]

Supporters of a broader form of judicial activism, such as Ronald Dworkin, David A. J. Richards, and Michael Perry, likewise support judicial supremacy. According to Dworkin, "The courts in general and the Supreme Court in the last analysis have the power to decide for the government as a whole what the Constitution means."[41] This principle, which he contends was established in *Marbury*, is now "beyond challenge as a proposition of law, and the constitutional wars are now fought on the territory it defines. The capital question now is not what power the Court has [as to finality], but how its vast power should be exercised."[42] Furthermore, Dworkin distinguishes principle from policy, or law from politics, and then argues that the Court has a greater competence for discerning constitutional principles and thus for protecting rights. He asserts: "The United States is a more just society than it would have been had its constitutional rights been left to the conscience of majoritarian institutions."[43] The other branches, or "majoritarian institutions," he concludes, are more competent in the realm of policy.[44]

Despite favoring a very broad sphere of judicial supremacy, Dworkin does advocate civil disobedience for individual citizens who disagree with the law. However, it is difficult to see how citizens (except perhaps the sturdiest of souls) could base their civil disobedience on an alternative reading of the Constitution in a political and legal context where the Court dominates the polity's discussion of constitutional meaning. Just as unused muscles atrophy, it seems likely that the capacity of citizens to discuss constitutional meaning would diminish if Dworkin's principle/policy distinction were strictly followed.[45]

According to David A. J. Richards, judicial review (or judicial constitutional interpretation) would be "nugatory" without judicial supremacy.[46] Overlooking even the possibility that judicial supremacy has eroded constitutional authority, Richards concludes that "overall such judicial supremacy will tend to secure a greater balance of fidelity to enduring constitutional values."[47] Richards does maintain that public examination and debate about judicial decisions characterize a healthy polity. He claims that "the tension between judicial supremacy and public arguments of judicial mistake is fundamental to the integrity of democratic constitutionalism. . . . Judicial supremacy is thus working correctly when overall it tends to vindicate the best arguments of principle. Public debate over constitutional issues is most reasonable when most engaged by comparable critical arguments against which the state (including judicial power) can be searchingly tested."[48]

It is unclear how the public's role in the process of interpretation will be maintained (or why the public should remain interested in interpretation) in the context of judicial supremacy. Noting that congressional challenges to judicial supremacy would amount to giving Congress the power to reverse judicial decisions, Michael Perry contends that such initiatives should be rejected and that the polity should continue to adhere to judicial supremacy lest the Court and the power of judicial review be rendered meaningless.[49] In sum, judicial restraintists and judicial activists agree that the people's representatives should not challenge judicial supremacy. They may disagree about the proper range of judicial power, but they all agree that judicial power is absolute and unchallengeable within that range.

The widespread acceptance of judicial supremacy has vastly constricted the contemporary constitutional debate. Scholarly and political agreement about judicial finality and its dilemma for democracy has led scholars to demand an objectively verifiable—or at least an intersubjectively verifiable—standard to ground the Court's use of judicial review. Instead of broadly discussing the meaning of the Constitution, most scholars accept judicial supremacy[50] and thus the judiciary's political unaccountability to the other branches and its electoral unaccountability to the people. Within this context the Constitution means simply "what the judges say it is,"[51] which focuses the debate on "the role of the Supreme Court" in American democracy rather than on constitutional meaning as distinguished from judicial interpretation. Consequently, most scholars agree with John Hart Ely: "The central function is at the same time the central problem of judicial review: a body that is not elected or otherwise politically responsible in any significant way is telling the people's elected representatives that they cannot govern as they'd like."[52]

Under judicial supremacy, the Court's word is final and its decisions are free from public validation or rejection. To avoid being charged with illegitimate use of power, the Court must attain, or at least give the appearance of attaining, infallibility.[53] It must provide an acceptable foundation for its decisions. Toward that end, leading judicial activists, including Justices Benjamin Cardozo and Earl Warren, Ronald

Dworkin, Michael Perry, Laurence Tribe, and John Hart Ely, have tried to provide a grounding for a broad range of judicial power.[54] However, critics of judicial activism contend that activist arguments appeal to judicial, not constitutional, authority: they advocate a narrower, more restrained use of judicial power. Jurists such as Rehnquist and Frankfurter and scholars such as Berger, Bork, and Christopher Wolfe have advanced arguments that favor judicial self-restraint and legislative resolution of constitutional disagreements.[55] Yet critics of judicial self-restraint contend that restraintist arguments appeal to democratic, not constitutional, authority. In either case, constitutional scholars regularly assert that none of the theories adequately grounds judicial review.

The judicial activist versus judicial restraintist debate has been recast into several different discourses, the most prominent of which are the "interpretivist versus noninterpretivist" and the "originalist versus nonoriginalist" debates.[56] Although these terms do serve to distinguish subtle theoretical differences, they overlook or obscure a belief that most of the interlocutors share—an adherence to judicial supremacy. As long as the widespread acceptance of judicial supremacy remains largely unnoticed, its influence on the shape of the contemporary constitutional debate will be undiscussed. The categories used in these debates, and thus the shape of the debates, would likely be broadened if scholars examined and reconsidered their attachment to judicial supremacy.[57]

The unresolved disagreement between advocates of judicial self-restraint and judicial activism has led other influential theorists, such as those involved in the Critical Legal Studies Movement, to assert that judicial review cannot be reconciled with liberal democracy. Paul Brest, for example, states that the central issue of the "fundamental rights" controversy, or the central problem of liberal constitutional adjudication, "is not susceptible to resolution within its own terms."[58] Therefore, he concludes, that problem will not be solved "until despair or hope impels us to explore alternatives to the world we currently inhabit."[59] Those influenced by the insights of the continental hermeneuticists also assert that further efforts to ground judicial review through reasoned constitutional argument are futile.[60] These scholars largely embrace postmodern skepticism about textual meaning, which makes a successful appeal to constitutional authority even more difficult than usual.

If judicial supremacy continues to be widely accepted, judicial authority will continue to subsume constitutional authority, and constitutional authority will continue to erode. It would appear, then, that we may soon face a choice between two problematic alternatives: a willful imposition of some sort of partisan use of judicial power (that is, an outright appeal solely to judicial authority)[61] or an abandonment of judicial review in the name of a willful imposition of legislative power (that is, an outright appeal solely to democratic authority).[62] Both alternatives seem to assume that attempts to justify power in reasonable and constitutional terms are futile; they only disagree about whose interpretation (the judiciary's or the legislature's) ought to be determinative. Presumably, in the event of actual conflict, the stronger force would prevail.[63] From the point of view of limited government or constitutional democracy, both of these alternatives are unacceptable. Both would demean the independent authority of the constitutional text, as well as replace constitutionally limited government with theoretically unlimited government and ultimate rule by the strongest institution or greatest force.

It does seem, therefore, that scholarly argument about constitutional interpretation has reached a critical juncture, though not necessarily an impasse, despite some scholars' characterization of these differences as unbridgeable polarities. It is true that advocates of judicial activism, as well as those of judicial self-restraint, continue to assert and reassert their incommensurate and seemingly unpersuasive justifications for judicial power, while other scholars have simply abandoned all efforts to give a reasoned justification for judicial review. Yet an examination and reconsideration of judicial supremacy—the key, unstated assumption that these scholars share (despite their other differences)—may serve to bind these discussions together.

Many scholars have argued that the people, and the people's representatives, have become increasingly less informed about constitutional meaning and therefore increasingly less able to follow or participate meaningfully in constitutional debates. Consequently, these scholars assert (*without any mention of the influence of unexamined beliefs about institutional arrangements such as judicial supremacy*), the people and the people's representatives are simply less able than the judiciary to interpret the Constitution.[64] This argument results in large part from the "competency debate." In this debate, scholars and public officials typically judge Congress (to say nothing of the people) to be incompetent or incapable of solid constitutional interpretation, for various structural reasons—for example, representatives and senators are elected by the people. Although these critics are somewhat sensitive to the institutional features that make the judiciary better suited than the legislature for constitutional interpretation, they do not usually give due consideration to the influence that judicial supremacy has had within those institutions. In short, those in the competency debate seem to accept judicial supremacy as a given. Their conclusions, perhaps even the focus of the competency-debate literature, might be different if these scholars examined the effect widespread acceptance of judicial supremacy has had on them.[65]

CHALLENGING JUDICIAL SUPREMACY: THE DEPARTMENTAL ALTERNATIVE

Recently, a few scholars and public officials proposed an alternative to the judicial activism versus judicial self-restraint discourse that promises to move the interpretive debate beyond its alleged impasse, to broaden constitutional authority, and to improve congressional and popular participation in constitutional interpretation. Adherents to this emerging school of thought—called departmentalism[66]—argue that each state and branch of government has a right to interpret the Constitution on its own, even if its interpretation challenges that of the judiciary.[67] Unlike judicial, legislative, or executive supremacy, departmentalism maintains constitutional authority independent of any single interpreter by leaving open the possibility that any particular constitutional interpretation may be errant—and thus challengeable. In sum, departmentalism, at least theoretically, seems most compatible with constitutional supremacy, limited government, and the rule of law.

Some scholars have argued that departmentalism may also change the tenor of the scholarly debate about the nature and extent of legitimate judicial review.[68] Since departmentalists reject judicial finality as inconsistent with constitutional supremacy,[69] serious study of their arguments may cause some scholars to abandon, or at least reconsider, their adherence to judicial supremacy. If scholars would abandon their belief in judicial finality, the interpretive debate would be transformed from a defense of various degrees of judicial review (essentially, more activism versus more restraint) into a reinvigorated dialogue about constitutional meaning.[70] Rather than centering on the role of the Court, the new debate might focus attention on the meaning of the Constitution with respect to specific substantive issues.

Although the growing literature on departmentalism emphasizes its theoretical consistency with constitutional supremacy and its import for reconstructing the scholarly debate about judicial review and democracy, in this book I focus on the empirical consequences of departmentalism as it is practiced in the American political context.

The Benefits of Departmentalism

Some scholars have suggested that the nation can benefit from practicing departmentalism, that is, from further developing the right of each institution to formulate its own interpretation of the Constitution. They contend that if Congress practices departmentalism: (1) Congress' destructive attacks on the judiciary (for example, on the Court's power of judicial review or on its personnel) would be replaced by constructive criticism of the judiciary's constitutional interpretation of particular cases;[71] (2) the quality of the judiciary's constitutional interpretation would be improved;[72] and (3) congressional as well as public sensitivity to constitutional issues would deepen.[73] Gary J. Jacobsohn, Sanford Levinson, and Stephen Macedo, among others, argue that departmentalism will produce these benefits even if the Court remains an active participant in constitutional interpretation. On the other hand, J. B. Thayer, John Agresto, and Robert Nagel, among others, believe that these benefits will occur only if the Court practices self-restraint.

Benefit 1: Debate about Constitutional Meaning Will Replace Congressional Attacks on the Judiciary. Departmentalists of both camps—those who favor judicial activism and those who favor judicial self-restraint—agree that when Congress challenges judicial supremacy, legislative attacks on the judiciary will be replaced with debate about constitutional meaning. Walter Murphy, for example, claims that departmentalism should alter the nature of the conflict by lessening the stakes of congressional-judicial disagreement. He contends that when the polity accepts a judicial monopoly on constitutional interpretation, conflict centers on the Court's powers rather than on the Court's decisions. Thus, under judicial finality, disagreements about constitutional meaning appear largely as attacks upon judicial review. Murphy suggests that since departmentalism allows the elected branches to disagree openly and directly with specific judicial decisions, it may, at least in the long run, reduce conflict between the judiciary and the elected branches, thereby "soften[ing] the current and largely misguided debate about judicial review and democracy."[74] In sum, departmentalism should make disagreement about constitutional meaning less threatening to the judiciary.

Although the "modified departmentalism" that Murphy calls for seems to advocate judicial activism or self-restraint depending upon the matter being dealt with, some scholars suggest that departmentalism is more likely to improve the constitutional discussion when it is practiced in a context solely, or at least largely, characterized by judicial activism. Gary Jacobsohn, for example, contends that even under departmentalism the Court can and should remain active, and perhaps in most instances it should be the leading constitutional interpreter in the political system. Yet Jacobsohn also argues for increased congressional participation in constitutional interpretation. He contends that "the Court may have a special role in this process, but it was never intended for that institution to go it alone."[75] According to Jacobsohn, if the leadership within Congress becomes sensitive to the constitutional dimensions of public policy issues, it may sensitize the institution as a whole to constitutional issues, which may in turn prompt a judicial response and sensitize the public as well.

Stephen Macedo agrees that departmentalism practiced in the context of judicial activism should heighten constitutional·consciousness. He argues that "principled [judicial] activism in no way implies that the Supreme Court is the final interpreter of the Constitution (except for the parties to the cases that come before it, and for inferior courts) or that Supreme Court interpretations of the Constitution are binding on Congress, the president, or the citizenry."[76] He argues further that "denying judicial interpretive supremacy helps engage the interpretive responsibilities of the other branches and the public."[77]

Other scholars have suggested that departmentalism would be more likely to improve the constitutional debate when it is practiced in a context of judicial self-restraint. They argue that only judicial restraint will prompt Congress to forego its "traditional" passivity in constitutional interpretation and become more active. Some time ago J. B. Thayer argued that as judicial power expands, legislative responsibility declines. He contends that

> the courts . . . enter into the harvest thus provided for them with a light heart, and too promptly and easily proceed to set aside legislative acts. The legislatures are growing accustomed to this distrust, and more and more readily inclined to justify it, and to shed the consideration of constitutional restraints,—certainly as concerning the exact extent of these restrictions,—turning that subject matter over to the courts: and what is worse, they insensibly fall into a habit of assuming that whatever they can constitution-

ally do they may do—as if honor and fair dealing and common
honesty were not relevant to their inquiries.[78]

Thayer further states that judicial supremacy would decrease the
legislature's already waning sensitivity to the constitutional dimensions of policy questions and would further induce Congress to pass responsibility for constitutional matters to the Court. He argues: "No
doubt our doctrine of constitutional law [judicial supremacy] has had a
tendency to drive out questions of justice and right, and to fill the
minds of legislators with thoughts of mere legality, of what the Constitution allows. And moreover, even in the matter of legality, they have
felt little responsibility; if we are wrong, they say, the courts will correct it."[79] Thayer's argument implies that challenging judicial supremacy would stimulate congressional responsibility for constitutional interpretation by encouraging broader thinking and debate in Congress.

John Agresto agrees with Thayer. Agresto claims that legislative
constitutional interpretation will improve the public's sensitivity to
constitutional issues. Although he states that "only through a reinvig-
oration of the political interaction of all branches can the vision of a
Court engaged in a continuing colloquy with the political institutions
and with society at large be fully realized,"[80] he nevertheless implies
that the Court must restrain itself in order to reintegrate the other
branches into the constitutional dialogue. Agresto may finally occupy
a middle ground between restraintists such as Thayer and activists
such as Jacobsohn and Macedo. Even though Agresto states that "judicial self-restraint rigorously applied, seriously minimizes the possibility of [the] contribution [of judicial review to] the healthy gover-
nance of the nation," he seems to favor the legislature over the
judiciary when push comes to shove. He believes that "the perils of judicial supremacy are actually much worse than those of unchecked
legislative omnipotence."[81] Therefore, though coequality of and activism by all the branches is the ideal, in practice the judiciary must restrain itself in order to prompt Congress to act. Eventually, when congressional constitutional interpretation becomes the norm rather than
the exception, the Court can once again be judicially active without
dominating the constitutional discussion.

In any case, Agresto believes that the current judicial monopoly on
constitutional interpretation encourages the elected branches to attack the institutional powers of the Court because the elected
branches cannot disagree with its decisions on the basis of an alternative constitutional interpretation. Since judicial authority subsumes

constitutional authority, the elected branches can express disagreement with judicial constitutional interpretation only by attacking the personnel of the Court (for example, impeaching a justice), by attacking the institutional powers of the Court (for example, limiting the Court's jurisdiction), or by attempting to change the meaning of the Constitution through amendment. However, under departmentalism, Agresto contends, the elected branches will no longer need to attack the Court to voice disagreement with its constitutional interpretation because they can legitimately express their criticism more directly. Their discontent will be vented on the true source (the specific judicial interpretation in question), which will focus discussion on the meaning of the Constitution rather than on the powers of the Court.[82]

Several scholars have expressed skepticism about departmentalism's ability to shift conflict from the institutional to the constitutional level. For instance, Gary Jacobsohn asserts that even though departmentalists claim not to question the legitimacy of judicial review, departmentalism nevertheless risks increasing attacks on the Court rather than on specific judicial decisions. Jacobsohn cites as an example Lincoln's challenge to the judiciary's constitutional interpretation in the *Dred Scott* case. Jacobsohn argues that "Stephen Douglas' charge that Lincoln was engaged in an attempt to discredit the Court cannot so easily be dismissed. Indeed, to the extent that the work of the Taney Court had wrought real damage, *the Court had to be discredited*, at least in the eyes of those who Lincoln felt misunderstood the Court's role in the interpretation of constitutional principles."[83] Paul Brest also believes that departmentalism may increase institutional attacks on the judiciary. He argues that since departmentalism threatens the tradition of judicial finality and leaves the elected branches "free to disregard the Court's rulings," it is "likely to encourage disrespect for the courts."[84] It remains to be seen whether Congress can challenge judicial supremacy without threatening judicial review.

Benefit 2: The Quality of Judicial Constitutional Interpretation Will Be Improved. Only those scholars favoring the practice of departmentalism in a context of judicial activism argue that challenging judicial supremacy would improve the quality of judicial constitutional interpretation. They predict that Congress' discussion of constitutional meaning will increase the importance of reasoned argumentation in judicial decisions and thus improve the quality of the constitutional dialogue. Since departmentalism challenges automatic or traditional deference to judicial authority in constitutional interpretation, the elected branches can choose whether to accept or reject the Court's constitutional interpretations. Several scholars have argued that whether the elected branches choose to accept or reject the Court's interpretation will depend upon whether they find the Court's supporting reasoning persuasive. These scholars say that since the judiciary will not be able to rely on automatic deference to its decisions, the Court will be compelled to state more carefully the reasons underlying its interpretations, perhaps by acknowledging and addressing objections or counterarguments raised in other contexts. For example, Murphy contends that the quality of judicial interpretation will improve because appeals to traditional sources of judicial authority (such as precedent) will decrease and appeals to reasoned argument (such as scientific or philosophic evidence) will increase. He argues that "by decreasing the scope of judicial authority to bind other branches of the federal government, [departmentalism] underlines the value, even necessity, of reason in persuading other branches to accept any particular constitutional interpretation."[85] Thus, Murphy concludes, the Court will provide new and better reasons for its decisions, thereby contributing to an improved constitutional dialogue.[86]

Benefit 3: Public Sensitivity to Constitutional Issues Will Be Heightened. Scholars favoring the practice of departmentalism in the context of both judicial activism and judicial self-restraint have argued that challenging judicial supremacy will deepen public sensitivity to constitutional issues. For example, Gary Jacobsohn and Stephen Macedo argue that judicial activism is compatible with departmentalism and increased constitutional sensitivity. Jacobsohn contends that the new institutional dialogue between the Court and the elected branches about constitutional meaning will lead to a heightened popular consciousness about substantive constitutional issues. Because departmentalism is premised on the notion that the Constitution has meaning independent of judicial interpretation, Jacobsohn suggests that the elected branches and the public will be able to distinguish constitutional meaning from judicial constitutional interpretation.

Jacobsohn notes the importance of maintaining civic virtue, or popular participation in constitutional discourse: "In a republican polity the realization of substantive ideals must engage the people as active participants in a common quest."[87] According to Jacobsohn's conception of departmentalism, Congress, the executive, and the people are important participants in the interpretive process; however, the judiciary would be the dominant partner. He contends: "The Court may have a special role in this process, but it was never intended for that institution to go it alone."[88] And since judicial finality in constitutional interpretation breeds public indifference to moral and constitutional argument, Jacobsohn continues, "the only way to break this destructive cycle and to redirect public sentiment (and thus eventually the Court as well) toward the fulfillment of constitutional aspirations [is] through the initiative efforts of nonjudicial institutions [that is, through departmentalism]. . . . Public sentiment *is* everything; in the end it is the consent of the governed that undergirds the legitimacy of the constitutional polity."[89]

Stephen Macedo agrees that a vigorous institutional discussion about constitutional meaning would prompt energetic public discussion as well. He contends that under departmentalism citizens would act as "conscientious interpreters" who would "review the acts of public officials for conformity with the Constitution and be prepared to act in politics themselves as pursuers of constitutional ideals and not as promoters of narrow interests."[90]

Other scholars claim that departmentalism will heighten public sensitivity to constitutional concerns only if it is practiced in the context of judicial self-restraint. J. B. Thayer argues that as judicial power expands, legislative responsibility and popular sensitivity to constitutional issues decline. Thus

> the people, all this while, become careless as to whom they send to the legislature; too often they cheerfully vote for men whom they would not trust with an important private affair, and when these unfit persons are found to pass foolish and bad laws, and the courts step in and disregard them, the people are glad that these few wiser gentlemen on the bench are so ready to protect them against their more immediate representatives. . . . Meantime they and the people whom they represent, not being thrown back on themselves, on the responsible exercise of their own prudence, moral sense, and honor, lose much of what is best in the political experience of any nation; and they are belittled, as well as demoralized.[91]

Thayer believes that judicial self-restraint would encourage a reemergence of congressional constitutional interpretation, which would in turn heighten popular sensitivity to substantive constitutional questions.[92] The improved congressional debate would enlarge the ideas, strengthen the moral fiber, deepen the moral education, and improve the political understanding of the citizenry.

Robert Nagel also argues that "excessive reliance on judicial review is undermining both fidelity to constitutional principles and the general health of the political culture."[93] He believes that the Court should strike down laws only when they are clearly unconstitutional. Contending that judicial self-restraint will lead to a broader, more organic development of constitutional principles, as well as to the preservation of constitutional authority, he states that "one main enemy of the constitutional order, whether conceived of as a public morality or a political theory, is the routinization of judicial power. . . . Excessively concerned about tangible accomplishments, courts close themselves off from the *wisdom* available in the political constitution and undermine long term support for basic principles."[94]

According to Sanford Levinson, departmentalism's emphasis on the Constitution as a "public source of social understanding" may draw citizens to participate in constitutional debates. However, he also cautions that departmentalism actually presupposes a certain amount of constitutional consciousness. He contends that departmentalism cannot create constitutional consciousness or a shared aspiration to understand and meet the Constitution's ideals, although it may heighten preexisting constitutional consciousness. Levinson's analysis implies that civic virtue may be lacking and that citizens may therefore view challenges to judicial supremacy as willful assertion and reassertion of institutional powers rather than as disagreement about constitutional meaning. Under those circumstances, the rule of law would be threatened, not strengthened.[95] Levinson alternately embraces a postmodern skepticism about and an abiding hope for shared meaning and public interestedness centered around a constitutional discussion.[96]

The Costs of Departmentalism

Scholars have identified at least three objectionable consequences or costs that departmentalism may produce and that may challenge the nation's commitment to a stable, knowable, unified rule of law: (1) legal and political confusion would deepen, perhaps leading to chaos;[97] (2) the legislature would gain supremacy and become lax in safeguarding individual rights;[98] and (3) the executive would gain supremacy.[99] In general, if Congress practices departmentalism, skepticism about constitutional authority and the rule of law would deepen. Critics contend that departmentalism will produce these costs whether it is practiced in a context of judicial activism or judicial self-restraint.

Cost 1: Political and Legal Confusion Would Deepen. The first cost of departmentalism—the deepening of political and legal confusion—causes scholars the most concern. They contend that because departmentalism tolerates conflict between the branches about what the Constitution means, it may engender legal and political confusion about which standard governs at any given time, which may in turn result in chaos or even anarchy. Laurence Tribe, for example, states that "chaos would be the *inevitable* result" of challenging judicial supremacy.[100] Rex Lee argues that in certain circumstances departmentalism might lead to anarchy: "For some purposes it would be tantamount to anarchy to take the position that Supreme Court decisions have no effect outside the context of the particular case in which they were developed."[101] However, he believes without a doubt that it would "lead to nothing less than constitutional chaos. *Orderly* government under a constitutional system requires that the final authority to say what the Constitution means be vested somewhere."[102]

Paul Brest, on the other hand, claims that departmentalism will lead to something more severe than chaos: "Anarchy would prevail if every official and agency were free to disregard the Court's rulings."[103] Ramsey Clark, former attorney general of the United States, agrees that "any other rule [than judicial finality] would be anarchy."[104]

Several of these same scholars claim further that the rule of law requires a single sovereign, the Court, to maintain several principles fundamental to the rule of law, namely stability, predictability, knowability, and certainty. For example, Burt Neuborne contends that departmentalism would lessen the predictability and knowability of the law. He states: "It would be utterly destructive of the guiding value of constitutional law for the organs of government to speak with more than one authoritative voice about its meaning."[105] Neuborne concludes that "it is impossible for law to influence primary behavior effectively when individuals are subject to inconsistent and conflicting signals about the law's meaning."[106] Paul Brest argues that judicial supremacy "reflects our dedication to the rule of law," whereas departmentalism threatens the stability necessary for maintaining the rule of law.[107] Anthony Lewis claims that departmentalism is more befitting a system based on will, or the rule of man, than on the rule of law.[108] Laurence Tribe also claims that challenges to judicial supremacy would signal "a grave threat to the rule of law."[109]

Cost 2: Congress Would Gain Supremacy and Become Lax in Safeguarding Individual Rights. Scholars also suggest that since the legislature may challenge the constitutional interpretations of the insu-

lated judicial branch, departmentalism may lead to legislative supremacy and thus to a less vigorous protection of individual rights.
Walter Murphy, for example, notes that constitutional democrats fear
that the majority will abuse rights and thus argue against giving popularly elected legislatures the final say in defining which substantive
individual rights are worthy of protection.[110] Thomas Emerson argues
more forcefully that allowing the legislature to challenge judicial supremacy would "completely undermine the historic powers of the
courts to protect our system of individual rights against legislative en-
croachment."[111] For example, Emerson contends, Congress' attempt to
redefine the scope of the right to privacy and the right to choose abortion may encourage it to attempt to redefine the scope of other constitutional rights, citing its initial actions as precedent. If Congress were
to challenge *Roe v. Wade* by establishing fetal rights, "it could also, for
example, overrule *Brown v. the Board of Education* by asserting that
racial segregation in the public schools is constitutional because the
right of association overcomes the right to equal protection of the
laws."[112] Emerson fears that this could open the door to general lax-
ness in safeguarding individual rights. John Agresto, on the other
hand, seems to discount this possibility. He contends that departmentalism would promote more secure equal liberty with popular consent
as a grounding.[113] Furthermore, he argues that the Court can, and has,
abridged individual rights as much as, or perhaps even more than,
Congress has—particularly in the area of civil rights.[114]

Cost 3: The Executive Would Gain Supremacy. Several
scholars have suggested that departmentalism may create or reinforce
executive supremacy. Robert Scigliano claims that departmentalism
seems to greatly increase the president's power over the other
branches. He argues that although in theory departmentalism favors
no particular branch, in practice it favors the executive since the latter either retains the initiative to act (as in foreign affairs) or performs
its function last (as is usually the case in domestic affairs). Thus the
executive may either order actions that then become fait accompli or
seize finality by vetoing proposals that the other branches have approved. Although departmentalism seems to support alternative solu-
tions to the question of who should interpret the Constitution, it actually promotes only one—the choice between executive or judicial
supremacy.[115] Scigliano contends: "the doctrine [departmentalism] is
one of executive supremacy, the President acting outside the law" by
frustrating or ignoring the Court and Congress.[116] This leads Scigliano

to embrace judicial supremacy because "there is no practical alternative if the constitutional plan is to be followed."[117]

For Christopher Wolfe, although departmentalism begins by giving each branch an "absolute veto," unless Congress forces the president to recognize the legislature's power (perhaps by persuading lower executive officials to enforce its decisions rather than those of the president), an executive-congressional conflict will likely end in victory for the executive branch.[118] Wolfe accepts Scigliano's argument that the practice of departmentalism leads in the end to a choice between executive supremacy or judicial supremacy. He contends that sustained conflict would ultimately be resolved by executive supremacy because the executive can unilaterally force compliance with its interpretation. Thus "it, not the judiciary, has the sword."[119]

LEVELS OF CONSTITUTIONAL
CONSCIOUSNESS: AN ALTERNATIVE
TO THE BENEFIT-COST FRAMEWORK

In the following chapters I explore whether challenging judicial supremacy broadens or narrows constitutional authority by reconstructing the abortion and war powers debates. Both debates reveal that constitutional authority deepened to a certain extent when Congress practiced departmentalism. The quality of each constitutional debate improved significantly when Congress practiced departmentalism, although not to an ideal level. Yet the benefit-cost framework[120] used to evaluate departmentalism prevents one from capturing these more subtle advances toward ideal constitutional consciousness and constitutional authority because it downplays the benefits and exaggerates the costs.[121]

The framework's rigid standard of evaluation leads scholars to assume that a given benefit will either emerge fully or not at all. Following that assumption, departmentalism would fail as a viable alternative to judicial supremacy if any evidence indicates that a given benefit has not fully emerged. In addition to creating this remarkably high standard for departmentalism's benefits, this approach also creates a remarkably low threshold for departmentalism's costs: If a risk even threatens to appear, it would mean that departmentalism should not be pursued as an alternative to judicial supremacy. Although an ideal standard can be useful in measuring levels of improvement in constitutional debates, the benefit-cost approach goes further and interprets any result that falls short of the ideal as unqualified evidence that departmentalism should be rejected. In short, the rigidity of the framework leads one to reject departmentalism as a viable alternative to judicial finality and to support the continued practice of judicial supremacy.

Historically, departmentalism tended to emerge as an alternative to judicial supremacy during periods of political and legal strife; circumstances today are no different. Contemporary contexts of conflict should inform any evaluation of departmentalism as an alternative to judicial supremacy. Yet the benefit-cost approach analyzes departmentalism in a vacuum. Extreme contention over a woman's role in the "public" and "private" spheres (in the home and the workplace, as well as in a variety of supporting institutions) informs the political and legal discourse about abortion, just as the demise of the bipartisan consensus about foreign policy goals (such as containment) informs the political and legal discourse about the war powers.

Intense and bitter cleavages characterize the abortion and war powers debates. Advocates of opposing positions in these debates constitute distinct language communities. Although they are discussing the same issues, they talk past each other in incommensurate discourses rather than with each other in a dialogue of common terms. Issues such as abortion and the war powers, which reflect deeper cleavages in American politics and society, seem intractable in this context of conflict. Thus in both the scholarly and popular presses it is regularly asserted that the abortion debate is polarized or that alternative viewpoints in the foreign policy debate are diametrically opposed. The best contribution that departmentalism might make to improve the quality of these debates is not simply to achieve a positive accounting on an abstract benefit-cost sheet but to locate a common language, with the Constitution as its referent, so that disputants may speak with each other rather than past each other—even though they may continue to hold opposing positions on the issue in question. Before participants can locate this common constitutional language, they must distinguish constitutional authority from judicial authority in the abortion debate and constitutional authority from executive authority in the war powers debate. Only then will the Constitution be able to provide common terms for a shared debate. This common constitutional language should broaden constitutional authority and remind disputants of their similarities, even as they strive to clarify the grounds for their differences.

To arrive at a less rigid, more contextually sensitive, and thus more accurate and even-handed evaluation of departmentalism as an alternative to judicial finality, the theoretical claims about the benefits and costs must be recast to capture advances toward ideal constitutional consciousness and take into account the social and political context in which departmentalism is practiced. Thus, I have developed a more flexible model I call the levels of constitutional consciousness. I use the term "constitutional consciousness" because it captures the idea of the Constitution as a focus and shaper of the parameters of the community's political and legal discourse and because it reveals an awareness on the part of participants in a debate that the Constitution has authority and meaning independent of judicial authority and interpretation. Clearly, constitutional consciousness differs from the scholarly or public consciousness that supports the practice of judicial supremacy by elevating the Court's authority to an absolute or "cultlike" level.[122] Terms that evoke a similar meaning include "civic virtue," "shared value," "community values," "constitutional aspiration," and "constitutional frame of mind."

My model locates six levels of constitutional consciousness (see Table 1.1). The supremacy of the dominant branch is still accepted at the lowest three levels of constitutional consciousness (the nonparticipating, the deferring, and the attacking levels). However, as one moves up through the levels, the authority of the dominant branch will become distinguished from the authority of the Constitution. At the lowest level of constitutional consciousness, the *nonparticipating* level, participants do not express any opinions about the meaning of the Constitution. The authority of the dominant branch completely subsumes constitutional authority. At the next level, the *deferring* level, participants may actively interpret the Constitution until the traditionally dominant branch rejects that position. At that point, participants indicate that they will defer to the authority of the dominant branch rather than continue to discuss constitutional meaning. At the next highest level, the *attacking* level, participants do not express disagreement by articulating an alternative constitutional position. Rather, they reject positions that differ from their own by attacking their opponents' legitimacy or by ridiculing their opponents' arguments. Instead of deepening constitutional authority, the challenge serves only to narrow judicial authority.

If departmentalism successfully transforms the "cult of the Court" consciousness into broader constitutional consciousness, participants should at the very least be able to introduce an alternative constitutional interpretation and provide new arguments to support it. I call

Table 1.1. Levels of Constitutional Consciousness under Conditions of Judicial Activism and Judicial Self-Restraint

Levels	Judicial Activism			Judicial Self-Restraint		
	Congress	**Judiciary**	**Public**	**Public**	**Congress**	**Judiciary**
Engaging	Engages opposing arguments	Majority opinion engages new and opposing arguments	Engages opposing arguments	Engages opposing arguments	Engages opposing arguments	Engages opposing arguments
Recognizing	Recognizes but does not engage opposing arguments	Majority opinion recognizes but does not engage opposing arguments	Recognizes but does not engage opposing arguments	Recognizes but does not engage opposing arguments	Recognizes but does not engage opposing arguments	Recognizes but does not engage opposing arguments
Introducing	Introduces new arguments; expresses disagreement through discussion of constitutional meaning	Majority opinion introduces new arguments	Introduces reasons to ground own position	Introduces reasons to ground own position	Introduces new arguments to ground increased congressional participation; accepts responsibility for decisions; expresses disagreement through constitutional discussion	Accepts wider role for Congress and introduces reasons to ground own position
Attacking	Expresses disagreement through attacks on Court's powers or personnel	Concurring opinion(s) introduces new arguments	Attacks Court's powers or personnel	Attacks Court's powers or personnel	Attacks executive at policy, rather than constitutional level; accepts authorization for executive decisions cannot be assumed	Does not accept some executive decisions
Deferring	Accepts judicial supremacy; may interpret Constitution until Court speaks, or through constitutional amendment	Dissenting opinion(s) introduces new arguments	Largely accepts judicial supremacy	Largely accepts judicial supremacy	Accepts executive supremacy; may discuss Constitution or policy until executive speaks	Largely accepts executive supremacy
Nonparticipating	Accepts judicial supremacy; acquiesces completely to Court; no discussion of constitutional dimensions of policy	Entire Court relies on precedent to dismiss new arguments	Acquiesces completely to Court	Acquiesces completely to Court	Accepts executive supremacy; acquiesces completely to executive; no discussion of constitutional dimensions of decision making	Acquiesces completely to executive

this the *introducing* level of constitutional consciousness. In this higher quality debate, the discourse should be cast into increasingly commensurate constitutional terms. At the next highest level, participants should be able to recognize opposing arguments and claims, though they may still dismiss them without serious consideration or fail to fully address the important objections or concerns that their opponents raise. In this manner, participants continue to locate common constitutional terms for their discussion (despite their continuing disagreement). I call this the *recognizing* level of constitutional consciousness. Finally, at the highest level of constitutional consciousness, the *engaging* level, participants will move beyond mere acknowledgment of opposing arguments and sympathetically engage such claims in a dialogue. Rather than dismissing opposing arguments, as was possible at the recognizing level, participants will view the opposition's alternative position as a contending, yet legitimate constitutional reading and therefore seriously consider and sympathetically address their arguments and concerns, with the Constitution as a common referent. Even though participants in a debate continue to adhere to opposing interpretations, they will have indicated that they share the goal of discussing the meaning of the Constitution.

These levels help evaluate the extent to which Congress' practice of departmentalism contributed to distinguishing constitutional authority from judicial authority in the abortion debate and from executive authority in the war powers debate, creating a common constitutional language and broadening constitutional authority in both debates. The levels take into account the polarized social and political context in which the abortion and war powers debates took place. A discourse that successfully broadens constitutional authority will move through several levels of constitutional consciousness rather than simply attaining one level and remaining there. At each level, concerns and resistances arise that must be resolved before participants can move on to the next level. In this light, what some scholars characterize as "costs" appear to be a normal part of a vigorous and developing discourse.

The levels of constitutional consciousness provide a basis for rigorous comparisons of the abortion and the war powers cases, as well as for future explorations of departmentalism. However, unlike the more "systematic" benefit-cost approach, my framework, as well as other social scientific research, remains sensitive to the socio-political contexts that influence the practices being researched and the judgments that researchers must make while exploring those practices. On the other hand, arbitrary and capricious interpretation that bases reconstruction simply on personal predilection and that contends that a dialogue can mean anything and everything must and can be avoided.[123] The levels of constitutional consciousness strive to avoid these two extremes—full systematization that abandons context and arbitrary interpretation that abandons rigor—since both would lead to incomplete or errant evaluations of departmentalism as an alternative to judicial supremacy. The levels avoid the panhistorical assumptions and claims of the benefit-cost approach by exploring the practice of two congressional challenges to judicial authority within their particular societal and historical contexts, which, of course, have been shaped in part by judicial supremacy. My approach to reconstructing and interpreting the debates promises to shed light on the relationship between challenging judicial supremacy and improving constitutional authority, without necessarily promising to resolve what the Constitution means with respect to abortion and the war powers.

CHAPTER TWO

Departmentalism and
Judicial Activism:
The Abortion Debate

ROE'S INTERPRETATION
OF THE FOURTEENTH AMENDMENT

The debate about the constitutional status of a woman's right to abortion and a fetus' right to life did not arise with *Roe v. Wade*.[1] However, I begin with *Roe* because it prompted Congress to challenge judicial supremacy. *Roe*'s interpretation of the Fourteenth Amendment favored the woman's right to choose. The Court decided that the Constitution or, more specifically, the constitutional right to privacy "is broad enough to encompass a woman's decision whether or not to terminate her pregnancy."[2] Refusing to say that life begins at conception, or at any specific point during pregnancy, the Court declared that it could not determine when life begins. Noting the conflicting and thus inconclusive evidence, the Court argued that it "need not resolve the difficult question of when life begins when those trained in the respective disciplines of medicine, philosophy, and theology are unable to arrive at any consensus . . . at this point in the development of man's knowledge."[3] Justice Douglas's concurring opinion reiterated the Court's decision not to define life. He stated: "When life is present is a question we do not try to resolve. While basically a question for medical experts . . . it is, of course, caught up in the matters of religion and morality."[4]

The *Roe* Court also argued that fetuses were not independent legal persons. The absence of both a precedent and a constitutional definition of personhood, as well as the traditional "liberality" regarding abortion, persuaded the Court "that the word 'person', as used in the Fourteenth Amendment, does not include the unborn."[5] Noting that "the Constitution does not define 'person' in so many words,"[6] the Court claimed that it could not find a single case which held that a fetus is a person within the meaning of the Fourteenth Amendment.[7] Further, the Court argued that "the unborn have never been recognized in the law as persons in the whole sense."[8] The Court also suggested that "a woman enjoyed a substantially broader right to terminate a pregnancy [throughout Anglo-American history] than she does in most states today."[9] The Court concluded that the word "person" by and large "has application only postnatally" and that Fourteenth Amendment protections apply only after birth.[10]

Despite arguing that fetuses were not independent legal persons, the Court contended that the woman's right to choose abortion was not absolute, in part because the states retained an interest in protecting potential life. However, since the right to abortion is a fundamental right,[11] states can regulate or proscribe abortion to further their interest in protecting potential life only when that interest becomes compelling.[12] On the basis of "both logical and biological justification," *Roe* held that the state's interest in potential human life becomes compelling at viability, or at about the third trimester of pregnancy, since at that point the fetus can survive relatively independently outside the womb.[13] The Court argued that this holding did not depend on a specific definition of when life begins:

> Logically, of course, a legitimate state interest in this area [prenatal life] need not stand or fall on acceptance of the belief that life begins at conception or at some other point prior to live birth. In assessing the state's interest, vis-a-vis the woman's constitutional right to choose freely, recognition may be given to the less rigid claim that as long as at least *potential* life is involved, the state may assert interests beyond the pregnant woman alone.[14]

Finally, the *Roe* Court argued that states could not resolve the conflict between the woman and the fetus by favoring the fetus' life over the mother's life, even during the third trimester, if a physician determines that an abortion must be performed to maintain maternal health.[15] Thus the Court indicated that the woman's right to life was paramount over the state's interest in potential life.

THE HUMAN LIFE BILL'S INTERPRETATION
OF THE FOURTEENTH AMENDMENT

During hearings on the human life bill in 1981, Congress debated the constitutionality of *Roe v. Wade* and offered an alternative reading of the Fourteenth Amendment that favored fetal rights rather than the woman's rights.[16] The human life bill made several findings and offered a constitutional interpretation that challenged *Roe* with respect to when life and personhood begin, when the state's interest in potential life becomes compelling, and how to resolve conflicts over fetal and maternal rights.

On the basis of new scientific and legal evidence, the human life bill claims that life begins at conception. Taken together, Sections 1(a) and 1(b) recognize fetuses as legal persons whose constitutional rights and liberties are protected by the Fourteenth Amendment. Section 1(a) states that "Congress finds that the life of each human being begins at conception,"[17] and Section 1(b) states that "Congress further finds that the Fourteenth Amendment of the Constitution of the United States protects all human beings."[18] The human life bill expressly states that Section 5 of the Fourteenth Amendment empowers Congress to enforce the due process clause for *"each human life exist[ing] from conception*, without regard to race, sex, age, health, defect, or condition of dependency, and for this purpose *'person' includes all human beings."*[19] The human life bill also recognizes that states have a compelling interest throughout pregnancy "in protecting the lives of those whom the state *rationally regards* as human beings."[20]

In sum, the human life bill finds that life begins at conception, that fetuses are legal persons whose constitutional rights and liberties are worthy of protection, and that states have a compelling interest in protecting potential life throughout pregnancy. Finally, the human life bill allows the states to favor the fetus' life over the woman's life, even if the woman's life is threatened by carrying the fetus full term. In contrast, *Roe* declines to determine when life begins, declares that fetuses are not legal persons, argues that the states' interest in potential life becomes compelling only during the third trimester or at viability, and favors the woman's right to life in instances of conflict.

Several members of Congress, both opponents and supporters of the human life bill,[21] noted the conflict between Congress' constitutional interpretation in the bill and the judiciary's constitutional interpretation in *Roe*. For example, Senator John East (R-N.C.), a leading supporter of the bill, contended: "Congress has constitutional power to enact S. 158 [the human life bill] despite the holding of *Roe v. Wade* that unborn children are not persons and there is a right to abort them."[22] According to Senator Robert Packwood (R-Ore.), who opposed passage, the human life bill challenged *Roe* because it would make abortion a criminal act. Thus, Packwood argued, if the bill passed, "the Court would then be faced with the constitutional issue of whether or not the constitutional right of a woman to have an abortion can be overridden by a statute making abortion murder. I doubt that the Supreme Court would find the statute constitutional."[23]

RESISTANCE TO BROADENING
CONSTITUTIONAL AUTHORITY

Several aspects of the human life bill debate suggested that, to a limited extent, Congress did not distinguish constitutional from judicial authority or replace a discussion of institutional powers with a discussion of the constitutionality of abortion. Resisting the bill's attempt to distinguish constitutional from judicial authority, representatives such as Packwood, Max Baucus (D-Mont.), Daniel Moynihan (D-N.Y.), and Millicent Fenwick (R-N.J.) attempted to adhere to judicial finality. They questioned Congress' right to interpret the Constitution in conflict with the judiciary and insisted that judicial constitutional interpretation could be changed only through constitutional amendment. Rather than discussing the constitutional status of the right to abortion others, such as Senator East and Representative Henry Hyde (R-Ill.), responded by attacking the Court's institutional powers. To the extent that members of Congress continued to debate about departmentalism (to discuss who should interpret the Constitution) rather than to practice it (to discuss constitutional meaning), replacement did not occur and Congress did not significantly heighten its constitutional consciousness, broaden constitutional authority, or improve the quality of the debate.

Yet, despite some strong resistance, the hearings continued, in part because Congress also displayed some significant replacement by asserting its right to question judicial constitutional interpretation and by introducing new arguments and concerns that cast doubt upon the constitutional status of the right to abortion.

The Deferring Level:
Congressional Adherence to Judicial Finality

Baucus, Moynihan, Fenwick, and Packwood, among others, argued that Congress should not offer an alternative constitutional interpretation to *Roe* or challenge judicial supremacy. Rather, Congress ought to defer to the Court and express disagreement only by changing the constitutional text itself through constitutional amendment. Of course, these arguments are somewhat ironic. Despite declaring their allegiance to the Court's monopoly on constitutional interpretation, these representatives were actually engaging in constitutional interpretation. Their need to argue for judicial supremacy seems to belie the argument—at least to a certain extent. In any case, those arguments do suggest a lack of congressional displacement and a low, deferring level of constitutional consciousness. Baucus, for example, contended that "all members of this Subcommittee should satisfy themselves that S. 158 represents responsible congressional action."[24] Clarifying his concern, Baucus questioned whether Congress can "define personhood [assuming a consensus exists about when life begins], or is that only for the Supreme Court or constitutional amendment?"[25] Packwood also questioned whether "S. 158 [is] a legal and proper method" to ban abortion.[26]

Others argued that the human life bill's constitutional interpretation challenged that of the Supreme Court in *Roe* and unconstitutionally threatened judicial finality. For example, Moynihan declared: "In my view this legislation constitutes a *direct* assault upon the constitutional processes and concepts of the United States government."[27] Furthermore, Moynihan argued, the human life bill would abridge judicial supremacy, which he claimed was established and supported by settled judicial precedents such as *Marbury v. Madison, Cooper v. Aaron,* and *U.S. v. Nixon.*[28] In Moynihan's view, *Marbury* established that "it is for the Court to decide what the Constitution says. . . . Congress can set in motion a process for amending the Constitution, but with respect to the interpretation of the words of the Constitution, the Court is the supreme branch of government."[29] Thus, for Moynihan, the human life bill raised the central question of whether it was "within Congress' constitutionally prescribed power to declare that a fetus is a person after the Supreme Court has declared that it is not. In other words, can an Act of Congress overturn the Supreme Court's interpretation of the Constitution? I believe the answer is, unequivocally, that it cannot."[30] Fenwick also argued that the nation had accepted judicial finality as a legitimate principle of government since *Marbury v. Madison.*[31] Further, she stated that "it is wrong to try to change a decision of the Supreme Court taken on grounds of constitutionality and try to reverse it by law."[32]

Several members of Congress also charged that the human life bill intruded on the Court's institutional power and abridged the separation of powers. According to Fenwick, when Congress challenges judicial finality, it invades the judicial institution, abridges the separation of powers, and destabilizes the balance of powers in the government.[33] Baucus agreed that Congress' constitutional interpretation invades the Supreme Court and abridges the separation of powers. He argued that "the more the Congress utilizes the statutory process to overturn Supreme Court decisions, the less there is a meaningful distinction between the Supreme Court and Congress."[34] Baucus contended that the human life bill would cause the branches to begin to "merge," contrary to the principle of separation of powers enunciated in *Marbury*.[35] Moynihan argued even more forcefully that the human life bill "would commence, for the first time in history, a serious invasion by the legislative branch of the judicial branch."[36]

Members of Congress who accepted judicial finality typically contended that Congress should express its disagreement with Supreme Court decisions only through constitutional amendment or outside of the normal political process. By doing so, Congress could express disagreement without challenging judicial supremacy. Yet, even an amended Constitution would still mean "what the judges say it means," since the Court would retain the last word in interpreting it.

Moynihan agreed that constitutional amendment was the route that Congress should follow to correct or alter Supreme Court decisions. According to Moynihan, any other alternative would "undermine the Constitution."[37] Baucus also stated that when the Supreme Court interprets the Constitution, short of constitutional amendment, it "generally" has the last word.[38] He added: "Under our constitutional form of government, the proper way to alter the constitutional decisions of the Supreme Court is by constitutional amendment."[39] Baucus's position is a bit more subtle than it might appear at first glance. He did contend that Congress has a responsibility to consider the constitutionality of statutes and to reject unconstitutional statutes, rather than simply abdicating that responsibility by relying on judicial interpretation. Although Baucus supported judicial finality, he admitted that Congress has "a legislative responsibility not to enact statutes which are blatantly unconstitutional."[40]

However, given Baucus's adherence to judicial finality, Congress presumably would have to follow judicial precedent when considering a statute's constitutionality. Unless the Court had not previously spoken about a particular issue, Congress' responsibility to consider the constitutionality of statutes would be greatly restricted by judicial constitutional interpretation. Despite Baucus's talk of congressional responsibility, in his view, once the judiciary had spoken on a constitutional matter, Congress would be obliged to defer. Thus, though Baucus's position initially seems to indicate improved constitutional consciousness, upon closer inspection it largely amounts to continued deference to judicial authority. Following Baucus's understanding, the Constitution again seems to mean only "what the judges say it means." As is generally the case under judicial supremacy, Congress' responsibility to consider the Constitution reduces to Congress' obligation to defer to judicial authority.

Many of these advocates of deferring to the Court grounded their position by appealing to the authority of legal experts who supported judicial finality. For example, Moynihan noted that the General Accounting Office, twelve legal scholars, eighty law professors,[41] the Congressional Research Service, and even the legal counsel to Catholic Charities accepted judicial finality. The materials that Moynihan submitted to back up his claim indicate that many groups and individuals supported judicial finality even though they opposed *Roe v. Wade*. Despite their dismay with *Roe*, they refused to challenge it on constitutional grounds.

Packwood also cited several authorities who supported judicial finality and who questioned Congress' power to challenge judicial constitutional interpretation. He noted that six attorneys general and twelve constitutional scholars had said that the human life bill is "an unconstitutional way to reverse a Supreme Court decision."[42] He noted that, at the level of principle, there were both supporters and opponents of legal abortion among these scholars. Moynihan found only two authorities, John Noonan and Stuart Galebach, who supported the human life bill's challenge to *Roe*. Moynihan and Packwood's citation of these authorities is important, since it shows the widespread adherence to judicial finality in the legal profession, even among those who disagree significantly on particular political issues. However, as should be obvious by now, far more than two authorities could be cited to support the human life bill as a practical application of the idea that Congress may challenge judicial constitutional interpretation.[43]

Yet, even if no legal experts or authorities could be found to support congressional challenges to judicial finality, that alone, of course, would not prove the constitutionality of judicial finality. It would only show that judicial finality is widely accepted by legal experts, not necessarily sanctioned by the Constitution. In any case, these arguments signaled Congress' adherence to the discussion about the proper role of the Court—not a shift toward a broader discussion of constitutional meaning—and thus suggested a low level of constitutional consciousness at this point in the debate.

The Attacking Level:
Judicial or Constitutional Supremacy?

Rather than centering the discussion immediately on the constitutionality of *Roe*, several members of Congress contended that the Court, not the legislature, had invaded or usurped powers. They attacked the alleged activism of the Court, as well as its personnel. These discussions exemplified an attacking level of constitutional consciousness. Since these representatives began to disagree with the Court, challenge judicial supremacy, and thus differentiate constitutional from judicial authority, they displayed a deeper level of constitutional consciousness than representatives at the deferring level, all of whom accepted judicial supremacy. Yet discussion at the attacking level still focused largely on institutional powers rather than on constitutional meaning. Thus, although judicial supremacy was challenged at this level, constitutional consciousness and constitutional authority were not greatly heightened.

East and Hyde charged the Court with usurpation. East contended that "the separation of powers problem is that the Court has usurped its power. Hence, we are trying to restore the balance in terms of the legislature."[44] He added that "many people" think that the judiciary has overstepped constitutional limitations and usurped legislative power in recent years, and he hoped that "the Court would take note of it. Maybe the dialog itself would cause them to put on the brakes. That ... would make the[se] hearings useful."[45] Instead of discussing the constitutionality of *Roe* or the constitutional status of a right to choose abortion, Hyde attacked the Court more broadly for practicing judicial activism and for legislating rather than adjudicating. Citing John Hart Ely's *Democracy and Distrust*,[46] Hyde claimed that the judiciary had illegitimately substituted its will for the judgment of popularly elected legislatures.[47] East attacked the Court directly by noting that scholars often cite *Roe* as the "most extreme example of a case in which the Supreme Court substituted its own judgment for the judgment of elected legislatures."[48]

East and Hyde also repeatedly charged that the Court had illegitimately fabricated an allegedly constitutional argument in the *Roe* decision. According to East, "The Court *stated by fiat* that [unborn children] are not protected as persons under the fourteenth amendment. . . . Then the Court *created* judge-made rules governing abortion."[49] East added that the Court gave "no constitutional or factual bases for its holdings or their precise scope."[50] Hyde also accused the Court of illegitimately creating a constitutional right to privacy. He argued that "the fuzzy notion of a right to privacy, which nobody found in the Constitution for two hundred years, [is] now used in justifying the killing of 1.5 million preborn children a year."[51] Additionally, Hyde claimed that the Court was not speaking in good faith when it refused to determine when life begins. He suggested that the Court was able to define life and perhaps even did so indirectly by ruling out the possibility that life began at conception. Thus, Hyde continued, a "great void was left by the Court's *declared inability* to decide when life begins. They said it was not anything they needed to decide, as though personhood was an independent ambulatory term not necessarily associated with human life."[52]

Hyde also attacked the Court's personnel rather than the constitutionality of *Roe*. For example, he chided Justice Douglas for recognizing corporations as persons, despite his liberal, antibusiness leanings, and then went on to wonder "why, if a liberal luminary of the Court [like Douglas], can recognize corporations as persons, cannot other liberals and supporters of judicial activism recognize fetuses as persons?"[53]

CLEARING THE PATH FOR DEBATING
THE CONSTITUTIONALITY OF *ROE V. WADE*

Despite the arguments explored above that suggest various levels of congressional resistance to a broader constitutional discussion, other arguments suggest that Congress also discussed constitutional meaning at length during the human life bill hearings. Yet, even here traces of resistance to departmentalism remained and had to be addressed before the broader debate about the constitutionality of abortion could begin. Within the discussion of constitutional meaning, particularly with regard to pinpointing when life begins, several members of Congress temporarily regressed and discussed institutional powers, or the relative competence of Congress and the judiciary.

East rejected several alternatives—namely tightening Congress' control over the nomination process, restricting the judiciary's appellate jurisdiction, and simply obtaining a constitutional amendment outlawing abortion—that would have amounted to debating about institutional powers rather than about the constitutionality of abortion. Directly challenging *Roe* without attacking the Court, East respectfully contended that the human life bill *"invited* the Court to *reconsider* what it had done" in *Roe*.[54]

East argued further that Congress has a right and a duty to interpret the Constitution, even if that leads to conflict with judicial constitutional interpretation. Thus East contested Moynihan's claim that *Marbury* required "automatic [congressional] deference" to judicial decisions. Rather, East argued, support for the Constitution might sometimes obligate members of Congress to challenge judicial constitutional interpretation: When a representative is "confronted with a proposed law that is consistent with his own honest construction of the Constitution and with his view of sound policy that conflicts with what he regards as an erroneous Supreme Court decision, [he] has at least the right and perhaps the duty to vote for the bill. To do otherwise would be to close his eyes on the Constitution and see only the case."[55] Citing Lincoln's position on the *Dred Scott* ruling, East conceded that judicial decisions are binding on particular parties to a case. However, like Lincoln, East rejected judicial finality, or the idea that other branches are bound to follow the general constitutional principles enunciated by the Court in any particular case.[56] East argued that although the other branches must accept the Court's decision as it applies to the particular litigants in the case at hand, the branches remained free to challenge the constitutional interpretation underlying the Court's decision.

Expressly denying that the human life bill attacked the Court in any way, East claimed that the bill aimed to "encourage the Court to reexamine the results and reasoning of *Roe*."[57] East also contended that rather than attacking the Court, the human life bill was designed simply to prompt the Court to discuss further when life and personhood begin under the Constitution. He argued: "All we are doing here is trying to enlist [the Court] in a little dialog on this very profound public issue and get them to look at it again."[58] He added that the human life bill was not an attempt to exclude the judiciary from the discussion or to attack its powers. Instead, it was an attempt to create a dialogue with *Roe*. Thus, he contended, "if we say we can [determine when life begins] we are not overruling the Court. They will have another shot at it. We have not taken away their appellate jurisdiction. We are simply suggesting, well, let us try. This is a gentle prodding of the Court to reconsider."[59]

Representative Charles Dougherty (R-Pa.) also claimed that the human life bill should be understood as a response to *Roe v. Wade* and subsequent judicial abortion decisions, not simply as an attack on judicial power.[60] Similarly, Senator Jeremiah Denton (R-Ala.) directly confronted the *Roe* decision. He argued that "the 1973 decision of *Roe v. Wade* was a serious mistake which must be corrected as soon as possible."[61]

Regression to Institutional Competence in Congress' Discussion of *Roe*

In the midst of this discussion of constitutional meaning, several members of Congress claimed that Congress could define life because the *Roe* Court declared itself not competent to do so. Furthermore, they suggested that the Court *invited* Congress to enter the debate. Even though these representatives intended to challenge the constitutionality of the abortion right, in claiming that the Court thought that it was Congress' right or responsibility to determine when life begins, they were discussing relative institutional power and competency and not the constitutional status of the abortion right. For example, Denton stated that the *Roe* Court refused to decide when life begins and whether the unborn are persons because that power belonged to Congress. He argued: "This decision as to when human life begins involves the very sort of considerations that are appropriate for Congress, but *not for the Courts* as was recognized in [*Roe v. Wade*]."[62]

Dougherty agreed that since in *Roe* the Supreme Court did not define when life begins, Congress should.[63] Dougherty cited *Baker v. Carr*[64] on the "political question" doctrine[65] to support his position that the Court did not consider itself competent to determine when life begins. On this reading, the *Roe* Court left it to Congress to resolve the question of when life begins, and *Roe*, widely cited as the broadest and most active use of judicial review since *Brown v. Board of Education,* is thought to exemplify adherence to the political question doctrine, a doctrine usually associated with judicial self-restraint. Leaving aside for the moment this dubious claim, the argument clearly attempts to narrow the scope of judicial power and therefore represents an attack on the judiciary as well as a regression to a narrower debate about who should interpret the Constitution.

Dougherty and Denton tried to downplay the challenge that the human life bill posed to *Roe* by arguing that in that decision the Court had recognized Congress' superior ability to deal with issues of life and personhood. This was not true, however. The *Roe* Court did not claim that it lacked the institutional competence necessary to address those questions or suggest that Congress might somehow have greater competency in such matters than the judiciary. The Court said simply that various experts presented conflicting versions about the beginning of life and personhood and that available information did not conclusively resolve those conflicts. The Court implied that should Congress choose to introduce new scientific, legal, or philosophic arguments, the Court would be happy to consider them.

Senator East understood this difference. Unlike Dougherty and Denton, who tried to exclude the judiciary from the abortion discussion, East set the scene for a renewed congressional-judicial dialogue. The problem was not that *Roe* did not address the issues of life and personhood, East argued, it was simply that *Roe* did not *resolve* either the scientific question (the medical and biological question of when life begins) or the value question (the legal and constitutional question of whether fetuses have rights) that surround a woman's right to abortion.[66] In contrast to Dougherty and Denton, East refrained from diminishing the Court's powers. East contended that the "purpose of this legislation is not to impair the Supreme Court's power to review the constitutionality of legislation, but to exercise the authority of Congress to disagree with the result of an earlier Supreme Court decision based on an investigation of facts and on a decision concerning values that the Supreme Court has declined to address."[67]

Finally, East, again unlike Dougherty and Denton, refused to exclude the Supreme Court from further discussions of life and personhood. He concluded: "Congress is entirely justified in expressing its view on such questions, subject to Supreme Court review."[68] In short, if Congress could offer new findings about life or personhood that would help to resolve the issues,[69] the Court might reconsider *Roe*, but *Roe* did not *expressly* invite or encourage Congress to enter the dialogue.

Additionally, Baucus and Moynihan reminded Dougherty and Denton that *Roe* said that fetuses are not persons under the Fourteenth Amendment.[70] Fenwick reminded Congress that *Roe* did not explicitly suggest that Congress should decide when life begins or when fetuses become persons, specifically noting that *Roe* said that "person" as used in the Fourteenth Amendment does not include the unborn.[71] To resolve *Roe*'s meaning definitively, Baucus read directly from the decision: "The word 'person' as used in the Fourteenth Amendment does not include the unborn."[72] Obviously, Baucus's clarification did not resolve the "legal" and "value" questions *Roe* raised about life and personhood. It did, however, clarify the conflict between the human life bill and *Roe* about the constitutionality of abortion.

THE INTRODUCING LEVEL:
DEBATING THE MEANING OF THE CONSTITUTION

On several occasions during the human life bill hearings, representatives vigorously debated the constitutionality of abortion and *Roe*. To prove that the Fourteenth Amendment protected fetal rights and liberties, several members introduced new scientific and philosophic arguments into the debate. On the basis of these arguments, the human life bill found that life began at conception and that fetuses were persons with constitutional rights worthy of protection under the Fourteenth Amendment. These findings challenged *Roe* and provided Congress with an opportunity to discuss the constitutional status of the right to abortion. Thus these representatives improved the quality of the constitutional discourse about abortion by inserting an interpretation of the Fourteenth Amendment that grounded the constitutional protection of fetal rights and liberties and provided supporting scientific, legal, and philosophic arguments, thereby casting a previously polarized debate into common constitutional terms. However, they did not recognize or engage opposing arguments about women's rights. Most advocates of a fetal rights interpretation of the Fourteenth Amendment did not consider the arguments supporting women's rights, just as most advocates of women's rights did not consider the arguments supporting fetal rights. Consequently, the discussion still remained somewhat intractable. In short, these members of Congress attained only an introducing level of constitutional consciousness.

In this part of the debate, several representatives discussed Congress' power to enforce the Fourteenth Amendment by defining, redefining, and expanding the scope of rights and liberties protected therein. Section 5 of the Fourteenth Amendment states: "Congress shall have the power to enforce, by appropriate legislation, the provisions of this article."[73] This section appears to call for Congress to consider what the Fourteenth Amendment or the "provisions of this article" mean. Furthermore, in order to pass legislation to enforce

Fourteenth Amendment protections, Congress would necessarily have to consider what those protections were.[74] Thus Dougherty concluded that Congress "certainly has the power to expand rights by declaring that all human beings are persons."[75]

Members of Congress supporting the human life bill argued that the bill addressed two questions: a "scientific" one (When does life begin?) and a "legal" one (Does the Constitution recognize fetuses as persons and thus protect their rights?). They suggested that the first was a *factual* question, whereas the second was a *value* question. Of course, this differentiation unself-consciously assumes the validity of the fact/value distinction. It overlooks the possibility that even researchers in the hard sciences construct hypotheses, conduct experiments, and make discoveries in a social context whose values may influence their own values, which in turn may influence the choices and interpretive judgments they make as they work. In this light, scientific discoveries are not simply factual, if what one means by factual is that scientists discover knowledge free of any reasoned judgment or interpretation. In any case, those exploring the scientific question, like those exploring the legal question, cannot successfully finesse the problems of value and social context simply by asserting that their results are "factual."[76]

On the claimed basis of new scientific and legal argument, Section 1 of the human life bill found that life begins at conception and that the Fourteenth Amendment protects all human beings, including fetuses.[77] The Fourteenth Amendment, which guarantees certain constitutional protections to *persons*, was the constitutional referent that structured the human life bill debate.[78] Supporters of the human life bill sought to challenge *Roe*'s understanding of the Fourteenth Amendment by establishing that fetuses qualified as persons and thus were worthy of Fourteenth Amendment protection. Since the Constitution undoubtedly protects the rights and liberties of persons, in this part of the human life bill debate representatives sought to determine whether science or philosophy, at their current state of development, could convincingly establish that fetuses were persons. Thus Hyde contended that if Congress could establish, as fact, that fetuses are living human beings, then the Constitution, as well as the judiciary, would be obligated to protect fetal rights and liberties.[79] He argued that "passing S. 158 would be a reassertion of the explicit words of the Constitution that there is a right to life, a constitutional right, and that Congress has the right and the constitutional duty to implement the Fourteenth Amendment by appropriate legislation."[80]

Dougherty also noted that as long as the status of unborn children remains unresolved, "the Supreme Court will not protect [fetuses] as persons."[81] Like Hyde, Dougherty asserted that once Congress found that life begins at conception, the Court would have to reconsider *Roe* in light of that finding. Although Dougherty finally conceded that *Roe* did not expressly say that it would equate the beginning of life with personhood, he argued that a congressional finding would compel the Court to draw such a conclusion.[82] East agreed. He argued that "*Roe v. Wade* would be vitiated" by the human life bill's finding that fetuses were persons from the moment of conception.[83] East underscored that it is "appropriate for Congress as well as the Supreme Court to ask whether a particular class of individuals are human beings."[84]

In an attempt to ground the human life bill's claims that life, personhood, and thus constitutional protection begin at conception, supporters such as East integrated new scientific evidence and legal arguments into the abortion debate. East questioned several physicians and scientists at length about when human life begins. Although these scientists largely agreed that scientific evidence had conclusively shown that life begins at conception, they claimed that the present state of scientific knowledge was largely inconclusive with respect to the beginning of personhood.

For these scientists the possibility remained that a gap existed between the beginning of life and the beginning of personhood. Even scientists and members of Congress who had no difficulty accepting as *fact* that human life begins at conception were often unable to declare, with the same level of certainty, precisely when human life attains personhood and legal rights worthy of constitutional protection. As Thomas Emerson points out, the human life bill rests on the assumption that human life and personhood are indistinguishable. He states that "according to the theory of the Bill, [human life] is endowed with the attributes of a human person, possessing a soul or at least entitled to the special status accorded human beings in our society."[85]

Several scientists supported the human life bill's claim that life begins at conception.[86] For example, Dr. Jerome LeJeune argued that scientific evidence indicated that life begins at conception or fertilization.[87] Dr. Hymie Gordon also argued that science had established, as fact, that the fetus is a living organism at conception.[88] Thus LeJeune and Gordon contended that science, independent of philosophical or theological argument, established as *fact* that life begins at conception. However, Dr. Micheline M. Mathews-Roth noted that in the scientific literature, conception refers to fertilization rather than implantation, which usually occurs approximately one week after fertilization. Mathews-Roth contended that although an individual life is created at conception, current technology cannot *prove* that life exists until implantation occurs.[89]

Several other scientists expressed doubt about Congress' use of "new" scientific arguments to challenge *Roe*. They argued that no significant scientific developments regarding when life and personhood begins had occurred that would alter the Court's conclusions in *Roe*. Furthermore, new scientific developments, findings, or arguments could not prove as *fact* when life begins because that problem, at bottom, is value laden or metaphysical.[90]

Although several human life bill supporters, including East, seemed to assume rather than provide evidence for an indisputable connection between the beginning of life and personhood, several scientists who had confidently argued that life begins at conception hesitated to define personhood or to claim that scientific evidence about the beginning of life could establish as fact the beginning of personhood. For example, Dr. Watson Bowes argued that life begins at conception or fertilization, but that personhood may begin later.[91] Mathews-Roth argued that although conception creates a genetically distinguishable individual, personality may not be present at conception.[92] Dr. McCarthy DeMere suggested that since personhood is difficult to define as scientific fact, and since previous state attempts to define personhood have led to abominations, such as Nazi Germany's exclusion of the Jews and the U.S. Supreme Court's exclusion of blacks in the *Dred Scott* case, the state ought to refrain from authoritatively defining personhood.[93] DeMere emphasized that he made this argument despite his conviction that scientific evidence had established as fact that life begins at conception.

Ultimately, East withdrew his initial claim that scientific evidence proved as fact that life begins at conception, doubting that scientific arguments alone could ever conclusively resolve that question. He speculated that "perhaps science can only help us in a very limited way and ultimately we get into a moral and ethical judgment here."[94] Following that logic, East claimed that every definition of when life begins, *even conception*, inevitably would be controversial and thus seem arbitrary. Therefore, he argued, *Roe*'s viability standard was no more accurate a place to recognize a state interest in potential life than conception would be.[95] East also contended that uncertainty about the beginning of life led the human life bill to allow states to recognize a compelling interest in potential life throughout pregnancy, regardless of the status of the woman's right to choose. Despite East's claim about uncertainty, the final version of the human life bill stated with extreme confidence that "the life of each human being begins at conception."[96]

East offered other legal and philosophic arguments to support his claim that fetuses were persons with rights and liberties worthy of constitutional protection. These arguments also seemed to assume rather than ground the connection between life, personhood, and constitutional protection. For example, East asserted that the Constitution, tradition, history, the framers of the Fourteenth Amendment, Abraham Lincoln, the Declaration of Independence, and Justice Brennan's opinion in *Furman v. Georgia* (408 U.S. 238 [1972]) all recognized the "sanctity of human life" and supported the idea that fetuses deserve legal protection.[97] He stated further that since the Declaration of Independence recognized that all men were created equal and have rights, fetuses must also have rights unless the lives of certain human beings, such as fetuses, are not worthy of legal protection.[98] Finally, East appealed to "common sense," contending that "*commonsensically*, there is such a thing as human life. We are here."[99]

In sum, by introducing the fetal rights interpretation of the Fourteenth Amendment, as well as new scientific, philosophic, and legal arguments to support that interpretation, Congress reached an introducing level of constitutional consciousness in the human life bill hearings, thus significantly broadening constitutional authority as distinguished from judicial authority in the abortion debate. However, most members of Congress on opposing sides of the abortion issue did not recognize or engage the arguments of their opponents. Although they introduced new arguments that grounded their own constitutional interpretations, they failed to recognized and engage the constitutional arguments of the opposition.

To attain the recognizing level, Congress must acknowledge the arguments that support the opposing constitutional interpretation and thus begin to consider the latter as a legitimate alternative reading of the Constitution. Before they can engage in a dialogue, representatives must indicate not only that they recognize opposing claims, but also that they are able to recognize those claims as serious grounds for a viable alternative constitutional interpretation. Although engaging in a dialogue does not require participants to change their position on the abortion issue, it does require them to exhibit a deepened understanding of their opponents' argument.

More specifically, members of Congress favoring women's rights could begin to engage opposing arguments by considering abortion from the fetal perspective. They might reconsider the status of the fetus, perhaps by considering the argument that a potential child, rather than mere protoplasm, is involved in the abortion decision. From this perspective, the constitutional argument that the Fourteenth Amendment protects fetal life becomes a more plausible alternative constitutional interpretation. Although prochoice advocates might still oppose the fetal rights reading of the Constitution, they would now be able to consider it to be a serious alternative interpretation of the Fourteenth Amendment rather than dismissing it outright.

Similarly, representatives favoring fetal rights could begin to engage opposing arguments by considering abortion from the woman's perspective. They might consider that a woman's psychological as well as physical health may be at risk if an abortion is denied and that restricting reproductive choice may restrict the scope of a woman's public (and private) identity. From this perspective, the argument that the Fourteenth Amendment protects the woman's right to choose becomes a plausible constitutional reading. Again, prolife advocates might not embrace this constitutional interpretation, but their understanding of the opposition's position, and of constitutional meaning, would now be quite improved. Although advocates might still disagree on the issue, they would now be engaged in a dialogue about the constitutional status of the woman's and the fetus' rights and liberties, thereby heightening constitutional consciousness and broadening constitutional authority.

Unfortunately, both recognition and dialogic engagement were largely absent in the human life bill debates. Senator Packwood dismissed the fetus' perspective, or prolife position, without seriously considering its merits, just as Representative Hyde and Senators Denton and East dismissed the woman's perspective, or prochoice position, without seriously considering the arguments supporting it. However, the human life bill's challenge to judicial supremacy did allow members of Congress to introduce new arguments, and a few, such as Senator Baucus and Representative Fenwick, were able to engage those arguments. Their ability to engage both the fetus' and the woman's perspectives in a sympathetic dialectic suggests that a broader constitutional dialogue in which participants talk with rather than past each other about alternative constitutional interpretations might be possible in Congress in the future. Nevertheless, in the human life bill debate most of the participants failed to achieve that higher (engaging) level of constitutional consciousness.

For example, rather than reconsidering the status of the fetus, Packwood, a strong supporter of *Roe*, simply dismissed representatives supporting fetal rights as tyrannic, religious fanatics. He asserted: "Every generation witnesses a new group of citizens who believe themselves the keepers of the faith, ... moralists who are so convinced they are right that they choose to impose their morality on us. There is a growing force in this country fueled by a Cotton Mather mentality. ... [T]he danger to the liberties of all Americans is most threatened by those who want to compel conformity of thought and deed."[100]

Hyde, a supporter of the human life bill, also refused to recognize and engage the opposing position by repeatedly dismissing, without any serious consideration, any arguments supporting the woman's right to abortion. For example, he stated that he would "not spend much more time on the euphemisms that are used in the subject: prochoice."[101] Hyde's unwillingness to engage opposing arguments can also be seen in the numerous attempts he made to ridicule his opponents. For instance, he offered the following characterization of prochoice supporters: "Centuries ago we had alchemists, people who sought to change base metal into gold. We today have our alchemists who have successfully turned what was once a crime, the crime of abortion, into the gold of an act of compassion and humanity. *Roe v. Wade* is certainly the keystone of that result."[102]

Denton, also a supporter of the human life bill, rightly noted that many of his prochoice opponents, such as Packwood, refused to engage the prolife arguments that supported fetal rights. However, Denton did not perceive his own failure to engage opposing arguments. For example, he could not conceive that those who support abortion might also do so from a position of regard or respect for life. Thus he contended that "the abortion issue is a prime example of the *total lack of regard of others for human life*."[103] Similarly, throughout the debate East repeatedly asserted that most abortions are sought by women who are selfishly trying to relieve stress and that such selfishness is not an adequate grounding for *Roe*'s protection of abortion on demand.[104]

However, as I stated earlier, some representatives did engage opposing arguments, even as they offered reasons for adhering to a contrary position. Their discussion indicated that they were aware of their opponents' reasoning and that they considered it a viable alternative interpretation. In short, they recognized opposing claims and connected the woman's and the fetus' rights perspectives by offering counterreasons to explain why they continued to adhere to their own positions despite the admittedly strong claims of the opposition. For example, by acknowledging that abortion could be tragic, Baucus moved beyond the incommensurate arguments that some prochoice advocates offered—namely that the fetus is simply protoplasm and that the choice of abortion is therefore emotionally uncomplicated or morally unambiguous. Instead, he recognized that the abortion decision may entail a practical conflict between two abstract goods: between that which the fetus needs to flourish and that which the woman needs to flourish.[105] He stated: "Certainly there are instances where a fetus might be aborted under circumstances that most Americans would consider tragic."[106] Baucus also addressed the prolife claims by providing a different perspective on abortion—he argued that the woman's needs and the fetus' needs can tragically conflict. He concluded that pregnant women are keenly aware of that conflict and of the moral dimensions of the abortion decision. Thus he argued that "women who are faced with such a decision agonize very deeply in their own conscience and soul and in their own religion. And I believe they do want to make their own decision."[107]

Similarly, although she stated her own very strong view, Fenwick, in recognizing the tragedy involved in abortion also recognized and sympathetically engaged arguments made from the perspective of protecting the fetus. She contended that "we are dealing here with a tragic and very important subject. . . . I do not think anything can be called an inconvenience that causes human beings, women, to tear themselves apart and risk their lives. You do not do that for an inconvenience. It has saddened me in the House to hear people sometimes refer to the desire to terminate a pregnancy as a desire to get rid of a little inconvenience."[108] Fenwick's recognition that the conflict between the woman's needs and the fetus' needs might result in a tragic loss of life in the abortion decision, not simply a removal of mere protoplasm, displayed her ability to engage the opposition's claim that fetuses are human life. Thus she added that "for those who object on principle, I have the highest respect."[109]

For his part, Dougherty displayed his inability to engage opposing arguments when he responded to Fenwick's argument as follows: "When she talked about the agony of the person involved, the woman. I would just like to go on record saying that there is an agony involved for the unborn child, too."[110] Dougherty appears to have overlooked Fenwick's earlier acknowledgment of the fetus' needs. Rather than overlooking the fetus' perspective, as Dougherty charged, her statements suggested that abortion is tragic *because of* the conflict between the fetus and the woman in the decision. East, a leading sponsor of the human life bill, also displayed an inability to engage Fenwick's arguments. He claimed that he did "not find . . . a great deal of agony constitutionally or otherwise in understanding, because of new knowledge, that we might have a differing conception of how a right might be applied in a particular context."[111] East's statement suggests that he was not willing or able to discuss fetal rights while also seriously engaging the woman's perspective and the import that fetal rights might have for women.

Conclusions on the Human Life Bill Hearings

Significant replacement occurred during the human life bill hearings. Members of Congress debated the constitutionality of *Roe* and offered an alternative interpretation of the Fourteenth Amendment that would protect fetal rights, introducing new legal, scientific, and philosophic arguments to support their position. Rather than deepening skepticism about constitutional authority and the rule of law as the critics of departmentalism had feared, constitutional consciousness heightened and constitutional authority broadened when Congress challenged judicial supremacy in the human life bill hearings. However, these debates revealed little recognition of opposing arguments, let alone willingness to engage in a dialogue. Therefore, the human life bill debates suggest a mixed result for the departmentalist claims. Congressional debate improved to an introducing level of constitutional consciousness, but room for improvement to higher levels remained.

IMPROVING THE QUALITY OF JUDICIAL CONSTITUTIONAL INTERPRETATION

Some scholars predict that the quality of judicial constitutional interpretation should improve when Congress challenges judicial supremacy in a political and legal context characterized by judicial activism. They argue that when Congress challenges judicial constitutional interpretation with new arguments, the Court should acknowledge and respond to those arguments and thereby contribute to broadening constitutional authority and to locating a common constitutional language. Thus the Court should not rely solely on precedent by automatically equating constitutional reasoning with precedential reasoning or dismiss alternative constitutional readings simply by declaring that the Constitution means what the justices said it meant in *Roe*. However, the Court would not necessarily have to overturn *Roe* or reject precedential reasoning to improve the quality of its constitutional discussion. It could adhere to the precedent of *Roe* and display improved quality if it seriously considered the new arguments as rival, potentially compelling constitutional readings. The Court would have to supply additional constitutional reasons that explained why it decided to adhere to the precedent of *Roe*, despite the new, somewhat compelling arguments. In this way, the Court itself would make a theoretical distinction between its own rulings (precedent) and the Constitution.[112]

The Recognizing Level: The *Akron* Case

In 1983, two years after the human life bill hearings, the city of Akron passed an ordinance that challenged *Roe*. Several aspects of Akron's ordinance paralleled the human life bill's challenge to *Roe*.[113] For example, like the human life bill, the Akron ordinance found that life began at conception. The ordinance stated: "It is the finding of the Council that there is no point in time between the union of sperm and egg, or at least the blastocyst stage and the birth of the infant at which point we can say the unborn child is not a human life and that changes occurring between implantation, a six-week embryo, a six-month fetus, and a one-week-old child, or a mature adult are merely stages of development and maturation."[114]

Again like the human life bill, viewing abortion from the fetal perspective, the city of Akron attempted to regulate abortions further than *Roe* allowed. For example, Akron's informed consent provision required physicians to inform the woman, before the abortion, "that the unborn child is a human life from the moment of conception."[115] Consequently, *Akron v. Akron Center for Reproductive Health* provides an opportunity to observe whether the Court recognizes and engages new scientific arguments similar to those introduced in the human life bill debates, thereby improving the quality of constitutional interpretation, or whether the Court relies solely on the force of precedent to strike down Akron's ordinance.

From the outset the *Akron* majority relied on the logic of *Roe* and failed to engage Akron's finding that life begins at conception. The Court dismissed Akron's finding without much consideration simply *because* it challenged *Roe*. Writing for the majority, Justice Powell stated that "the doctrine of *stare decisis* [adherence to precedent], while perhaps never entirely persuasive on a constitutional question, is a doctrine that demands respect in a society governed by the Rule of Law. We respect it today, and reaffirm *Roe v. Wade.*"[116] The Court assumed the constitutionality of *Roe* and failed to consider Akron's argument as a potentially compelling constitutional interpretation. Equating the precedent of *Roe* with the rule of law, the Court stated that informing women that life begins at conception is a "requirement inconsistent with the Rule of Law."[117]

Thus the Court struck down Akron's ordinance on the grounds that the informed consent provision, contrary to *Roe*, obstructed the woman's right to choose abortion. Following *Roe*'s trimester framework, the Court argued that to be upheld, Akron's informed consent and hospital regulations had to address the state's interest in safeguarding the health of pregnant women.[118] The Court used precedent to foreclose consideration of arguments outside of the logic of *Roe* (for example, that life may begin at conception). Refusing to take the fetal perspective into account, the court contended that, contrary to *Roe*, the informed consent provision was designed "not to inform the woman's consent but rather to persuade her to withhold it altogether."[119] The Court argued that informing women that life begins at conception is "a requirement inconsistent with the Court's holding in *Roe v. Wade* that a state may not adopt one theory of when life begins to justify its regulation of abortions."[120] In short, the *Akron* majority relied solely on the precedent of *Roe* each time it struck down parts of Akron's ordinance that attempted to regulate abortion.[121] Each time, the Court failed to acknowledge and engage Akron's finding that life begins at conception or the new scientific arguments upon which the findings were based.

However, Justice O'Connor's dissent did consider the constitutionality of the new arguments and *Roe*, thereby keeping the discussion of the fetal rights perspective alive in the abortion debate and improving judicial constitutional interpretation. According to O'Connor, scientific advances have blurred the lines of *Roe*'s trimester/compelling state interest analysis.[122] Since medical technology has made abortion safer, *Roe*'s framework demands that states are less free to regulate abortion in the interest of the woman's health. Thus, O'Connor stated, "the State's compelling interest in maternal health changes as medical technology changes."[123] As medical technology continues to make abortion less threatening to maternal health than normal childbirth, the right to choose abortion without state interference will extend beyond the first trimester. At the same time, O'Connor argued, advances in medical technology have also made viability possible before *Roe*'s third trimester estimate. Consequently, states might be able to prohibit abortion to protect their interest in fetal life much earlier than the third trimester. O'Connor noted that because the point at which these interests become compelling varies, future medical advances may challenge the right to abortion by causing the interest in maternal health and the interest in potential life to conflict. Therefore, O'Connor concluded, *Roe* should be reconsidered in light of new scientific advances, because its "framework . . . is clearly on a collision course with itself."[124]

Rather than simply rejecting the precedent of *Roe*, O'Connor directly addressed the problem of defining when life begins, which, of course, was raised by Akron's challenge to *Roe*. Like East in the human life bill hearings, O'Connor argued that scientific evidence did not support the *Roe* framework. Again like East, she challenged the arbitrary nature of placing life at viability, despite the fact that *Roe* said states have a compelling interest in fetal life beginning only at viability. O'Connor argued that "*potential* life is no less potential in the first weeks of pregnancy than it is at viability or afterward."[125] She added that "although the Court refused to 'resolve the difficult question of when life begins' the Court chose the point of viability . . . to permit the complete proscription of abortion. . . . [This point] is no less arbitrary than choosing any point before viability or any point afterward."[126] Thus, O'Connor argued, "the State interest in potential human life is likewise extant throughout pregnancy,"[127] not simply at an arbitrary and changing viability point. In conclusion O'Connor offered an alternative standard to adjudicate the constitutionality of regulating or proscribing abortion. This new standard would give the states broader power to protect the fetus: "State action 'encouraging childbirth except in the most urgent circumstances' is 'rationally related to the legitimate governmental objective of protecting potential life.' "[128]

Although O'Connor's dissent prompted the Court to acknowledge that the new scientific developments challenged the very basis of Roe's analytic framework, it failed to engage these findings, arguing that "prudence dictates" an adherence to the precedent of *Roe*.[129] The Court may have had good reasons for its action. "Prudence" connotes that there are other, unspoken grounds for the Court's decision. For example, the Court might have thought that it was better to adhere to the trimester framework rather than act as a "science review board" to determine the varying points at which the relevant interests would become compelling, given progress in medical technology. However, the Court failed to explain *why* it was prudent to adhere to *Roe*. Rather,

the Court simply applied the *Roe* framework to Akron's ordinance
without engaging Akron and O'Connor's arguments. Since the *Akron*
majority failed to divulge the reasons for its decision and to address
the scientific challenge to *Roe*, the quality of the Court's interpretation improved only to the recognizing level rather than to the engaging level of constitutional consciousness.

The Deferring Level: Congress and the Abortion Funding Restriction Act Debates

In 1976 Congress passed the Hyde Amendment, which prohibited states from using federal Medicaid funds to subsidize abortion
costs. Congress gained approval for this restriction by amending it to
the Health, Education, and Welfare (later renamed Health and Human Services) Department's budgetary appropriation each year. Thus
supporters of the Hyde Amendment had to obtain approval for the prohibition on a yearly basis. In 1985 several senators unsuccessfully attempted to make that prohibition permanent through the Abortion
Funding Restriction Act. If Congress had passed this act, the Hyde
Amendment would have become a permanent part of the Federal
Code, and supporters of the prohibition would no longer have had to
obtain annual approval for the funding restriction. The Abortion
Funding Restriction Act also proposed to amend the Civil Rights Act
of 1964 so that it would cover fetuses and, presumably, protect their
civil rights. The Abortion Funding Restriction Act stated: "Nothing
contained in the Civil Rights Act of 1964 shall be construed to authorize the use of Federal financial assistance for abortions and no such
assistance shall be used to perform abortions except where the life of
the mother would be endangered if the fetus were carried to term."[130]

Although supporters of the Abortion Funding Restriction Act contended repeatedly that the act did not challenge *Roe*, they nevertheless premised their actions on a definition of the beginning of life that
conflicted with that decision. For example, Senator Orren Hatch (R-
Utah), the main sponsor of the act, noted that the bill answers Ronald
Reagan's request to Congress for legislation to "end the killing."[131]
Hatch argued that the act would prevent federal subsidization of a
"practice that the President notes may well be . . . the taking of a human life."[132] However, Hatch felt compelled to add that the act did not
conflict with *Roe*. Senator Dennis DeConcini (D-Az.) also asserted that
in the Abortion Funding Restriction Act "the issue is life."[133] Supporters of the act maintained that they were not challenging judicial

supremacy or *Roe*. They argued that they were making a decision
about funding, not abortion, and that such decisions were well within
the bounds of congressional power.[134] They believed that they had discretion over funding decisions unless the Supreme Court struck down
the Hyde Amendment.[135]

Other members argued that the act did challenge *Roe*. However,
they did not discuss *Roe* or concerns about fetal rights. They claimed
to oppose the act on the grounds that Congress should accept judicial
supremacy rather than challenge *Roe* through statute. They argued
that the appropriate way for Congress to express its disagreement
with the Court was by proposing a constitutional amendment.

Although Senator Hatch claimed that the bill did not confer personhood on the unborn, Senator Packwood disagreed, contending that
the act challenged *Roe* by indirectly granting the unborn status as
persons.[136] Packwood argued that the Fourteenth Amendment does not
recognize fetuses as persons. Thus, Packwood continued, if one were to
accept Hatch's assertion that the Abortion Funding Restriction Act
did not grant fetuses the status of personhood, one would have to conclude that the Act would extend civil rights "to cover *entities* that are
not persons within the meaning of the Fourteenth Amendment."[137]
However, contrary to Hatch's disclaimer, Packwood contended that the
act actually recognized fetuses as living persons from conception, and
as such, possessors of constitutional rights worthy of protection.[138]
Packwood also noted that regardless of various judicial and legislative
challenges to the right to choose abortion, the Court had reaffirmed
Roe and the Senate had rejected the human life bill, which attempted
to overturn *Roe*.[139] Packwood contended that although Congress did
control funding decisions, constitutional law protects the right to
choose to have an abortion "and if this body is to change that law, we
are changing constitutional law."[140] Nevertheless, Hatch continued to
assert that the act did not conflict with *Roe* "in the slightest."[141] Thus
Hatch and other supporters of the act refused to recognize the challenge that the act posed to judicial supremacy and *Roe*. They continued to center debate on Congress' funding powers rather than on the
constitutionality of *Roe*.

Even though Packwood recognized the challenge that the act posed
to *Roe*, he focused his discussion on institutional powers rather than
on constitutional meaning. He stated: "If who should interpret the
Constitution is to be the subject of the debate, let us start that debate."[142] Supporting judicial supremacy, Packwood contended that the
act was "an [illegitimate] effort to give Congress, rather than the Su-

preme Court, the right to determine what is constitutional."[143] Packwood also contended that if Congress or the people disagree with a judicial decision, they ought to pursue constitutional amendment, not congressional constitutional interpretation. Senator Howard Metzenbaum (D-Ohio) agreed that the Abortion Funding Restriction Act represented an illegitimate "attempt to amend the Constitution through the back door of legislation."[144]

The Abortion Funding Restriction Act debates suggest a regression in the constitutional debate about abortion. Leading supporters of the act declined to address constitutional meaning, arguing that the act did not challenge *Roe* directly or indirectly. These members of Congress failed to continue the human life bill's discussion about the constitutionality of abortion and instead renewed the discussion of institutional powers, or who should interpret the Constitution. Some opponents of the act did recognize that it challenged *Roe*. But they argued that it was not proper for Congress to challenge the Court through ordinary legislation. They contended that judicial opinion could only be challenged through constitutional amendment. Rather than contesting Congress' constitutional interpretation in the Abortion Funding Restriction Act on the grounds that it was errant, they objected to Congress interpreting the Constitution. Rather than providing further grounding for *Roe* and broadening constitutional authority, opponents of the act simply asserted the supremacy of the judiciary in constitutional matters. Thus in the Abortion Funding Restriction Act debates, Congress achieved only a deferring level of constitutional consciousness, in contrast to its actions in the human life bill debates, where it achieved an introducing level.

The Deferring Level: The *Thornburgh* Case

In 1982 Pennsylvania passed a bill that attempted to regulate abortion more strictly than *Roe*. The bill included an "informed consent" provision that obligated physicians to inform women about the anatomical and physiological stages of fetal development; the physical and psychological risks associated with abortion; and the medical, paternal, and state aid that might be forthcoming should the woman decide to carry the fetus to term. The bill obligated physicians to use the abortion procedure most likely to preserve the life of the fetus in postviability abortions and required that a second physician be present to care for the fetus should it survive the abortion procedure. The Court struck down these provisions in *Thornburgh v. American*

College of Gynecologists and Obstetricians[145] on the grounds that they unconstitutionally obstructed the woman's fundamental right to choose abortion freely (without state interference).

Although the constitutional dialogue regressed during the Abortion Funding Restriction Act hearings, the *Thornburgh* majority still might have addressed the new constitutional arguments and scientific evidence discussed during the human life bill hearings—especially since the dissents served to present those arguments to the majority. Yet, the *Thornburgh* majority relied on the logic of *Roe* to avoid acknowledging or engaging new arguments that challenged the constitutionality of that decision.

In *Thornburgh* the Court reaffirmed *Roe* and relied solely on the force of precedent to overturn Pennsylvania's statute further regulating abortion. Writing for the majority, Justice Blackmun stated:

> In the years since this Court's decision in *Roe*, States and municipalities have adopted a number of measures seemingly designed to prevent a woman, with the advice of her physician, from exercising her freedom of choice. *Akron* is but one example. But the constitutional principles that led this Court to its decision in 1973 *still provide the compelling reason* for recognizing the constitutional dimensions of a woman's right to decide whether to end her pregnancy.[146]

Yet the court declined to discuss those constitutional principles in light of the new arguments about the beginning of life; it simply asserted the primacy of *Roe*, mechanically applied the *Roe* framework, and thus declared that Pennsylvania was attempting to intimidate women into continuing their pregnancies. For example, the Court struck down Pennsylvania's informed consent provision on the grounds that it attempted to influence the woman's decision.[147] Rather than using this provision as an opportunity to engage the fetal perspective, the Court simply dismissed Pennsylvania's regulation as "an outright attempt to wedge the Commonwealth's message discouraging abortion into the privacy" between a woman and her physician.[148] Furthermore, citing *Cooper v. Aaron*,[149] the Court argued that it was "sworn to uphold the law even when its content gives rise to bitter dispute."[150]

Unlike the *Thornburgh* majority, Justice White in his dissent was willing to consider arguments that challenged the constitutionality of *Roe*. And unlike the other dissenters (Burger, Rehnquist, and O'Connor), White stated directly that recognizing an interest in potential life throughout pregnancy challenged *Roe*. White claimed that the Court had misinterpreted the Constitution in *Roe* when it declared that state interest in potential life becomes compelling only at viability. He stated that "this venture has been fundamentally misguided since its inception" in *Roe*.[151] Adherence to precedent, or *stare decisis*, is important, White argued, but the Court should correct "constitutional decisions that, on reconsideration, are found to be mistaken."[152]

White used arguments similar to those raised in the human life bill hearings to contest *Roe*'s declaration that state interest in fetal life should become compelling only at viability rather than throughout pregnancy.[153] For example, incorporating new scientific information discussed at the human life bill hearings, White contended that

> however one answers the metaphysical or theological question whether the fetus is a "human being" or the legal question whether it is a "person" as that term is used in the Constitution one must at least recognize, first, that the fetus is an entity that bears in its cells all the genetic information that characterizes a member of the species from all others, and, second, that there is no arbitrary line separating a fetus from a child, or indeed, an adult human being.[154]

Arguing that life is a developmental, not a static, concept, he concluded that despite *Roe*'s statement to the contrary, the Constitution allows states to retain an interest in protecting potential life throughout pregnancy, not just at viability. He claimed that "the state's interest is in the fetus as an entity in itself, and the character of this entity does not change at the point of viability under conventional medical wisdom."[155]

White also argued that if abortion is a fundamental right, it must follow the *Palko-Griswold* line of reasoning about the Fourteenth Amendment's due process clause, which states that all fundamental rights must be necessary to ordered liberty and entrenched in tradition. According to White, the Fourteenth Amendment does not protect the woman's right to abortion since free and egalitarian democratic society does not presuppose the right to choose abortion.[156]

Although White's dissent provided the *Thornburgh* majority with a direct opportunity to acknowledge and engage new arguments about when life begins, the Court reasserted judicial supremacy and used the precedent of *Roe* to dismiss White's challenge without serious con-

sideration. In *Akron*, the majority recognized that scientific developments may have challenged the *Roe* framework. In that case the majority said only that "prudence dictated" continued adherence to *Roe*
despite the new developments. The *Thornburgh* majority made no
such recognition. Justice Stevens, in a concurring opinion, contended
that White's view could not be held without adopting "the religious
view that a fetus is a 'person' . . . [without which] there is a fundamental and well-recognized difference between a fetus and a human being."[157] Stevens asserted that "Justice White is . . . surely wrong in
suggesting that governmental interest in protecting fetal life is
equally compelling during the entire period from the moment of conception until the moment of birth."[158] Stevens reiterated *Roe*'s trimester framework and contended that White's theory abridged it.[159]
Stevens concluded that the Court should strike down the Pennsylvania statute because rather than following the logic of *Roe* by pursuing
legitimate compelling interests, the state "wholly subordinates constitutional privacy interests and concerns with maternal health [to concern for the fetus] in an effort to deter a woman from making a decision that, with her physician, is hers to make."[160]

    Thornburgh suggests a mixed result for departmentalist claims.
The *Thornburgh* majority adhered to the *Roe* framework without addressing new arguments and improving the quality of judicial constitutional interpretation. Yet White's dissent presented new scientific
arguments, reexplored the *Roe* framework, and thus improved the
quality of judicial constitutional interpretation. However, since the
Thornburgh majority refused to recognize these new arguments, it attained only a relatively low, deferring level of constitutional consciousness.

PUBLIC SENSITIVITY AND THE LEVELS
OF CONSTITUTIONAL CONSCIOUSNESS

    Some scholars have argued that improvements in Congress'
constitutional discussion will filter down into the general population
and deepen public awareness and understanding of the different arguments in the abortion debate. Senator East, a leading sponsor of the
human life bill, argued that a broader congressional debate should
broaden the public's debate about abortion. At the conclusion of the
human life bill hearings he stated that "whatever happens, at least we
have been allowed now to begin a public discussion on a very vital,

critical, important matter of moral, ethical, sociological, and economic consequence."[161] East added that, in his judgment, the human life bill hearings made "a very excellent contribution to the public discussion on the matter."[162] Of course, East also intended to encourage public doubt and criticism about *Roe* in order to prompt the Supreme Court to reconsider the decision. He hoped that "one might, through suffi- cient dialog in this country, generate enough consensus and doubt about *Roe v. Wade* that we might find an alternative to it. If these hearings did nothing else I would consider that a positive contribu- tion."[163] Finally, East argued that the legislature, rather than the Court, was best equipped to initiate the public dialogue about abor- tion. He claimed that the legislature could "air these differences [about abortion] and probe public feeling and sentiment on it. . . . I would hope this is the great virtue of the legislative deliberative process."[164]

Senator Baucus, an opponent of the human life bill, also hoped that the hearings would improve the public dialogue about abortion. He thought that Congress' discussion of *Roe* might lessen polarization surrounding the abortion issue and lead the public to consider and en- gage opposing arguments in a sympathetic rather than an adversarial manner. He stated:

> The debate [about abortion] has [often] not been informative, but confrontational. Some of the rhetoric has been inflammatory. Like most highly charged issues, the result has been that public atten- tion has become focused on the actions of those who are advocates of one side or another. These hearings could mark a turning point in the debate on abortion. They could offer an opportunity for a national dialog, a dialog that is responsible, thoughtful, and edu- cational.[165]

For public sensitivity to deepen, respondents would have to indicate a growing understanding of the arguments behind their own positions (the introducing level), an awareness of the arguments grounding the opposition's position (the recognizing level), and a willingness and ability to engage the opposing arguments sympathetically (the engag- ing level). Ideally, survey research would tap each of these three levels of constitutional consciousness with a series of open- and closed-ended questions. Unfortunately, to a great degree available survey research does not focus on the people's awareness and engagement of various arguments in the abortion debate. Most public opinion polls tap respondents' attitudes about *Roe* or about whether abortion should be legal. Rather than exploring whether citizens are following and understanding the public debate about abortion, these surveys ask respondents for their reactions to or feelings about decisions that the Court has already made.[166]

One exception is the National Opinion Research Center's (NORC) General Social Survey of 1982.[167] The survey asked respondents to supply the main arguments for and against abortion. Eighty percent of the respondents were able to supply at least one reason in favor of abortion, 53 percent were able to supply two reasons, and 28 percent were able to supply three reasons. Conversely, 86 percent of the respondents were able to supply at least one reason against abortion, 48 percent were able to supply two reasons, and 14 percent were able to supply three reasons.

Although the NORC survey is important because it suggests, contrary to much scholarly speculation,[168] that most people are fairly aware of different arguments in the public debate about abortion, some problems with the survey remain. First, one cannot determine which respondents favored or opposed abortion. Thus it is impossible to determine whether the NORC results signify awareness of respondents' own arguments, recognition of their opponents' arguments, or both. Furthermore, NORC conducted this survey only in 1982. Therefore, one cannot compare levels of public awareness at various key points in the abortion debate (for example, before and after the human life bill debates). Finally, the NORC survey does not include an item to tap engagement, the highest level of constitutional consciousness.

Other surveys conducted during the departmental period are even less helpful. Rather than tapping public engagement of the various arguments in the abortion debate, they tap public attitudes about whether abortion should be legal. This data may indirectly suggest higher or lower levels of public awareness and engagement. However, because these materials provide information that is only indirectly related to heightened public sensitivity to various arguments in the abortion debate, they should be used cautiously.

One way to use this research is by examining whether respondents with attitudes that began at the polar extremes (abortion should be legal/illegal in all circumstances) change their position during the departmental period, or following Congress' 1981 challenge to judicial supremacy in the human life bill debates. Respondents who previously believed that abortion should be legal in all circumstances should seriously consider arguments that support making abortion illegal in some circumstances. Respondents who previously believed that abortion should be illegal in all circumstances should seriously consider arguments that support making abortion legal in some circumstances. Change of that sort might suggest that respondents who once considered only the fetus' perspective or only the woman's perspective had begun to consider or engage the viability of the opposing perspective. If respondents on the polar extremes of the debate did change attitudes, either by embracing the opposing position or by accepting a move toward the middle (abortion should be legal/illegal under certain circumstances), that might indicate a greater level of public awareness and engagement of the opposing perspective in the debate.

Of course, using survey research materials in this manner remains somewhat problematic. Since these polls directly tap only public attitudes about the legality of abortion, they may conceal deepened public awareness and engagement. Respondents could recognize and engage opposing arguments without necessarily changing their position on the legality of abortion. Furthermore, it is possible, though less likely, that individuals moved between categories even though aggregate percentages remained stable. In sum, the absence of change in attitudes does not necessarily indicate a lack of public awareness or engagement.

In any case, survey research conducted during the departmental period reveals a nearly unwavering level of stability at the polar extremes. Available public opinion polls indicate that attitudes about abortion remained almost absolutely stable throughout the predepartmental and departmental periods (see Table 2.1).

Table 2.1 suggests that, in large part, the movement the departmentalists anticipated toward the middle position (abortion should be legal in some circumstances) did not occur. Percentages in each column remained remarkably stable throughout the period. Respondents who initially thought that abortion should be legal or illegal in all circumstances did not seem to be considering opposing arguments. However, comparing the 1981 and 1983 Gallup polls suggests that, following the human life bill debates, 5 percent of those respondents who previously thought that abortion should be illegal in all circumstances may have been considering selected circumstances in which abortion should be legal. This movement may indicate that a small number of previously extreme respondents may have deepened their sensitivity to new arguments and the opposing perspective in the abortion debate.

Although respondents on the extremes showed little change, polls indicated that respondents who previously were uncertain of their po-

Table 2.1. Attitudes about Abortion in the United States, various years, 1975–1983 (in percentages)

	Legal in All Circumstances	Legal in Some Circumstances[a]	Illegal in All Circumstances	Don't Know
1975	21	54	22	3
1977	22	55	19	4
1979	22	54	19	5
1980	25	53	18	4
1981	23	52	21	4
1983	23	58	16	3

Source: Data compiled from *Gallup Opinion Index*, Reports 178 (June 1980), 190 (February 1981), and 215 (August 1983), published monthly by Gallup Poll, Princeton, N.J. These polls represent a random sampling rather than follow-up interviews with the same group.
[a]Attitude that abortion should be illegal in all but "hard" cases, such as pregnancies due to rape or incestuous rape or pregnancies that would endanger the woman's life.

sition may have been giving more consideration to the legality of abortion for pregnancies connected with "hard" circumstances (see Table 2.2). Since respondents in these polls were asked to indicate whether they favored or opposed *Roe* in the first trimester (the period when states cannot restrict abortion), Table 2.2 can be interpreted as summarizing public attitudes about abortion at the extremes (respondents either favored legal abortion in all circumstances or opposed it in all circumstances—at least in the first trimester). For the most part, Table 2.2 reveals remarkable stability. However, it also shows that a small number of previously undecided respondents changed positions. This may indicate that institutional debates about abortion had some effect on public awareness of various arguments surrounding the issue. But

Table 2.2. Attitudes about *Roe v. Wade* in the United States, various years, 1973–1985 (in percentages)

	Favor	Oppose	Undecided
1973	52	41	7
1975	54	38	8
1976	54	39	7
1977	53	40	7
1979	60	37	3
1981	56	41	3
1985	56	42	2

Source: Data compiled from the Harris Survey, made available by the Roper Center, Storrs, Conn. These polls represent a random sampling rather than follow-up interviews with the same group.

these polls reveal little significant change in the "extreme" attitudes, contrary to departmentalist predictions.

The data in the two tables suggest that the benefits of departmentalism evident at the institutional level may not have filtered down and improved the public debate, again contrary to departmentalist expectations. However, the public opinion did not directly tap public awareness and engagement. Although the available data are inconclusive at best, they may indicate that the improvement in constitutional consciousness found at the institutional level was not significant enough to affect the public debate.

To more adequately address public sensitivity to constitutional issues, survey research should more directly tap whether the public attained the three highest levels of constitutional consciousness, namely introducing, recognizing, and engaging. Such an inquiry could be undertaken as follows. First, respondents would be asked whether they thought that women should have the right to abortion under the U.S. Constitution. Respondents answering "yes" would be coded as favoring the woman's perspective, while "no" answers would be coded as favoring the fetus' perspective. Then, to tap the respondents' ability to recognize the arguments that grounded their own positions (or perhaps to introduce new arguments into the debate), those who favored the woman's perspective would be asked an open-ended question: Why should women have the right to choose abortion under the Constitution? Those who favored the fetus' perspective would be asked: Why should women not have the right to choose abortion under the Constitution? Again to tap the respondents' recognition of the arguments that grounded their own positions, respondents would be asked whether they had heard certain key arguments in the public debate. Those who favored the woman's perspective would be asked whether they had heard that some people thought that women should have a right to choose abortion under the Constitution because they thought that (1) the fetus is not as fully developed a human being as the woman; (2) the Constitution protects the woman's right to privacy; and (3) full equality for women depended on a woman's ability to make choices about when to have children. Those who favored the fetus' perspective would be asked whether they had heard that some people thought that a woman should not have a right to choose abortion under the Constitution because they thought that (1) life begins at conception; (2) the fetus has a right to life; and (3) the Constitution protects all persons, including fetuses.

To explore whether they recognized arguments that grounded their opponents' positions, the respondents would be asked in an open-ended question to identify the arguments that grounded their opposition's position. Those favoring the woman's perspective would be asked whether they had heard any reasons that others have given to support their position that women should not have the right to choose abortion under the Constitution. Those favoring the fetus' position would be asked whether they had heard any reasons that others had given to support their position that women should have the right to choose abortion under the Constitution.

Respondents would then also be asked whether they had certain arguments that grounded their opponents' position. Those favoring the woman's perspective would be asked whether they had heard that some people thought that a woman should not have a right to choose abortion under the Constitution because they thought that (1) life begins at conception; (2) the fetus has a right to life; and (3) the Constitution protects all persons, including fetuses? (Note that these are the same three awareness questions asked earlier of those favoring the fetus' perspective.) Those favoring the fetus' perspective would be asked whether they had heard that some people thought that women should have a right to choose abortion under the Constitution because (1) they thought that the fetus is not as fully developed a human being as the woman; (2) they thought that the Constitution protects the woman's right to privacy; or (3) they thought that full equality for women depended on a woman's ability to make choices about when to have children? (Note that these are the same three awareness questions asked earlier of those favoring the woman's perspective.)

Finally, in order to tap whether respondents were willing and able to engage opposing arguments, respondents would be asked whether they thought certain opposing arguments had any validity. The interviewer would explain that he or she understood that the respondent opposed that position, present two arguments that opposed the respondent's position, and then ask the respondent whether either one had any validity. Those who favored the woman's perspective would be asked the following: (1) Even though you support the woman's right to choose abortion, do you think it makes any sense when others talk about "fetal rights" or "rights of the unborn"? and (2) Even though you support the woman's right to abortion, do you think the woman has any responsibility to consider the potential life or well-being of the fetus when she considers abortion? Those who favored the fetuses perspective would be asked the following: (1) Even though you support the fetus' right to life, do you think denying women the right to choose abortion would in any way limit the ability of women to participate equally in society? and (2) Even though you support the fetus' right to life, do you think that circumstances like a woman's financial situation, life plan, or current relationship with the father should have any influence on her choice?

Until such questions are asked that more directly tap the public's ability to introduce, recognize, and engage arguments in the abortion debate, scholars should not begin to make definitive conclusions about the public's (in)sensitivity to the constitutional dimensions of public issues.

CONCLUSION

When Congress challenged judicial supremacy in a legal and political context previously characterized by judicial activism, constitutional consciousness heightened and constitutional authority broadened. When Congress directly challenged *Roe* in the human life bill hearings by introducing an alternative reading of the Fourteenth Amendment, Congress improved its constitutional consciousness to an introducing level. The Court followed in *Akron* by improving its constitutional consciousness to an even higher, recognizing level. When Congress indirectly challenged *Roe* in the Abortion Funding Restriction Act hearings and failed to introduce an alternative constitutional interpretation to support the challenge, Congress' level of constitutional consciousness fell to a deferring level, as did the Court's in the *Thornburgh* case. The more directly Congress challenged judicial supremacy, the more constitutional authority broadened. Rather than deepening skepticism about constitutional authority or the rule of law, as the detractors of departmentalism predicted, challenging judicial supremacy broadened constitutional authority by locating a common constitutional referent—the Fourteenth Amendment—that began to bridge discussions of women's rights and fetal rights, hitherto conducted in incommensurate terms. Despite this significant broadening of constitutional authority, the debate still remained somewhat intractable since most participants were unwilling to engage opposing arguments in a sympathetic dialogue. It may be that departmentalism practiced in a legal and political context of judicial self-restraint may more readily foster the higher levels of constitutional consciousness. In the next chapter I investigate the debate about the constitutional allocation of the war powers, which took place in a context of judicial self-restraint.

CHAPTER THREE

Departmentalism and Judicial Self-Restraint: The War Powers Debate

JUDICIAL SELF-RESTRAINT AND EXECUTIVE DOMINANCE IN FOREIGN AFFAIRS: POLITICAL AND LEGAL CONTEXT OF THE WAR POWERS

The Supreme Court has in large part restrained itself from adjudicating foreign policy cases—particularly those that raise questions about committing troops to foreign territories. The Court has consistently argued that such cases raise "political questions" that are "nonjusticiable," or beyond judicial scrutiny.[1] Early on, the Court developed the political question doctrine and argued that the political branches alone (the executive and Congress) should cooperatively address foreign policy concerns.[2] In the modern era, particularly after World War II, the executive branch came to largely dominate decisions about foreign affairs and military commitments.

Executive dominance became pronounced as the United States became a world power in the twentieth century.[3] When the Court applied the political question doctrine in the modern period, the doctrine often served to uphold both executive supremacy in foreign affairs and the executive's decision in each particular case. Although in theory the political question doctrine supported the idea that the president and Congress would cooperatively decide questions about foreign affairs and troop commitments, in practice the doctrine led to executive dominance. As the executive began to dominate troop commitment decisions and Congress began to withdraw, the Supreme Court's political question doctrine had the practical effect of supporting executive preeminence.[4] More recently, in *Goldwater v. Carter*,[5] the Court rejected

Senator Barry Goldwater's argument that it was unconstitutional for President Carter to terminate the United States–Taiwan Mutual Defense Treaty without Senate approval, using the political question doctrine in a manner that supported executive dominance in foreign affairs.

In *Crockett v. Reagan*[6] a federal court used the political question doctrine again to uphold the executive's decisions. Twenty-nine members of Congress sought declaratory judgments regarding President Reagan, Secretary of State Alexander Haig, and Secretary of Defense Caspar Weinberger's support for military assistance to El Salvador despite Congress' statements to the contrary in the War Powers Act and the Foreign Assistance Act. Even though the Court found that congressional authorization of such acts had to be specific rather than inferred, it declared the issue nonjusticiable, claiming that it could become justiciable if Congress specifically required the president either to report his actions in El Salvador to Congress or to withdraw U.S. forces immediately. Similarly, in *Sanchez-Espinoza v. Reagan*,[7] several legislators, as well as citizens of Nicaragua and Florida, argued that the executive's actions to subvert the Nicaraguan government abridged the War Powers Act. The lower court dismissed the case through the political question doctrine. In *Lowry v. Reagan*[8] 110 members of Congress requested a declaratory judgment that would obligate the president to comply with the War Powers Act by formally reporting troop movement into the Persian Gulf in 1987. Again the Court used the political question doctrine to reject the request.

Occasionally the Court went further and actively supported executive dominance by arguing that the president did and should dominate foreign policy decision making—as, for example, in *U.S. v. Curtiss-Wright*.[9] In that case, the Court declared that the president "is the sole organ of the federal government in the field of international relations—a power which does not require as a basis for its exercise an act of Congress."[10] However, such direct statements are actually exceptions to the Court's general policy of adhering steadfastly to the political question doctrine. In either case, however, the result is the same: judicial support for executive supremacy.

More specifically, judicial self-restraint and the application of the political question doctrine to cases that challenged the legality of the Vietnam War had the effect of upholding the president's decisions to continue escalating American involvement. The Supreme Court consistently refused to grant certiorari to suits contesting the war's constitutionality. For example, in *Mora v. McNamara*[11] the Court refused to review a case in which draftees challenged the legality of U.S. military involvement in Vietnam. In their dissents, Justices Stewart and Douglas claimed that the Supreme Court should examine whether American involvement in Vietnam was a war within the meaning of Article I, Section 8, of the Constitution and whether the executive could constitutionally order draftees to participate if Congress had not declared war.[12]

On the lower federal level, the courts ruled that Congress had acquiesced to the president's decision to escalate the war. For example, in *Velvel v. Johnson*[13] a district court rejected the notion that Congress had been forced against its better judgment to appropriate money for military operations in Vietnam. *Berk v. Laird*[14] also said that Congress acquiesced in continuing the war. In *Orlando v. Laird*,[15] a case in which soldiers attacked the authority of the executive to wage war in Vietnam, the lower court said: "As we see it, the test is whether there is any action by the Congress sufficient to authorize or ratify the military activity in question."[16] It argued that Congress had authorized the war through the Tonkin Gulf Resolution and through continued appropriations. The lower court therefore concluded that "the war in Vietnam is a product of the jointly supportive actions of the two branches to whom the congeries of the war powers have been committed. Because the branches are not in opposition, there is no necessity of determining boundaries."[17] A few decisions indicated that congressional authorization in such matters was difficult to determine indirectly. For example, in *Mitchell v. Laird* the judiciary said that Congress' decision to continue funding the war effort may indicate its reluctance to abandon previously committed troops rather than a desire to continue to support or even to have begun the war.[18] In *Atlee v. Laird* the judiciary also said that congressional intent regarding the war could not be inferred from funding decisions.[19] Nevertheless, these decisions must be understood as exceptions. Generally, the federal judiciary claimed that Congress had clearly committed itself to the president's decision to escalate the war.

CONGRESS CHALLENGES JUDICIAL SUPREMACY
AND EXECUTIVE DOMINANCE:
THE WAR POWERS RESOLUTION

In a climate of judicial self-restraint and executive dominance, Congress challenged executive preeminence in foreign affairs.

Toward the end of American military involvement in Southeast Asia, the congressional-executive consensus on containment broke down. The War Powers Act, Congress' initial departmental challenge to executive supremacy in foreign policy matters, was a product of that breakdown, as well as a reaction to the unilateral and unlimited power that the executive had used to pursue containment goals. With containment an apparent failure and President Nixon ordering secret bombing raids on Cambodia without congressional support, Congress sought a more effective way to check unlimited and unauthorized uses of executive power regarding military commitments. First, on January 12, 1971, Congress repealed the Tonkin Gulf Resolution.[20] Even more important, in 1973, Congress adopted the War Powers Act over Nixon's veto.[21]

The War Powers Act contains several provisions that challenge executive supremacy in foreign affairs and that aim to reintegrate Congress into decision making about military commitments and troop movements. Section 8(a) challenged the judicial rulings that sustained the constitutionality of the Vietnam War by inferring congressional support from appropriations and other forms of support for previously committed troops. It states that congressional authorization to introduce troops into hostilities should not be inferred from any laws or treaties unless they expressly authorize such commitments.[22] Furthermore, the War Powers Act (or Resolution) states that the president, in every possible instance, must consult with Congress before introducing troops into hostilities.[23] The War Powers Resolution also requires the president to report any troop commitments to Congress within forty-eight hours.[24] Finally, the Resolution states that the president must terminate the use of military force in sixty days if Congress does not declare war or extend the sixty-day period by law.[25] The president can extend the sixty-day period up to thirty days, as necessary, to withdraw troops.[26] However, Congress at any time may pass a concurrent resolution that directs the president to remove armed forces from foreign lands.[27]

Although the War Powers Act states that it does not alter the constitutional authority of the president and Congress, its preamble takes for granted Congress' power to interpret the constitutional allocation of war powers.[28] Furthermore, the act's leading sponsors understood themselves to be repudiating a long-standing precedent of executive dominance in foreign affairs. Some sponsors contended that the framers intended for the Constitution to place the war powers under congressional control. Section 2(a) of the act states:

It is the purpose of this joint resolution to fulfill the interest of the framers of the Constitution of the United States and insure that the collective judgment of both the Congress and the President will apply to the introduction of the United States Armed Forces into hostilities, or into situations where imminent involvement in hostilities is clearly indicated by the circumstances, and to the continued use of such forces in hostilities or in such situations.[29]

Several other sections of the War Powers Act emphasize congressional power. Section 2(b) notes that the necessary and proper clause gives Congress the power to make all laws necessary and proper for carrying its own powers into execution, as well as the powers of other officers or departments. Section 2(c) limits the commander in chief's power to introduce forces into hostilities to situations where there is "(1) a declaration of war, (2) specific statutory authorization, or (3) a national emergency created by attack."[30]

In the War Powers Act Congress challenges the executive's interpretation of the Constitution. Congress passed the act over President Nixon's veto. Nixon expressly argued that he had vetoed the act because it infringed on the president's ability to fulfill his responsibility to faithfully execute the laws, defend the country from foreign invasion, and uphold the Constitution. Furthermore, every president since Nixon has resisted the War Powers Act by claiming that Article II, Section 2, of the Constitution—the commander in chief clause—grants the president a wider authority than the War Powers Act.[31] However, no president has *formally* declared the act unconstitutional and nonbinding on the executive, and various presidential advisers have conceded that it is "the law of the land."[32]

Furthermore, presidents have frequently reported their actions in a manner that seems quite consistent with the War Powers Resolution. However, they all claimed that their actions and reporting stemmed from their constitutional authority as commander in chief rather than from a statutory obligation created by the War Powers Resolution. For example, when President Ford committed armed forces to Da Nang to evacuate Vietnamese and American citizens, when he used military forces to evacuate refugees from Saigon and Phnom Penh, and when he used armed forces to liberate the USS *Mayaguez* from Cambodia in 1975, he reported those troop commitments to Congress. After each incident, Ford claimed that his actions were supported by the Constitution—that they were "undertaken pursuant to the President's constitutional authority as commander in chief and chief executive in the conduct of foreign relations."[33] He also noted that he was reporting to Congress "in accordance with [his] desire to keep the Congress fully informed on this matter, and taking note of Sec. 4(a) (2) of the War Powers Resolution."[34] When President Carter sent American military equipment to aid in the evacuation of American citizens from Zaire in 1977 and when he used the military in an attempt to rescue American hostages from Iran in 1980, he also argued that his actions and his subsequent reports to Congress flowed from his constitutional authority as commander in chief.[35]

In 1981 President Reagan introduced military advisers into El Salvador without reporting to Congress; in 1982 he committed armed forces to Lebanon without reporting initially, and he committed forces to the Sinai without consulting Congress; in 1983 he invaded Grenada and sent troops to Chad without consulting Congress; in 1986 he used force against Libya without consulting Congress; and in 1987 he sent forces into the Persian Gulf without consulting Congress. Following each incident, Reagan argued that he had acted on the basis of "the President's constitutional authority with respect to the conduct of foreign relations and as Commander in Chief of the United States Armed Forces."[36] When he chose to report his actions to Congress, he noted that he did so on the basis of his constitutional authority, not because of any statutory obligation. Reagan consistently stated that he reported to Congress "in accordance with [his] desire that Congress be informed on this matter and consistent with the War Powers Resolution."[37]

In sum, the disagreement between the executive and Congress about the Constitution's allocation of the war powers continues, with the Court remaining steadfast in its contention that the war powers issue is a "political question." It refuses to address such questions until Congress and the executive have exhausted all possible alternatives that the political process makes available to them to express and resolve disagreement on these matters.[38]

THE TONKIN GULF PERIOD

On August 2, 1964, several North Vietnamese patrol boats attacked the USS *Maddox*, an American destroyer routinely patroling in international waters along North Vietnam's Tonkin Gulf. On August 3, President Johnson publicly announced that the *Maddox* had been attacked in international waters, that it had counterfired in self-defense, and that he had repositioned naval vessels in the region. Johnson instructed the USS *C. Turner Joy* and protective aircraft to join the *Maddox* and to "attack any force that attacks them."[39] Johnson also sent a note of protest to North Vietnam.[40] Finally, Johnson promised that North Vietnam would suffer grave consequences if it chose to undertake another unprovoked attack against the United States on the high seas.

On August 4, the North Vietnamese allegedly attacked the *Maddox* again. Whether this second attack actually occurred remains a matter of controversy. Francis Wormuth and Edwin Firmage note that the administration's contentions about the attack were never verified. They state: "On August 2 and 4, 1964, according to announcements by the Johnson administration—which the Senate Committee on Foreign Relations was later unable to verify—North Vietnamese torpedo boats made futile attacks on two American destroyers in the Gulf of Tonkin."[41] Larry Berman clarifies this point by arguing that "considerable doubt exists as to whether this second 'attack' even took place. While there is little doubt that North Vietnamese gunboats were operating in the area, weather conditions were so bad and tensions aboard ship so high that Johnson later quipped, 'For all I know, our Navy was shooting at whales out there.' "[42] Stanley Karnow uses even stronger language: "Subsequent research by both official and unofficial investigations has indicated with almost total certainty that the second communist attack in the Tonkin Gulf never happened."[43]

However, during congressional hearings, Robert McNamara, Johnson's secretary of defense, continued to maintain that he had seen "unimpeachable" proof of Communist plans to attack the *Maddox*. McNamara added that he could not reveal that proof for national security reasons.[44] Karnow concludes that the attack was not deliberately faked, but that the administration seized the alleged incident to obtain passage of the Tonkin Gulf Resolution and thus wide discretionary power for the president to use subsequently in Vietnam. Berman confirms that the resolution was discussed and drafted in a National Security Council meeting two months before the *Maddox* incident. Like Karnow, Berman argues that the incident provided Johnson with an opportunity to secure the passage of the Tonkin Gulf Resolution.[45]

In any case, the *Maddox* and the *C. Turner Joy* counterfired, sinking two North Vietnamese ships and severely damaging a third. The president and his principal advisers argued that North Vietnam had deliberately attacked American ships in international waters without provocation. For their part, the North Vietnamese later claimed that

South Vietnam had attacked them first, provoking them into attacking the *Maddox* since the United States had been aiding South Vietnam in previous attacks on North Vietnam and since American ships
had been sighted in the region of the South Vietnamese attack. However, McGeorge Bundy claimed that the *Maddox* was patroling at least
100 miles away; thus, even if South Vietnam had attacked North Vietnam, the United States had not provoked anything.[46]

On August 4, Johnson announced to high-ranking Democratic legislators that North Vietnam had attacked the *Maddox* a second time,
that he had decided to retaliate, and that he was about to ask Congress for a resolution supporting his actions. According to Karnow,
"Not a congressman present demurred."[47] The American retaliatory
attack destroyed or severely damaged twenty-five vessels and a major
oil storage depot. In the exchange, four North Vietnamese patrol boats
destroyed two American aircraft and damaged two other planes.[48]
Johnson announced the retaliation to the nation while the attack was
taking place. At that time he said: "Repeated acts of violence must be
met not only with alert defense, but with positive reply. That reply is
being given as I speak to you tonight."[49]

Executive Interpretation of the War Powers:
The Tonkin Gulf Resolution

On August 5, Johnson's Tonkin Gulf Resolution was introduced in Congress. Accompanying the resolution was a presidential
message entitled, "To Promote the Maintenance of International
Peace and Security in South East Asia." In it Johnson reminded Congress that he had spoken to the American people about North Vietnam's unprovoked attack against the United States in international
waters and about his decision to retaliate.[50] The Tonkin Gulf Resolution broadly interpreted the president's power to commit troops to foreign countries. It stated "that the Congress approves and supports the
determination of the President, as Commander in Chief, to take all
necessary measures to repel any armed attack against the forces of
the United States and to prevent further aggression."[51] Section 2 of
the resolution recognized the president's power to determine the extent of American military commitments: "Consonant with the Constitution . . . the United States is, therefore, prepared, *as the President
determines*, to take all necessary steps, including the use of armed
force" to assist foreign countries that request aid to defend their freedom.[52] Furthermore, Section 3 allowed the president to determine the

duration of American military commitments. The resolution would expire after the president had determined that the "peace and security of the area is reasonably assured."[53] Because the Tonkin Gulf Resolution seems to have allowed the executive to act unilaterally in military matters, his broad presidential powers would probably conflict with Congress' power to declare war.[54] Yet Section 3 also stipulated that Congress could, by concurrent resolution, terminate the Tonkin Gulf Resolution at any time.

On August 6, two representatives of the Johnson administration, Secretary of State Dean Rusk and Secretary of Defense McNamara, testified before the Senate Foreign Relations and the House Armed Forces subcommittees about the North Vietnamese attack, the American retaliation, and the Tonkin Gulf Resolution. The joint subcommittees reported the Tonkin Gulf Resolution favorably to the whole Congress. As chairperson of the Committee on Foreign Relations, Senator J. William Fulbright (D-Ark.), recommended "prompt and overwhelming endorsement" of the resolution, the "wise and necessary action of President Johnson," and future American retaliation against Communist aggression and violations of international law.[55] By a 502 to 2 vote, Congress approved the Tonkin Gulf Resolution on August 7.[56] President Johnson signed the bill into law on August 10.[57]

Johnson argued that the commander in chief clause[58] granted the president sole authority and responsibility to respond to North Vietnam's attack.[59] He claimed that only the president was empowered to make decisions about defensive military commitments. As commander in chief, Johnson doubled air and naval patroling in the Tonkin Gulf. He also ordered commanders to defend their vessels and to counterattack if they were fired upon. He argued: "As Commander in Chief, the responsibility was mine—and mine alone [to respond to the unprovoked aggression]. I gave the orders for [a prompt and unmistakable] reply, and it has been given."[60] Secretary of State Rusk agreed, arguing that the Tonkin Gulf Resolution would "declare the approval and support of the Congress for actions, in response to armed attack on United States forces, which the President has the authority and obligation to take in his capacity as Commander in Chief."[61] Rusk added that the Tonkin Gulf Resolution would "confirm and reinforce the powers of the Presidency."[62]

Apart from the discussion of the commander in chief clause, the executive branch engaged in very little, if any, additional discussion about the constitutional allocation of the war powers.[63] The executive did not discuss Congress' constitutional responsibility or authority in these matters. For his part, President Johnson asserted that the Tonkin Gulf Resolution "stands squarely with the four corners of the Constitution of the United States."[64] However, he did not provide additional arguments to support that statement. Rather, he and his administration contended that precedent supported the Tonkin Gulf Resolution's wide view of presidential power. Before Congress, Rusk argued that it was unnecessary to discuss the constitutional dimensions surrounding the Tonkin Gulf Resolution—at least to respond defensively to unprovoked attacks. He stated:

> I shall not take your time this morning to review the constitutional appeals or resolutions of this character. I believe it to be the generally accepted constitutional view that the President has the constitutional authority to take at least limited armed action in defense of American national interests; in at least eighty-five instances, Presidents of the United States have in fact taken such action.[65]

Rusk was correct in asserting that it was generally accepted that the president should be able to defend the country against attacks. However, the Tonkin Gulf Resolution's understanding of presidential power extended beyond self-defense to committing armed forces to war—in a manner that later appeared to conflict with Article I, Section 8, of the Constitution, which granted Congress the power to declare war.

Rusk also claimed that previous resolutions, such as the 1955 Formosa Resolution, the 1957 Middle East Resolution, and the 1962 Cuba Resolution, established a precedent of broad presidential powers in foreign affairs. He stated: "There can be no doubt . . . that these previous resolutions form a solid legal precedent for the action now proposed."[66] He added that the aforementioned precedents recognized the president's power "to take all necessary steps including the use of armed force."[67]

However, the Tonkin Gulf Resolution signaled a narrower role for Congress in making decisions about troop commitments. In the earlier resolutions, the president had asked Congress to authorize, not simply approve and support, his actions. As Jean Smith states: "This change in wording reflected more than presidential predilections; it involved a fundamental shift in the role of Congress."[68] Thus the Tonkin Gulf Resolution indicated that Congress approved and supported, rather than authorized, Johnson's decision. In this light, Johnson said that he had requested the Tonkin Gulf Resolution so that Congress could "express . . . the support . . . for all necessary action to protect our Armed Forces and to assist nations covered by the SEATO [Southeast Asia Treaty Organization] Treaty."[69]

Rusk contended further that the Tonkin Gulf Resolution recognized that broad presidential power and discretion was necessary to battle Communist aggression in Southeast Asia, as well as to contain the spread of Communism generally. In 1947 President Truman introduced the containment doctrine, which subsequent presidents, such as Johnson, followed. Containment policy sought to build "situations of strength" around the globe in order to contain Soviet power and the spread of communism. In this case, the Johnson administration was trying to build South Vietnam into a situation of strength.

Johnson and Rusk claimed that Communist aggression had prompted the United States to retaliate and had created a need for the Tonkin Gulf Resolution so that the president could continue to respond firmly to aggression, thereby containing the Communist threat. Johnson argued that the United States had not provoked North Vietnam's aggression, that the attack was part of a long-term Communist plan of aggression, and that it was illegal since the *Maddox* and the *C. Turner Joy* had been patroling on the high seas.[70] He further contended that the attack had violated nonaggression and collective defense pacts such as the 1954 Geneva Accords and the 1962 Laos Agreement, even though the United States was not a party to those agreements. Since North Vietnam was not willing to abide by the agreements, Johnson concluded that peace would require a firm response to North Vietnamese aggression.

Thus Rusk and Johnson concluded that an increased American military presence in the region would deter rather than provoke further Communist aggression. Johnson claimed that his administration would not use the Tonkin Gulf Resolution to broaden the war, but only to show North Vietnam and the Soviet Union that the United States was "united in its determination" to contain and then end Communist aggression in Southeast Asia.[71]

Although Johnson argued that the president alone possessed power to act, he did afford Congress the opportunity to approve his actions. He stated: "As President, there rested upon me still another responsibility—the responsibility of submitting our course to the representatives of the people, for them to verify it or veto it."[72] However, Johnson did not ask for congressional authorization of his actions. He argued only that congressional support was necessary to show congressional-executive unity to contain Communist aggression. He did not recognize any need to integrate Congress into the foreign policy decision-making process independent of a need to display a unified front. Claiming that the Tonkin Gulf Resolution would display unified congressional and presidential support for containing communism, and for establishing peace in the region, Johnson concluded that the resolution would show "all the world the unity of all Americans, to defend our own forces, to prevent aggression, and to work firmly and steadily for peace and security in this area."[73]

The Deferring Level: Congress Relinquishes
Responsibility and Accepts Executive Supremacy

President Johnson contended that after the administration submitted the Tonkin Gulf Resolution to Congress, "in each House there followed serious debate."[74] In reality, most members of Congress supported Johnson's Vietnam policy and accepted the Tonkin Gulf Resolution with little or no independent probing or consideration. They seemed to agree that the president did not need congressional authorization to commit military forces to Vietnam. However, during the Tonkin Gulf period, most members also supported the containment doctrine and accepted many of the "containing" goals behind Johnson's Vietnam policy. Thus congressional support for Johnson's actions may have indicated agreement about goals rather than simply deference to seemingly unlimited presidential power in foreign affairs. Congress' broad consensus about the goals of containment may have masked potential disagreement between Congress and the executive about the constitutional extent of presidential power being used to pursue those goals. Many representatives may have supported the Tonkin Gulf Resolution and its broad interpretation of presidential power because they thought that congressional-executive unity was necessary to battle Communist aggression effectively.

As noted earlier, the Johnson administration argued that the Tonkin Gulf Resolution's broad interpretation of presidential power would further several goals, such as repelling Communist and North Vietnamese attacks, maintaining the freedom of international waters, maintaining international peace, preventing further North Vietnamese and Communist aggression against neighbors and allies, and assisting Southeast Asia in protecting individual freedoms and self-determination. Senators William Fulbright (D-Ark.), Thomas Dodd (D-Conn.), George Smathers (D-Fla.), Strom Thurmond (D-S.C.), and

Frank Lausche (D-Ohio) accepted and reiterated the administration's key points about the *Maddox* incident and the need for the Tonkin Gulf Resolution. For example, Fulbright agreed that the United States intended to maintain international law, to respond to repeated Communist aggression with force when necessary, to uphold the Geneva Agreements, to protect vital American interests, to fulfill its obligation to Southeast Asian allies and partners, and to maintain Indochinese sovereignty against Communist threats.[75] Repeating the administration's contention that the United States was not interested in creating a new military or political sphere of influence, Fulbright indicated that he accepted the president's assertion that he had increased American troops in the region to counter the threat of heightened Communist aggression.[76] Fulbright also accepted that American resolve would deter future Communist incursions. He stated that the Tonkin Gulf Resolution "is designed to shatter whatever illusions our adversaries may harbor about the determination of the United States to act promptly and vigorously against aggression."[77]

Dodd, Smathers, and Thurmond supported the Tonkin Gulf Resolution because it affirmed the unlimited presidential power that the administration claimed was necessary to deter Communist aggression and uphold freedom. They appeared to support the Tonkin Gulf Resolution's containment goals as well as its broad grant of presidential power as a means to obtain those goals. This type of congressional response illustrates the difficulty of distinguishing adherence to containment from self-conscious deference to executive supremacy. However, the fact remains that each of these senators failed to challenge the seemingly unlimited powers that the Tonkin Gulf Resolution granted to the president to pursue containment goals.

Dodd argued that Johnson should possess whatever power is necessary to defend the freedom of the seas and to respond to Communist aggression. He contended that the United States needed to show the Communists that it was neither a "paper tiger" nor in an indecisive pre-election period. Thus he concluded: "I hope that Congress will move immediately to record its support for the action taken by President Johnson."[78] Smathers also argued that Congress should support the president's use of any means necessary to defend freedom and oppose Communist aggression.[79] Thurmond supported the Tonkin Gulf Resolution as a means of winning the war against international communism.[80]

For Lausche, since North Vietnam had attacked an American ship in international waters, the president had no choice but to retaliate.[81]

Yet Lausche conceded that alternatives to the military solution existed, thereby seeming to affirm the possibility of choice. For example, he noted that the West, Communists, and neutrals could form a three-headed coalition government. However, Lausche argued, because the Communists have always managed to gain control of such governments, and because they could not be trusted to keep either the spirit or the letter of their promises (as evidenced by their abridging the 1954 Indochina and 1962 Laos Accords), he would not trust them to participate fairly in a coalition government. Therefore, he concluded, the president's only viable choice was a forced one, namely retaliatory attack.[82]

Several members of Congress—for example, Senators Hubert Humphrey (D-Minn.) and Harvey Kuchel (D-Calif.)—accepted and reiterated Johnson's argument that the Formosa and Middle East resolutions had established solid precedent for the Tonkin Gulf Resolution.[83]

A more self-conscious acceptance of executive supremacy can be distinguished from consensus about containment in several other responses to the Tonkin Gulf Resolution. Several legislators said explicitly that Congress need not or should not discuss the scope of executive power contained in the resolution. Although these representatives supported Johnson's containment policy, they also believed that Congress need not be concerned that the Tonkin Gulf Resolution recognized seemingly unlimited presidential power as a means to further containment goals. Senators Fulbright, Thurmond, Kuchel, Hugh Scott (R-Penn.), Everett Dirksen (R-Ill.), and Bourke Hickenlooper (R-Iowa) and Representative Robert Kastenmeier (D-Wis.) accepted the Tonkin Gulf Resolution because it affirmed Johnson's broad discretionary power as commander in chief to commit armed forces to Southeast Asia. Some cited the Constitution to support the broad grant of presidential power, but none considered Congress' constitutional powers and responsibilities.

Fulbright, who shepherded the Tonkin Gulf Resolution through Congress for Johnson, noted that the resolution did not limit the president's discretionary power to commit American forces to Vietnam. He stated: "This provision is intended to give clearance to the President to use his discretion. We are not giving to the President any powers he has under the Constitution as Commander in Chief. We are in effect approving of his use of the powers that he has."[84] Fulbright affirmed Johnson's assertion that the president alone should judge whether an increased number of troops should be sent to foreign countries. He argued: "Whether or not that should ever be done is a matter of [the president's] wisdom under the circumstances that exist at the particular time it is contemplated."[85] Scott also supported the resolution's recognition of seemingly unlimited presidential power. He "was glad to hear . . . there is nothing in the resolution which limits the right of the President to repel any attacks or prevent further aggression within areas described in the resolution."[86]

Contending that executive supremacy had characterized foreign affairs for years, Thurmond argued that "the approval and support which the Congress now expresses for the President to take necessary measures to repel any armed attack is not new. This authority the President now has, and indeed he has been exercising this authority" in Southeast Asia all along.[87] Dirksen agreed that the president did not need congressional authority to commit armed forces to foreign lands. He argued that "the President could have taken this action in his own right as the Commander in Chief. He does not have to ask Congress about the deployment of troops, submarines, or fighter planes."[88] However, Dirksen contended, congressional support for Johnson was now necessary because the United States needed to show the Communists that Congress and the executive were unified in their intent to meet further aggression with firm resolve and retaliation. Unity, he argued, would deter further aggression.

Kastenmeier claimed that "the Chief Executive *alone* can conduct and coordinate our foreign policy in time of overseas crisis."[89] Also arguing that the president did not need to consult with Congress to commit troops, Hickenlooper claimed, "In this case there is not the slightest question in my mind that the President not only has full authority but has a responsibility to protect American institutions and interests when they are attacked, without having to come to the Congress for that authority."[90] Kuchel argued that passage of the Tonkin Gulf Resolution showed congressional support for Johnson's use of preexisting presidential power. He contended that Congress had "been called upon to recognize and to confirm in the President the authority, the duty, and the responsibility resting in him to take such steps as he deems appropriate under our Constitution to defend our country and our people, and to discharge America's solemn obligations as they may arise through our agreements for collective security."[91]

Several members of Congress contended that Congress had no general responsibility to participate in the making of foreign policy. For example, Fulbright and Senator Mike Mansfield (D-Mont.) argued that Congress' role in foreign policy was small at best. Fulbright noted that although Johnson consulted Congress regularly about important foreign policy matters, he was under no obligation to do so. Mansfield agreed: "We know that he is accustomed to consulting with the Joint Chiefs of Staff and with congressional leaders. But he does not have to do that."[92] Arguing that Congress' role in forming foreign policy was limited and advisory rather than a full or active partnership, Fulbright claimed that in foreign affairs the executive submits information to Congress, Congress advises the executive, "and that is *all*. We cannot direct or force [the executive]. . . . [O]ur role is of an advisory nature."[93] Fulbright noted that previous administrations had consistently reported and briefed Congress. Thus, he concluded, Johnson would include Congress in all major policy decisions. Fulbright asserted that he had "no doubt that the President will consult with Congress in case a major change in present policy becomes necessary."[94] Clearly, however, that decision would be made at Johnson's discretion.

Some legislators, including Senators Daniel Brewster (D-Md.), John Cooper (R-Ky.), George McGovern (D-S.D.), Gaylord Nelson (D-Wis.), and Allen Ellender (D-La.), signaled that they were inclined to challenge executive supremacy by debating the scope of executive power recognized in the Tonkin Gulf Resolution. This suggests that these men were aware of Congress' responsibility to challenge unlimited executive power and participate in important foreign policy decision making. However, their reluctance to sustain that line of questioning under pressure from strong supporters of the resolution suggests that agreement about substantive foreign policy ends outweighed their initial concern that the president should pursue those ends through limited, constitutional means.

For example, although Nelson supported the goals of containment, he did not want Congress to affirm, even if inadvertently, any "radical change in our mission or objective in South Vietnam," especially regarding landing armed forces.[95] Thus he considered introducing an amendment to the Tonkin Gulf Resolution that would have limited the president's ability to involve the United States in direct military combat in Southeast Asia without congressional approval. However, he never introduced this amendment because Fulbright persuaded him that the Tonkin Gulf Resolution was a moderate measure "calculated to prevent the spread of war." Fulbright added: "The last thing we want to do is become involved in a land war in Asia."[96] Fulbright was able to silence Nelson by arguing that united congressional support for Johnson and the Tonkin Gulf Resolution was necessary to counter Communist aggression effectively.

Similarly, Brewster wondered "whether there is anything in the resolution which would authorize or recommend or approve the landing of large American armies in Vietnam or in China."[97] Fulbright told him that Congress did not specifically intend to allow the executive to decide to commit new American forces to Southeast Asia without congressional participation. However, he added, since the Tonkin Gulf Resolution recognized vast presidential discretionary power, the executive could unilaterally commit new forces. Fulbright stated that there "is nothing in the Resolution, as I read it, that contemplates it. . . . However, the language of the Resolution would not prevent it. It would authorize whatever the Commander in Chief feels necessary."[98]

Cooper also questioned the extent of Congress' delegation of power. He asked Fulbright whether Congress was "giving the President advance authority to take whatever action he may deem necessary" regarding Southeast Asia. When Fulbright affirmed Cooper's suspicion, Cooper asked whether Congress would be delegating to the president the power to enter war. Fulbright again answered "yes." Neither Cooper nor Brewster further challenged the constitutionality of that interpretation of presidential power. Backing away from the implication that the broad grant of presidential power in the Tonkin Gulf Resolution conflicted with Congress' power to declare war, Cooper agreed that the Tonkin Gulf Resolution simply recognized that the president possessed the power to undertake any measures necessary to the nation's self-defense. He stated: "That is his [the president's] right and authority. If we have any power to confirm it, we do confirm it. We support him in his power to protect the security of our country and its honor."[99] As with Nelson, Fulbright succeeded in silencing Brewster and Cooper by arguing that questioning was divisive and that congressional-executive unity was necessary to maintain peace.

In similar fashion, Senator Frank Church (D-Ida.) persuaded Humphrey that congressional-executive unity was necessary to counter Communist aggression and that congressional questioning would threaten that unity. Church initially affirmed Congress' right and obligation to challenge executive policy. He stated that "there is not only a time, but there is an obligation on the part of the members of this Body to question policy, to express concern if we have a doubt, or to express approval."[100] However, he contended, although he had debated the administration's Southeast Asian policy in the past, the time to question "has passed. . . . [T]he President has a responsibility and the Congress has the duty to insist that our nation's right of protection from aggression will be observed."[101]

Senators Hickenlooper and Frank Carlson (R-Kans.) also argued that further debate about presidential power would be divisive and counterproductive and that the resolution would and should preempt further discussion. Thus Hickenlooper contended that "the use of American force may give rise to some persuasive arguments, perhaps on both sides of the question. However, a resolution of this kind fore-closes that argument and joins Congress with the President of the United States in unity."[102] Carlson also called for an end to congressional questioning of the president's Vietnam policy. He argued that a strong foreign policy required congressional-executive unity and that that unity required congressional support of the executive.[103]

In the face of majority pressure to discontinue debate, legislators who at first appeared willing to question the executive backed down from even mild questioning and asserted support for the Tonkin Gulf Resolution and Johnson's Vietnam policy. They frequently contended that their initial questioning had been fueled by a desire to engender wider congressional support for Johnson's policy rather than by a will-ingness to challenge the resolution's grant of broad presidential power or Johnson's Vietnam policy. When Ellender asked whether American naval and air presence in the region might have provoked North Viet-nam's attacks on the *Maddox* and the *C. Turner Joy*,[104] Fulbright in-sisted that the United States had not been provocative. Ellender im-mediately rescinded the question, saying that the United States was not at fault, that international law allowed the United States to patrol the Tonkin Gulf, and that American actions had not been provoca-tive.[105]

Furthermore, when McGovern questioned why North Vietnam would provoke the United States, Fulbright answered that although General Nguyen Khanh wanted to spread the war to the north, the Johnson administration had repeatedly rejected that route, preferring to concentrate on defeating guerrillas in the south. McGovern then asked Fulbright whether the resolution might escalate the war and thus increase American military involvement in Vietnam. Without elaboration or explanation, Fulbright answered "no."[106] McGovern then abandoned his challenge and agreed with Fulbright that the United States had no intention of increasing its military commitment to Vietnam, adding: "I did not want my remarks [that is, his question-ing of long-range American military plans] to be interpreted as preju-dicing the case for aid."[107]

Other members of Congress argued specifically against challenging the president's decision to send armed forces to foreign lands once troops had been committed. For example, Church argued that once troops were committed, Congress needed to support them through continued funding. However, he added, continued funding would signal Congress' acquiescence to the president's initial decision to commit troops, as well as Congress' partial responsibility for that decision. Church concluded that Congress and the executive had jointly committed the American military to Vietnam and should continue to fund the effort rather than abandon, and thus demoralize, the troops. Contending that U.S. policy in Southeast Asia "is more the product of our own addiction to an ideological view of world affairs" than a policy in the national interest, Church nevertheless felt compelled to support American troops already in Vietnam.[108]

Here Church raised a very important issue: the withdrawal dilemma. Although Congress might oppose Johnson's decision to escalate the war, it would be impossible for that body to effectively challenge him without endangering previously committed forces. Thus Congress' reluctance to discontinue funding the war for fear of endangering American soldiers in the region was interpreted by the judicial and executive branches as support for containment and for escalating the conflict.

One group of representatives stated that they disagreed completely with the policy of containment, but that they would defer to the executive's use of power in Vietnam. Senator George Aiken (R-Vt.), for example, seemed inclined to accept that Congress had some responsibility to participate meaningfully in important foreign policy decisions. However, at this point in the Vietnam conflict, a wider role for Congress in decision making was impossible or impracticable.[109] Aiken contended that Congress over the last several years had slowly relinquished responsibility for foreign policy decisions to the president. Thus, he concluded, Congress had no choice but to support the president even if it found the administration's Vietnam policy questionable.

In sum, the Tonkin Gulf period was characterized by congressional support for the substantive goals of Johnson's containment policy. Several members of Congress failed to actively review the Tonkin Gulf Resolution's grant of seemingly unlimited executive power. Others clearly were initially inclined toward challenging unlimited executive power in foreign affairs, but their attachment to containment seemed to overpower their concerns about executive supremacy. Finally, there were a few who specifically denounced containment, yet consciously deferred to executive supremacy in foreign affairs, thereby accepting the Tonkin Gulf Resolution. During the Tonkin Gulf period, few members of Congress distinguished executive authority from constitutional authority; consequently, they reached only a deferring level of constitutional consciousness.

The Recognizing Level: An Anomaly in the Tonkin Gulf Period

Sustained questioning about the extent of executive power in the Tonkin Gulf Resolution was rare during the Tonkin Gulf debates. Acceptance of Congress' responsibility to question, formulate, and authorize foreign policy was even rarer. However, despite their substantive agreement with the policy of containment, Senators Wayne Morse (D-Ore.) and Ernest Gruening (D-Alaska) challenged the executive's right to unilaterally commit troops to Vietnam. Additionally, they argued that Congress had the constitutional power and duty to participate meaningfully in decisions to commit troops to hostile areas. They also recognized several arguments and concerns raised by supporters of executive supremacy, namely unity, containment, precedent, and greater executive competency. Gruening and Morse offered an independent constitutional interpretation that challenged Johnson's interpretation of presidential power in the Tonkin Gulf Resolution, even though they largely agreed with many of his policy goals.

Morse countered the majority of Congress' pleas for silence and congressional-executive unity by pointing out that criticism and questioning of the executive's policy need not be viewed simply as negative, divisive, communistic, or unpatriotic. He argued that critical debate could strengthen foreign policy decision making. Noting Congress' resistance, Morse claimed that representatives seemed to "feel that if one raises any questions or expresses any criticism of the policies of our country in the field of foreign policy, one's very patriotism is subject to question."[110] Arguing that the international context was extremely complex, Morse criticized the administration's attempt to force all foreign policy issues into a simple "Communist versus freedom" dichotomy. He argued that vigorous congressional debate would lead to a better understanding of the complex circumstances that influence decisions about troop commitments.[111]

Although Gruening and Morse both supported containment goals, they did not support using unlimited executive power as a means to further those goals. For example, Morse explained that even though he deplored communism, he also deplored making war to resolve conflict with the Communists. Conceding that the Vietcong were attempting to subvert South Vietnam, he argued that the United States would fail strategically and morally if it attempted to counter the Vietcong militarily. Thus Morse claimed: "It is a tragedy that the Vietcong try to subvert South Vietnam but that is a reality. The solution is not the exercise of military might."[112]

Gruening explained that even though he deplored North Vietnam's "stupid and outrageous attack" on the *Maddox* and supported the administration's retaliatory policy, he opposed military intervention in Southeast Asia. He argued that such intervention would lead to war, that American lives would be lost, and, therefore, that he was opposed to the Tonkin Gulf Resolution because it allowed unchecked unilateral escalation.[113]

Morse and Gruening agreed with Johnson and the majority of Congress that precedent supported broad executive discretionary power in foreign affairs, but they challenged the legitimacy of that precedent. They contended that Congress should require further justification and consider the constitutionality of the resolution's interpretation of presidential power. Thus Morse argued that the precedent of executive supremacy in foreign affairs could have been mistakenly and unconstitutionally established in the past. He noted that

> several senators stated this afternoon that the United States was not asking for any more in the resolution now before the Senate than has already been asked for in the past, as though that were a sound argument. What has that to do with whether or not we pass the pending joint resolution? If we made mistakes in the past—as we have done, in my judgment—we should not make another one now.[114]

Morse added that the precedents that supported executive supremacy and the rule of man endangered the Constitution and self-government. He argued that

> if we continue to build up a wall brick by brick, precedent by precedent, which separates the Executive branch of the Government from the people, resulting in making the executive branch of the Government more and more inaccessible to direct control, we shall endanger the very survival and preservation of the Republic, and our constitutional system upon which it is based. . . . One of the great protections that the American people have in constitu-

tional theory, under our form of government, is that we are a government of laws and not of men.[115]

Rejecting any obligation to defer to executive supremacy, Morse emphasized Congress' responsibility to challenge executive supremacy, to review the president's decisions, and to decide whether or not to authorize or reject those decisions. In short, he argued that Congress should reassert and accept its responsibility to formulate the nation's policy in Vietnam. He contended:

> By long established practice, the executive conducts the Nation's foreign policy. But the Congress and particularly, by constitutional mandate, the Senate has a right and duty in these premises to "advise and consent." . . . Therefore we in the Senate would be derelict in our duty if we did not individually express our views if those views embody doubt or dissent, and where a vote is called for, to cast that vote as our conscience directs.[116]

Morse also claimed that automatic congressional deference to the executive in foreign affairs abridged the rule of law, the separation of powers, and checks and balances and allowed Congress to avoid its responsibility to participate in difficult decisions. He contended that there were

> many congressional politicians who would evade their responsibilities as to American foreign policy in Asia by use of the specious argument that "foreign policy is a matter for the executive branch of the Government. That branch has information no Congressman has access to." Of course, such an alibi for evading congressional responsibility may be based on lack of understanding or a convenient forgetting of our system of checks and balances that exists and should be exercised in the relations between and among our three coordinate and coequal branches of government.[117]

Like Morse, Gruening contended that most members of Congress deferred to the executive in foreign affairs to avoid responsibility for difficult policy decisions. He contended that "there are many in Congress who would prefer to pass the buck to the White House, the State Department, the Pentagon Building . . . and this resolution gives them the vehicle."[118]

Morse argued that Congress had an obligation to defend and uphold the Constitution and to oppose proposals such as the Tonkin Gulf Resolution. He argued that "there is no course of action that I could possibly follow in keeping with my conscience and my convictions in regard to any constitutional obligation under the oath that I took four times when I came into this body, but to vote against the joint resolution tomorrow."[119] More specifically, Morse objected to the broad powers that the Tonkin Gulf Resolution gave to the president. He claimed that the grant was unconstitutional because it overran Congress' constitutional power to declare war. He stated: "I shall not support any substitute which takes the form of a predated declaration of war. In my judgment that is what the pending joint resolution is."[120]

Morse also argued that the Tonkin Gulf Resolution unconstitutionally delegated Congress' power to declare war to the president. He contended that the Constitution "does not permit the President to make the war at his discretion. . . . The Commander in Chief, the President of the United States, has the inherent constitutional power immediately to defend the United States in case of an attack, but he does not have the inherent power after that immediate defense to proceed to make war."[121] Morse noted that Franklin Roosevelt had used his commander-in-chief power rightly to defend the country after the Japanese attacked Pearl Harbor. But, Morse continued, unlike Johnson, Roosevelt then asked Congress for a declaration of war rather than for unlimited presidential discretion to conduct war.[122]

Gruening and Morse also challenged the constitutionality of the Tonkin Gulf Resolution on the grounds that it unconstitutionally altered the constitutional system of checks and balances between Congress and the president. They claimed that the resolution denied Congress a role in the process of foreign policy decision making, and left Congress powerless to check the executive's decisions. Morse argued that the power to declare war, the power to authorize presidential decisions through legislation, and the power to appropriate funds "give the Congress a check and voice in determining American foreign policy." Morse also argued that "it is an elementary principle of constitutional law that the executive branch of government cannot spend taxpayers' money in the field of foreign policy, or for any other purpose except when the appropriations are passed by law."[123] Therefore, if the Tonkin Gulf Resolution passed, Congress would be accountable for acquiescing in unconstitutional executive supremacy and the executive would be responsible for overstepping the boundaries of its constitutional powers.

Gruening and Morse's acceptance of congressional responsibility to interpret the Constitution and to authorize or reject foreign policy de-

cisions—including the decision to commit armed forces—was exceptional in the Tonkin Gulf period. Also exceptional was their willingness to recognize the arguments that opposed their own position and
that supported executive preeminence in troop commitment decisions.
However, most members of Congress did not seize the opportunity that
Gruening and Morse's arguments presented to them. They failed to
distinguish constitutional from executive authority and broaden the
debate about the constitutional allocation of the war powers.

Several scholars contended that the 1974 War Powers Act would
change that dynamic by affording Congress another opportunity to
broaden constitutional authority. By passing the act in a legal and political context characterized by judicial self-restraint, Congress practiced departmentalism and challenged executive preeminence in foreign affairs. These scholars argued that Congress would exhibit
increased responsibility for challenging executive supremacy, for participating meaningfully in important foreign policy decisions, and for
deciding whether to authorize or reject presidential decisions about
committing troops to foreign lands; these actions would heighten Congress' constitutional consciousness and broaden constitutional authority. In the next section I examine the 1987 Persian Gulf debates and
explore whether Congress actually did improve the quality of the debate by exhibiting those behaviors.

THE PERSIAN GULF PERIOD

Executive Interpretation of the War Powers:
The 1987 Persian Gulf Decision

In September 1980 the war between Iraq and Iran began.
Commercial shipping in the Persian Gulf was quickly threatened. In
December 1986 Kuwait asked the United States to reflag several of
their tankers so they could fly under the American flag and thus re-
ceive full U.S. naval protection in the Persian Gulf. On March 14,
1987, the United States claimed that Iran had installed anti-aircraft
missiles near the Straits of Hormuz in the Gulf. The Reagan administration decided to send American warships into the Arabian Sea. On
March 23 the United States reportedly offered to reflag eleven of Kuwait's twenty-two tankers. On April 4 the Reagan administration
strengthened the U.S. naval presence in the Gulf. Hinting that it
might also provide a warship as an escort, the Soviet Union on April

14 agreed to lease three tankers to Kuwait. Between May 3 and May 11, Iran attacked three Kuwaiti tankers. Subsequently, Iran warned Kuwait not to seek superpower protection. On May 17 an Iraqi missile struck the USS *Stark*, killing thirty-seven sailors. Iraq apologized and offered reparations for the attack, which it claimed was due to pilot error. This was the first attack on a U.S. warship in the Persian Gulf. Two days after the *Stark* incident, on May 19, the Reagan administration publicly announced that it had decided to reflag Kuwait tankers and increase American naval presence in the Gulf to protect those tankers.

Various administration officials contended that the president had increased American military presence to further several important political and economic goals: to protect the unimpeded flow of oil,[124] to keep the sea-lanes open,[125] to secure the stability and cooperation of moderate Arab states in the region,[126] to limit Soviet influence and presence in the region,[127] to end the Iran-Iraq war,[128] to deter further hostilities,[129] and to prevent Iran from attacking Kuwaiti ships with their newly acquired Chinese Silkworm missiles.[130] Summing up, Under Secretary of State Richard W. Murphy stated: "Our purpose was to see to it that Iran did not succeed in becoming dominant in the Persian Gulf by intimidating and bullying the Gulf states and that the Soviet Union did not become, in a sense, the protector of those vital supply routes."[131]

However, the executive's reflagging decision was not implemented until July 18, 1987. Thus Congress had ample time to decide whether to authorize or reject the decision before the new naval forces were to be committed to the region. Also on May 19, the Committee on Foreign Affairs Subcommittee on Arms Control, International Security, and Science and on Europe and the Middle East began hearings on H.R. 2533. Although the War Powers Act seemed to obligate the president to report to Congress, the language of H.R. 2533 expressly obligated the secretary of defense to submit a report to Congress in seven days that would provide a military strategy that would "fully meet the security needs of our forces" in the Persian Gulf, assess the threat to American forces there, and discuss the rules of engagement and readiness conditions that American forces would follow.[132] Congress passed H.R. 2533 on June 15, 1987, and Secretary of Defense Weinberger did in fact submit a report to Congress.[133] However, by demanding a report about military strategy, Congress seemed to accept rather than review the president's reflagging decision.

The Deferring Level:
An Anomaly in the Persian Gulf Period

During the Persian Gulf period, only a few members of Congress unquestioningly deferred to the executive and opposed a broader role for Congress in foreign policy decision making. Consequently they reached only a deferring level of constitutional consciousness. For example, Representative Gerald Solomon (R-N.Y.) opposed H.R. 2533 because it would create a larger role for Congress in foreign policy. He noted that although he was initially inclined to vote for H.R. 2533 because it would affirm congressional support for the executive's reflagging decision, he had decided not to vote for the bill because it would allow "Congress to insert itself into foreign policy again and again and again."[134] He added that he had "a dislike for resolutions such as this because it can be construed as Congress, again, sticking its nose into foreign policy, and I resent that."[135] Although Solomon's position would not have been exceptional in the Tonkin Gulf period, it was rarely enunciated during the Persian Gulf debates. Most representatives challenged the administration's policy in the Persian Gulf.

The Attacking Level:
A Limited Challenge to Executive Supremacy

Many members of Congress attacked the administration's claims and arguments about the Persian Gulf. For example, Representatives Stephen Solarz (D-N.Y.) and Larry Smith (D-Fla.) questioned the administration's statement that the United States needed to increase its military presence in the Persian Gulf to keep the sealanes open. Smith argued that the administration falsely claimed that the increased American military presence had been protecting "vital interests" and "shipping" since over two hundred ships had been attacked in the region.[136] Under Secretary of State Edward Djerejian answered that the principles of freedom of navigation and maintaining a free flow of oil informed the administration's reflagging policy. Under Secretary of State Michael H. Armacost conceded that the United States did not offer protection to all neutral shipping. Like Djerejian, Armacost argued that protecting Kuwaiti ships was a limited means to the administration's larger goal of supporting the principle of free shipping.

Although Solarz largely agreed with the executive's policy goals in the Persian Gulf, he nevertheless contended that Congress should review the president's use of power. Solarz conceded that even though

Reagan said that American military force was necessary to maintain freedom of navigation and to prevent aggression against neutral shipping, the United States protected only American-flagged ships. Solarz argued that since non-Kuwaiti ships had been attacked and the United States had not responded, it was not actually protecting commercial shipping in the Persian Gulf.[137]

Representatives Gerry Studds (D-Mass.) and Toby Roth (R-Wis.) attacked the administration's claim that American and Soviet goals collided in the Persian Gulf region. Studds argued that the United States and the Soviet Union both aimed to preserve free navigation on the high seas, to resolve the Iran-Iraq conflict peacefully, and to avoid a superpower confrontation.[138] Roth also pointed out that the administration could not claim to be furthering the goal of free navigation if it also aimed to deny the Soviet Union a presence in the Persian Gulf. Secretary of State Weinberger maintained that the Soviet Union did not want to end the war. He confirmed Roth's contention that the United States sought to deny the Soviet Union a presence in the Persian Gulf. Yet Weinberger insisted that this was necessary because the Soviet Union would not maintain free shipping in the region, whereas the United States would (except in the case of the Soviet Union). Again, the executive's responses did not silence Congress' challenges.

Many members of Congress attacked the administration's claim that the United States could increase its naval presence in the Persian Gulf and maintain neutrality in the Iran-Iraq war. For example, Representatives Roth, Peter DeFazio (D-Ore.), and James Leach (R-Iowa) argued that reflagging would damage American neutrality in the Iran-Iraq war and increase disorder in the region. DeFazio pointed out that despite the administration's contention that the United States had remained neutral, it had in fact entered the war against Iran.[139] Roth also argued that reflagging Kuwaiti ships aligned the United States with Iraq, because Kuwait was allied with Iraq.[140] Leach agreed that reflagging Kuwaiti ships destroyed American neutrality.[141] He noted that although most legislators were opposed to withdrawal from the Persian Gulf, they also thought that maintaining American neutrality in the war would be the best way to keep the sea-lanes open.[142]

Representatives Robert Kostmeyer (D-Penn.), Robert Torricelli (D-N.J.), and Thomas Downey (D-N.Y.), among others, questioned the security arrangements for naval forces committed to the Persian Gulf. Rather than reviewing the decision itself or discussing whether the executive could constitutionally commit troops to the Gulf unilaterally, they debated how the executive's decision to commit forces to the region could be best implemented. Kostmeyer argued that Congress should concern itself mainly with naval response time, the rules of engagement that the navy would follow if Iran attacked a Kuwaiti ship, and allied contributions to the security forces in the region.[143] Downey contended that even though American interests in the Persian Gulf were undebatable, the administration had not carefully arranged protection for the forces that were to be sent there. Torricelli also maintained that the administration had not taken adequate steps to secure the safety of the naval forces that were to be committed to the Gulf. He argued that "the administration, having made a military decision without understanding the assets that were being used, used ships for missions for which they were not designed, without adequate protection, without the ability to ensure the safety of those aboard."[144]

Studds questioned the administration's claim that reflagging would deter Iran from engaging in further hostilities in the region. Studds argued that even though Congress and the executive agreed that the United States should pursue peace in the Persian Gulf, reflagging Kuwaiti tankers would further escalate tension in the region. He contended that the administration failed to consider the possibility that peace could be attained without an American military presence.

In sum, Congress was not reluctant to attack several claims and arguments that the executive branch made to ground its decision to reflag Kuwaiti tankers and increase American military presence in the Persian Gulf. Furthermore, executive arguments to the contrary did not silence these members. Even though several of them partially or fully agreed with the president's foreign policy goals in the Gulf, they still challenged some of his claims and strategies. However, since these representatives accepted the executive's unilateral decision with little or no consideration, they achieved only an attacking level of constitutional consciousness.

The Introducing Level: Congress on Hostilities and the Applicability of the War Powers Act

Several members of Congress questioned the executive's definition of hostilities and contended, despite the administration's claims to the contrary, that the War Powers Act applied to the Persian Gulf situation and that the president was obligated to consult with and report to Congress about committing naval forces there. This challenge led Congress to accept formal responsibility for foreign policy and to demand greater participation in decisions about troop commitments. The War Powers Act states that the president must, in every possible instance, consult with Congress before introducing armed forces into hostilities or imminent hostilities and report any such troop commitments to Congress within forty-eight hours. Thus debate about whether the War Powers Act applied to the Gulf situation and whether congressional participation in decisions about military commitments should be increased centered largely on whether hostilities had ensued or were imminent in the Persian Gulf.

Several administration officials—including Under Secretary of State Murphy; President Reagan; Secretary of Defense Weinberger; the legal adviser to the Department of Defense, Michael Matheson; and Under Secretary of State Armacost—consistently argued that hostilities were not imminent in the Persian Gulf and that therefore the War Powers Resolution did not oblige the president to consult or report to Congress. For example, Murphy contended that

> in light of all the surrounding circumstances, the protection accorded by United States naval vessels to these United States flag tankers transiting international waters or straits does not constitute introduction of our armed forces into a situation where "imminent involvement in hostilities is clearly indicated." The War Powers Resolution, accordingly, is not implicated by our actions. On the contrary, our actions are such as to make it clear that any prospect of hostilities is neither imminent nor clearly indicated.[145]

Murphy argued further that the *Stark* tragedy was an isolated incident rather than indicative of general hostilities. Citing the cases of Libya and El Salvador, Murphy noted that isolated instances had not been historically recognized as constituting imminent hostilities or as triggers for the War Powers Resolution.[146] According to Murphy, Section 4(a)(1) of the War Powers Resolution empowers the executive to determine whether hostilities are imminent. Thus, he stated, the executive had decided, subject to continual reevaluation, that hostilities were not imminent in the Persian Gulf and that the War Powers Resolution therefore did not apply.

It is highly doubtful that Section 4(a)(1) empowers the executive alone to determine whether hostilities are imminent. It merely states: "In the absence of a declaration of war, in any case in which United States Armed Forces are introduced (1) into hostilities or into situations where imminent involvement in hostilities is clearly indicated by the circumstances," the president shall report to Congress within forty-eight hours or provide other information that Congress may request.[147] Furthermore, the tone as well as the structure of the War Powers Resolution casts strong doubt upon any interpretation that would grant the executive unilateral decision-making authority.

In any case, Under Secretary of State Armacost agreed that imminent hostilities did not exist in the Persian Gulf. He stated that although "significant and worrisome" threats to U.S. interests existed, Congress should view them "in perspective."[148] Armacost argued, for example, that Congress should consider that less than 1 percent of the ships in the Persian Gulf had been attacked and that insurance rates as well as oil prices had remained stable.[149] He concluded that these signs of stability indicated that hostilities were not imminent in the Gulf and that the United States was definitely not involved in the Iran-Iraq war.[150]

The administration also contended that the United States was attempting to deter any outbreak of hostilities in the Gulf.[151] Thus Reagan argued that reflagging would "deter . . . potential attacks."[152] Weinberger contended that hostilities did not exist because the Persian Gulf "is not a war zone in the accepted meaning of that term."[153] According to Weinberger, no "imminence of hostilities in a recognized conventional sense of the term" existed in the Gulf because the United States had remained neutral in the Iran-Iraq war.[154]

Despite administration arguments to the contrary, several representatives did not simply accept the executive's contentions, nor did those contentions serve to silence congressional opposition or prevent Congress from reviewing the constitutionality of the executive's unilateral action and discussing how the Constitution allocates the war powers. Rather, the argument was introduced that the Constitution and the War Powers Act required greater congressional participation in decisions about committing forces abroad.

Representatives DeFazio and Theodore Weiss (D-N.Y.) argued that Congress should use the War Powers Resolution to compel the administration to discuss and assess the risks to American forces that existed in the Persian Gulf. Although DeFazio supported maintaining a U.S. presence in the region, he claimed that the administration was downplaying the risks there.[155] In order to highlight those risks, DeFazio favored formally invoking the War Powers Resolution. Weiss agreed. He contended that the War Powers Resolution would force the administration to reveal the heightened risks to American troops.[156] Armacost conceded that new Iranian actions increased the risk to Americans, but he contended that the United States could accept and manage that risk in order to secure its interests. DeFazio and Weiss, as well as others, continued to adhere to this position throughout the debate despite executive statements to the contrary.

Representatives Leach, Torricelli, Smith, Daniel Mica (D-Fla.), Dante Fascell (D-Fla.), Edward Feighan (D-Okla.), and Donald Bonker (D-Wash.) challenged the executive argument that hostilities were not imminent in the Persian Gulf. Leach argued that hostilities were "not only imminent, but they are quite present in the Persian Gulf."[157] He stated that thirty-seven men died when Iraq attacked the *Stark*, indicating that the Gulf was a zone of hostility. Centering discussion on how the Constitution allocates the war powers, as well as on Congress' right to participate meaningfully in decisions about committing armed forces, Leach asked Djerejian "why [the administration was] not responding to Congress in response to the War Powers Resolution, grant[ing that] it is a law that [they found] somewhat bothersome as administration?"[158]

Mica noted that the secretary of defense had conceded that daily attacks had been occurring in the Persian Gulf since 1984. Rather than ignoring the evidence of attacks and accepting Weinberger's argument, as would have been the norm during the Tonkin Gulf debates, Mica refused to be silenced and contended that, despite the administration's claims to the contrary, daily attacks indicated that hostilities were present and that the War Powers Resolution applied to the Persian Gulf.[159]

Fascell contended that even though Weinberger had argued that the Persian Gulf is not a war zone, Iran and Iraq were in fact at war there. Fascell noted that the context of war suggested at least the imminence, if not the presence, of hostilities in the region. Furthermore, Fascell challenged Weinberger's claim by arguing that recent incidents—Iran attacking Kuwaiti ships with increasing frequency, the Reagan administration deciding to reflag eleven Kuwaiti ships, the Soviet Union leasing three tankers to Kuwait, Iraq destroying the *Stark* with Exocet missiles and killing thirty-seven American servicemen, China selling Silkworm missiles to Iran that had three times the power of Exocet missiles, insurance rates rising, and Iran threatening to undertake suicide missions against American vessels in the Persian Gulf—all indicated that hostilities were imminent if not present in the region.[160]

Noting that thirty-seven Americans had died, the *Stark* had been crippled, and hundreds of ships had been attacked, Torricelli concluded that the War Powers Act applied to the Persian Gulf and that the executive should agree to increased congressional participation in decisions regarding military commitments there. He argued that hostilities "are not only imminent, they have transpired—and where forces are prepared for combat—which they are in that area, whether the policy be right or wrong—there is an obligation for notification of Congress."[161]

Feighan agreed. Challenging the administration's claim that the *Stark* attack was an isolated occurrence, he argued that the incident "clearly demonstrates the powder keg nature of events in that region of the world where violence now can strike with really little warning and where we find that mistakes can have very deadly consequences."[162] Therefore, he concluded, hostilities were imminent, the War Powers Act applied to the Persian Gulf, and Congress should be further integrated into the decision-making process for that region.

Furthermore, Smith contended that the administration's argument against the applicability of the War Powers Resolution was "ridiculous" when over two hundred hostile incidents had occurred in the Gulf, including the *Stark* tragedy.[163] He argued: "The problem is that this administration has refused consistently to honor what is in fact the law on the books, and the excuse used for this particular breach was that there was no imminent danger."[164] Bonker also challenged the executive by arguing that reflagging Kuwaiti ships involved American forces politically and militarily "in an area where hostilities definitely exist."[165] He added that the administration could not defend noncompliance with the War Powers Resolution when hostile actions were occurring in the Persian Gulf.

Several representatives, such as Torricelli and Howard Berman (D-Calif.), not only rejected the executive's contention that hostilities were not imminent but also pressed reluctant administration officials to discuss the circumstances that they thought would constitute imminent hostilities, thereby triggering the War Powers Act. Torricelli noted that although Iran had said that it would attack the Untied States and the United States had said it would defend against such an attack, the administration continued to insist that hostilities were not imminent in the Gulf. Thus Torricelli asked Under Secretary of State Murphy "what [would] constitute an imminent threat of hostilities as envisioned by you under the War Powers Act?"[166] Murphy refused to indicate what circumstances would trigger the act. Rather, he simply reiterated the administration's position that hostilities were not imminent in the Gulf. He stated that the administration did not "believe that anything that has happened to date, including the attack on the

U.S.S. *Stark*, has triggered the War Powers Resolution."[167] Torricelli refused to be silenced or to back down without an answer. He accused Murphy and the administration of "proposing an unacceptably high threshold for invoking the War Powers Act which is a poor precedent for the future. It is here where you have this direct conflict, [that] you were denying the applicability of the Act."[168]

Under questioning from Berman, Armacost also refused to indicate the circumstances that might constitute imminent hostilities.[169] He argued that the long-standing U.S. presence in the Persian Gulf suggested that hostilities had not suddenly become imminent; he continued, "Hypotheticals are hard [to discuss], but we have been there forty years" pursuing the same policy.[170]

Other members of Congress also continued to probe administration officials in an attempt to discover the particular circumstances that would trigger the War Powers Resolution. For example, Bonker wondered whether an Iranian attack against an American ship protecting the reflagged Kuwaiti vessels would trigger the resolution.[171] Berman asked whether an Iranian deployment of Silkworm missiles would trigger it.[172]

Unlike legislators of the Tonkin Gulf period, those of the Persian Gulf period did not unquestioningly accept and reiterate the executive's claims and arguments. Nor did they abruptly abandon their challenges because of pressure from the administration. Rather, many continued to question the executive's claims that hostilities were not imminent in the Persian Gulf and that the War Powers Resolution did not apply. Also unlike legislators of the Tonkin Gulf period, many representatives of the Persian Gulf period accepted the increased responsibility given Congress in the War Powers Act to be more active in foreign policy decision making. These legislators contended further that congressional silence would signal Congress' acquiescence in the executive's unilateral decisions to reflag Kuwaiti ships and to commit armed forces to the Persian Gulf. Unlike during the Tonkin Gulf period, legislators during the Persian Gulf period argued that Congress would bear at least a measure of responsibility for U.S. policy in the Gulf—even if it decided to remain silent.

DeFazio argued that congressional silence would constitute complicity or acquiescence in the executive's decisions. He stated that "silence is the most ringing endorsement [Congress] can give to an Administration stumbling toward war. Examining, debating and concurring on such a policy is a proper Congressional role. Under the requirements of the War Powers Resolution, we cannot do otherwise."[173] If Congress chose to remain silent, Defazio contended, it would still retain responsibility for Persian Gulf policy.

Representative Henry Gonzalez (D-Tex.) argued that Congress should participate in and take responsibility for Persian Gulf policy by applying the War Powers Resolution. He stated that "it behooves the Congress to act on its own laws. The President is in violation of the War Powers Limitation Act. At least, he ought to be stopped by the Congress."[174] Gonzalez argued that reflagging involved American forces in a wartime situation because Iran had acted hostilely against the United States, the United States was prepared for combat against Iran, and Secretary of Defense Weinberger had been discussing a preemptive strike against Iranian Silkworm deployment. Thus, he concluded, Congress should invoke the War Powers Resolution. He added that if Congress failed to invoke the resolution, the president would further involve American forces in the Persian Gulf and Congress would bear some responsibility for that development. He claimed that while "Congress diddles and dawdles, the President in the meanwhile involves the country, violating the very laws that the Congress has passed and refuses to oversee."[175]

Still other representatives, such as Solarz, Studds, Benjamin Gilman (R-N.Y.), and William Broomfield (R-Mich.), contended that the act would prompt the administration to discuss the principles underlying the policy and therefore deter the administration from thoughtlessly escalating American military presence in the Persian Gulf. Solarz claimed that Murphy's testimony showed that the administration had not carefully thought out all the contingencies of its policy. According to Solarz, H.R. 2533 would "obligate the administration to provide answers to some very fundamental questions before we find ourselves deeply involved in a commitment that could have very serious ramifications for vital American national interests."[176] Solarz concluded by offering his support for the administration's reflagging policy and for H.R. 2533's demand that the secretary of defense report to Congress. He argued that reflagging and reporting would contribute to building an accountable and defensible Persian Gulf policy.[177]

Gilman argued that the possibility of rapid escalation necessitated thoughtful and well-reasoned executive decision making. He stated:

> I think it is important that while we support maintaining a presence in the Gulf and keeping open international sea-lanes that we have at the same time signaled to the administration our strong concern and interest in having a well thought out plan and policy

to respond to all likely actions in the Gulf, and not merely react-
ing to emergency events as they take place. . . . Although the Congress has been consulted on the Gulf operation, it has become evident that the ramifications of this operation have not been fully
thought through.[178]

Studds argued that Congress should require the secretaries of state
and defense to indicate the principles underlying the administration's
Persian Gulf policy "before we get ourselves much more deeply involved in something from which there is no rationale or peaceful or
unbloodied extraction."[179] Broomfield claimed that the bill would improve congressional-executive consultation, strengthen U.S. policy in
the Persian Gulf, and

> ensure that Congress will be fully informed in all aspects of the
> United States' naval deployment in the Persian Gulf. . . . This bill
> reaffirms the critical importance of executive branch consultation
> with Congress on major foreign policy issues. . . . I don't think
> we've had enough consultation. . . . I think if we are going to have
> an effective policy, we have got to bring Congress in as full part-
> ners as far as consultation.[180]

He added that consultation would build "confidence [between] the administration and the Congress on foreign policy issues."[181]

Representative Mel Levine (D-Calif.) noted that the administration
was disseminating inadequate and internally inconsistent information, thereby indicating that it had not thought through its Persian
Gulf policy carefully enough. He claimed that if Congress forced the
administration to report, the executive would be compelled to think
out its Persian Gulf policy more carefully.[182] Representative Tom Lantos (D-Calif.) also supported increasing the role of Congress in foreign
affairs. Like the others, his discussion assumed an American presence
in the Gulf. He claimed that the *Stark* incident showed "the necessity
for the Congress and for the American people to examine the ramifications of the administration's actions in the Persian Gulf and to consider what the American policy in this area should be."[183]

Other representatives, including Lantos and Larry Smith, argued
that the executive should integrate Congress more fully into the process of making decisions about military commitments. Lantos contended that since the president had committed American forces to "a
war zone, reflagging is not a routine commercial transaction, but a

major foreign policy and military decision, and Congress, under our Constitution, must be a part of that decision making process."[184] Smith agreed. He argued that H.R. 2533 aimed to make Congress a fuller participant in the Persian Gulf decision-making process. According to Smith, it is "paramount that Congress be made a full partner in this debate. We must be in the loop at every stage. We must not be shielded from the tremendous dangers facing all vessels in the Persian Gulf, particularly United States ships. . . . [W]e must enter this policy with our eyes fully open to all possibilities and possible scenarios which will face us."[185]

Thus most members of Congress during the Persian Gulf period accepted responsibility for participating in foreign policy decisions. They frequently argued that increased congressional participation would improve the quality and cohesion of U.S. policy in the Persian Gulf. Despite this significant improvement, most of these legislators failed to accept responsibility to debate and decide whether to authorize or reject the executive's unilateral decisions to reflag Kuwaiti ships and to commit naval forces to the Persian Gulf to protect those ships. Consequently, Congress failed to pass a bill that would have expressly triggered the War Powers Resolution.[186] Supporters of the bill claimed that it would "reduce the chances of an overzealous President involving the United States in an unwanted war."[187] Opponents of the bill accepted executive supremacy in foreign affairs and effectively persuaded Congress not to invoke the War Powers Act. They reiterated the executive's claim that two hundred years of constitutional and statutory precedent supported the president's authority to unilaterally conduct foreign policy. They also contended that Congress did not have the authority to define the limits of executive power. Finally, they maintained that executive supremacy would secure stability in the Persian Gulf.[188]

However, even the supporters of the bill carefully pointed out that they did not want to withdraw the forces that the executive had previously committed to the Persian Gulf. They claimed that they intended to consider only whether reflagging could lead the United States into war. Seeming to accept the executive's unilateral decision as final, they stated that "the War Powers Act would . . . give Congress and the country an analysis of the possible ramifications of the policy in the Gulf."[189] Although these representatives may have thought that reflagging Kuwaiti ships was good foreign policy that needed no discussion, departmentalists argue that Congress still retained the responsibility to review, debate, and consciously participate in the decision.

Debating the Executive's Unilateral Decision:
An Anomaly in the Persian Gulf Debates

Only a few representatives indicated that they were willing to debate the president's initial decision to reflag and commit American naval forces to the Persian Gulf. They argued that Congress had a responsibility to review that decision and to decide whether to authorize or reject it. For example, Studds, Howard Wolpe (D-Mich.), and Michael Lowry (D-Wash.) argued that H.R. 2533 assumed that the administration's decision to reflag Kuwaiti tankers was final. They noted that the bill would oblige Secretary of Defense Weinberger to report about the security arrangements that were being undertaken to protect American ships in the Persian Gulf. However, they continued, this request for a security report assumed the legitimacy of the American naval commitment. Thus they refused to support the bill because they charged that it deflected Congress from questioning the executive's original decision to commit naval forces to the Persian Gulf and the security arrangements for those forces.

Wolpe noted that he originally was inclined to support H.R. 2533 so that the secretary of defense would be compelled to report to Congress about the Persian Gulf. However, he said that the H.R. 2533 hearings had revealed to him that the bill centered congressional questioning on security for forces already committed rather than on the decision to commit forces in the first place.[190] Arguing that the bill therefore "takes as a given" the reflagging policy, he opposed it on the grounds that it would signal congressional authorization of the executive's reflagging decision.[191] Studds also noted that although he was in favor of increasing congressional-executive consultation, he intended to vote against the bill because he did not want to signal support for the executive's initial decision to commit American forces to the Persian Gulf.[192]

Lowry explicitly argued that Congress should not authorize the executive's decision without directly reviewing the initial one to commit new forces to the Persian Gulf. He contended that Congress should vote to delay the reflagging, explore peaceful options at the United Nations, pursue European cooperation, discuss alternatives for responding to hostile Iranian attack, "and most important allow members of Congress with experience and expertise to participate in the decision-making process," thereby creating a "much sounder and more carefully thought out policy."[193] Lowry asserted, "Congress is reluctant to 'challenge presidential actions taken in the context of an international crisis.' Nonetheless, I think it would be absolutely wrong for us to let the President go it alone and wash our hands of responsibility. Congress must exercise thorough oversight of the policy-making process."[194] More specifically, Lowry argued that directly reviewing initial decisions to commit forces to foreign lands could avert tragedies, such as the Lebanon disaster. He noted that at first President Reagan had sent forces to Lebanon with only *tacit* congressional approval. However, Lowry continued, as time passed, circumstances changed in Lebanon and various Lebanese factions began to think that the United States had not remained neutral. Therefore, the risks to American forces increased. Yet Congress did not debate those changes.[195] Lowry contended that if Congress had monitored the effect a U.S. military presence would have in Lebanon, the administration might have been more aware of the erosion of support for the Marines there and perhaps been able to avoid the tragedy that ensued.[196]

From this analysis, Lowry concluded "that Congressional reluctance to second guess the administration contributed to the Lebanon disaster."[197] He argued further that, just as in Lebanon, U.S. forces committed to the Gulf had increased since the president's unilateral decision and American neutrality was again being questioned. Lowry called for Congress to review the executive's decision to commit forces to the Gulf and to decide whether to authorize or reject a continued American presence in the region.

Wolpe and Roth expressed concern that the administration would use the resolution as evidence of congressional support for its reflagging policy. Wolpe stated that Congress should not support the bill since historically the administration has taken "the most token consultations with the Congress as a rationale for the statement that Congress approves of its actions."[198] Roth suggested that rather than passing H.R. 2533, which the administration could later misleadingly use as formal legal evidence of Congress' authorization of reflagging, Congress should simply ask the administration to discuss the Persian Gulf situation through an informal letter. In that way, Congress could specifically distinguish its support for increased executive consultation from any decision to authorize or reject the administration's reflagging policy.[199] He stated that he "would be happy with the administration providing us information, but not in response to this resolution, because this resolution puts the imprimatur of Congress on an unknown policy we have in the Persian Gulf."[200]

Roth and Charles Bennett (D-Fla.) argued that the executive's unilateral decision abridged the constitutional allocation of the war powers, thus explicitly distinguishing constitutional from executive authority. For example, Roth contended that the executive's unilateral decision to commit forces to the Persian Gulf region might not deter further aggression but, rather, might lead to increased American involvement in an ongoing war—unilaterally and thus unconstitutionally directed by the president, as was the case in Vietnam.[201] More specifically, he argued that H.R. 2533 would grant the president unlimited power, which could lead to the executive conducting an undeclared war with American troops. Roth opposed the bill on the grounds that it was "a tune for marching off to war. This is the Tonkin Gulf Resolution of the eighties."[202] He added that the United States should not increase its commitment to the Persian Gulf "snake pit."[203]

Bennett also argued that if Congress supported the administration's reflagging policy it would be unconstitutionally delegating unlimited, unilateral war powers to the executive. Thus Bennett not only opposed the administration's reflagging policy, he also opposed H.R. 2533, because "it would give somebody else control of whether we go into a war, which may not be a winnable war."[204] Bennett added: "I think we should go into war like the Constitution says, when Congress decides we should go to war. . . . The United States should not back into a war like this."[205]

These few representatives were willing to accept congressional responsibility for Persian Gulf policy, to debate the executive's unilateral decision to commit forces to the Persian Gulf, and to decide whether to authorize or reject that decision. In doing so, they explicitly distinguished constitutional from executive authority, thereby broadening constitutional authority. However, as was the case with Gruening and Morse during the Tonkin Gulf debates, the arguments of Wolpe, Studds, Lowry, Roth, and Bennett were exceptions in the Persian Gulf debates.

Thus, although these individuals reached a very high recognizing level of constitutional consciousness, the rest of Congress did not follow suit. Contrary to departmentalist expectations, most legislators did not review the executive's decision to commit American forces to the Persian Gulf or directly challenge the executive's interpretation of the war powers. Nonetheless, during this period, constitutional consciousness was heightened to an introducing level and constitutional authority was significantly broadened. Congress did challenge several administration claims about the Gulf situation and introduced the argument that the legislative branch should participate more fully in, and accept greater responsibility for, decisions surrounding troop commitments.

PUBLIC SENSITIVITY AND LEVELS
OF CONSTITUTIONAL CONSCIOUSNESS

Departmentalists claim that improved congressional responsibility should, in turn, deepen public sensitivity to constitutional and political issues and lead to an improved public debate.[206] Comparing public opinion during the Tonkin Gulf period with public opinion during the Persian Gulf period, departmentalists would expect to find less deference to executive supremacy in foreign affairs and greater acceptance of a broader role for Congress in decisions regarding troop commitments and war during the Persian Gulf period.

As was the case with Congress, public support for containment in the Tonkin Gulf period may mask public disapproval of unlimited presidential power or executive supremacy. For public sensitivity, this problem is magnified. Whereas the statements of individual members of Congress helped to distinguish support for containment goals from support for the use of unlimited presidential powers to further those goals, most survey research during the Tonkin Gulf period allowed consideration of only the question asked and the closed-ended response. Unfortunately, the questions and responses do not adequately distinguish attitudes about containment with attitudes about the scope of presidential power. At best, then, the public opinion data must be understood to be suggestive rather than determinative regarding attitudes about the proper extent of presidential power.

The Tonkin Gulf Period

Public opinion polls conducted during the Tonkin Gulf period suggest that the public, like Congress, largely accepted executive dominance in foreign affairs and Johnson's Vietnam policy. Stanley Karnow claims that after the Tonkin Gulf incident, "85% of the American public stood behind the administration and most newspaper editorials faithfully reflected this support."[207] During the course of the Tonkin Gulf debates, Senator Fulbright also noted that "in addition to strong support in Congress ... [t]here have been ... expressions of widespread [public] support for the President's action in the country and in the press."[208] He submitted editorials from leading newspapers, such as the *Philadelphia Inquirer, Washington Post, New York Herald Tribune, New York Times,* and *Baltimore Sun,* to "illustrat[e] ... the general support for President Johnson's action in South East Asia."[209]

For example, the *Washington Post* contended that the Tonkin Gulf

Resolution did not create a predated declaration of war. Rather, in the *Post*'s view, the resolution allowed the president to respond quickly to attacks without advance congressional approval. George Herring noted that Johnson's approval ratings in the Harris polls increased from 42 percent to 72 percent overnight after the *Maddox* attack.[210] Of course, such increased support for the president after a military maneuver is typical. However, Gallup polls indicated that this level of support remained relatively stable well after the attack. A Gallup poll taken on June 24, 1965, indicated that Johnson still had a 69 percent approval rating. The work of Sidney Verba and his associates also confirms a high level of approval.[211] They found that a large majority of the public supported Johnson's unilateral commitment of troops to Vietnam. Furthermore, 81 percent of their sample said that they "would oppose withdrawal of our troops tomorrow."[212]

Verba and his associates also claim that even those who opposed Johnson's policy did so not because they opposed the vast presidential powers contained in the Tonkin Gulf Resolution but, rather, because they thought that Johnson was not using his powers aggressively enough: "The polls showed the American public firmly behind the President's policy. If he was under any pressure, it was from a growing group of opponents of this policy who wanted him to escalate the war."[213] Moreover, open-ended questioning of opponents of Johnson's Vietnam policy reveals no concern that the Tonkin Gulf Resolution abridged constitutional limitations by giving the president absolute authority.[214]

The public was not asked about Congress' role in troop commitment decisions during the Tonkin Gulf period.[215] This may indicate that acquiescence to executive supremacy in foreign affairs was so deep that pollsters did not design questions to tap public attitudes regarding Congress' role in foreign affairs generally, much less in committing troops to foreign lands. In sum, the polls suggest that during the Tonkin Gulf period, the public achieved at best a deferring level and at worst a nonparticipating level of constitutional consciousness.

The Persian Gulf Period

Public opposition to a presidential policy may indicate that the public is considering the policy rather than simply deferring to the executive in principle, which may suggest resistance to the unilateral or unlimited use of executive power. It is, of course, possible—even in a case of vast support for the president, such as during the Tonkin Gulf

period—that the public could be considering arguments and counterarguments, thus improving its political understanding. However, the
structure of the congressional-executive debate about the Tonkin Gulf
Resolution suggests that public understanding probably did not improve during that period. In the context of long-term executive dominance in foreign affairs, the substantial amount of disapproval exhib-
ited by the American public during the Persian Gulf period suggests
that citizens were willing to challenge the executive, to consider alternative arguments, and thus to improve their understanding of the constitutional dimensions of presidential power regarding troop commitment decisions in the Gulf region. Public acceptance of even a limited
role for Congress in such decisions suggests that citizens had moved
beyond the deference that characterized the Tonkin Gulf period toward
a broader consideration of the constitutional allocation of the war
powers.

Public opinion polls conducted during the Persian Gulf period indicate that less than a majority supported the Reagan administration's
decision to reflag and protect Kuwaiti tankers. A Gallup poll conducted on June 14, 1987, found that 47 percent approved the reflagging plan, 40 percent disapproved, and 13 percent were not sure.[216]
This suggests that a larger segment of the population was capable of
questioning and challenging executive foreign policy decisions than
was true during the Tonkin Gulf period, indicating an enlarged public
understanding of the foreign policy decision-making process. Nevertheless, just as was the case in Congress during the Tonkin Gulf period, the largest segment of the population supported the president's
reflagging decision. One could argue that the polling questions tapped
the public breakdown of the postwar foreign policy consensus rather
than public content or discontent with the extent of executive power in
foreign affairs. However, public disapproval of any sort entails at least
a limited challenge to the executive's dominance in foreign affairs, indicating, at this point, an attacking level of constitutional consciousness. To oppose the president, even at the policy level, the public would
have to consider whether or not he had erred and thus resist unself-
conscious deference to executive authority.

The public was not asked about Congress' role in foreign affairs during the Tonkin Gulf period; however, during the Persian Gulf period,
private citizens were regularly asked about Congress' role and the reflagging decision. This alone indicates a change in the structure of the
public debate and an enlarged understanding of the constitutional dimensions of presidential power in troop commitment decisions. Public

opinion polls during the Persian Gulf period indicate that a majority of the public accepted an increasingly wider role for Congress in decisions about military commitments. Seventy-five percent of a national sample said that Congress should be consulted in situations that might lead to war.[217] Another poll indicated that 63 percent of the public thought that the president should obtain Congress' approval to keep ships in the Persian Gulf rather than making that decision unilaterally.[218] These polls may support the departmentalist contention that heightened congressional sensitivity to constitutional issues (such as the constitutional distribution of the war powers) and improved congressional responsibility would improve the public debate. During the Persian Gulf period, then, the public seemed to challenge executive supremacy and accept greater congressional responsibility for important military commitments, thereby achieving an introducing level of constitutional consciousness and broadening constitutional authority.

CONCLUSION

A comparison of the Tonkin Gulf debates with the Persian Gulf debates reveals that constitutional consciousness did heighten to an introducing level and that constitutional authority did broaden when Congress challenged executive dominance in foreign affairs during the latter period. Thus Congress' challenge did not decrease constitutional authority or lead to greater skepticism about the rule of law, as critics of departmentalism had feared. During the Persian Gulf period, Congress accepted greater responsibility for participating in foreign policy decisions and for questioning and occasionally challenging executive claims and arguments. Furthermore, Congress contended that the executive should consult it more frequently and meaningfully. However, even though Congress had made significant strides since the Tonkin Gulf period in terms of assertiveness and constitutional consciousness, it remained largely unwilling to review the executive's unilateral decision to commit troops to the Persian Gulf and to accept responsibility for deciding whether to authorize or oppose that decision. Consequently, Congress achieved only an introducing level of constitutional consciousness during that period. Moreover, public opinion data suggest that the improved congressional debate during this period may have affected the public debate, since the public also reached an introducing level of constitutional consciousness. Whether

Congress practiced departmentalism in a context of judicial activism (as in the abortion debate) or in a context of judicial self-restraint (as in the war powers debate), constitutional consciousness was heightened and constitutional authority broadened significantly.

CHAPTER FOUR

Departmentalism, Constitutional Consciousness, and the Rule of Law

When Congress practices departmentalism, constitutional consciousness heightens and constitutional authority broadens. In the context of judicial activism, automatic deference to judicial authority recedes as constitutional authority is distinguished from judicial authority. In the context of judicial self-restraint, unself-conscious deference to executive authority recedes as Congress distinguishes constitutional from executive authority.

In the human life bill hearings, several members of Congress addressed the constitutionality of *Roe* directly by offering a fetal rights reading of the Fourteenth Amendment and introduced new arguments into the debate to support their position. They focused on constitutional meaning rather than simply on relative institutional powers and competencies. By discussing new scientific, philosophic, and legal arguments about when life and personhood begin they heightened constitutional consciousness to an introducing level and broadened constitutional authority. Despite continued disagreement, opponents discussed alternative readings of the Fourteenth Amendment, an important first step toward joining the woman's rights and the fetal rights discourses in a dialogue that has the Constitution as its common referent.

The majority of the *Akron* Court initially failed to confront the new arguments that supported fetal rights. The majority relied solely on the precedent of *Roe*, failed to engage the city of Akron's argument that life begins at conception, and thus failed to improve the quality of judicial constitutional interpretation. However, Justice O'Connor's dissent in *Akron* addressed the constitutionality of *Roe*, as well as the new scientific developments that challenged *Roe*'s analytic framework, and prompted the *Akron* majority to recognize scientific arguments that supported fetal rights. Thus the judiciary improved its constitutional consciousness up to a recognizing level in the *Akron* case and constitutional authority broadened further.

During the human life bill debates, Congress' level of constitutional consciousness heightened to an introducing level and constitutional authority broadened. On the other hand, the Abortion Funding Restriction Act challenged *Roe* indirectly, since supporters of the act did not wish to challenge judicial supremacy openly. Rather than acknowledging the challenge, most legislators involved in the Abortion Funding Restriction Act hearings claimed that the act did not threaten *Roe*. During those hearings, Congress achieved only a deferring level of constitutional consciousness and constitutional authority did not broaden.

Thus the abortion debates suggest that more directly expressed disagreement, such as in the human life bill hearings, leads to higher levels of constitutional consciousness, whereas less directly expressed disagreement, such as the Abortion Funding Restriction Act, leads to lower levels of constitutional consciousness. The latter occurs not because departmentalism has failed, but because members of Congress continue to pay lip service to judicial supremacy, even though they are challenging a judicial decision at the level of constitutional principle. Less direct forms of disagreement partake of both departmentalism and judicial supremacy and will accordingly lead to a more mixed result, or lower levels of constitutional consciousness. This suggests that practicing an even broader, more self-conscious form of departmentalism would heighten constitutional consciousness and strengthen constitutional authority. At the same time, it also suggests that continued adherence to judicial supremacy would narrow constitutional authority, thereby threatening the rule of law.

In the *Thornburgh* case, although the majority relied solely on the precedent of *Roe*, Justice White's dissent reintroduced new scientific and ethical arguments that supported fetal protection and reexplored the *Roe* framework. However, the majority did not recognize these new arguments. Thus the quality of judicial constitutional interpretation dropped to an attacking level of constitutional consciousness.

The only firm conclusions that can be drawn from public opinion polls about abortion is that scholars ought to conduct research that more directly explores public awareness and understanding rather than continue to tap public attitudes only about whether abortion should be legal. Until that occurs, even though the polls suggest re-markable stability in public attitudes, and perhaps a lack of deepened public understanding, it is not prudent to comment with confidence about departmentalism's effect at the popular level.

In the war powers debates Congress' constitutional consciousness improved from a deferring level to an introducing level when it chal-lenged executive dominance in foreign affairs. In the 1987 Persian Gulf debates, Congress introduced the idea that the executive should confer with Congress more frequently and meaningfully about the Gulf situation. Furthermore, Congress accepted greater responsibility for participating in important decisions and for questioning and chal-lenging executive claims and arguments about the region. Thus Con-gress began to distinguish constitutional from executive authority, achieved an introducing level of constitutional consciousness, and broadened constitutional authority during that period.[1]

Opinion polls suggest that a large majority of the public supported broadening Congress' role in foreign policy decision making, as well as the idea that Congress should be responsible for authorizing or reject-ing the executive's initial decision to commit forces to foreign lands. These opinion polls suggest that public sensitivity had heightened sig-nificantly after Congress challenged executive dominance in the War Powers Act, rising from a deferring level to an introducing level of con-stitutional consciousness. However, the same caveats that apply to public opinion polls in the abortion case also apply here. Public opin-ion about executive supremacy in foreign affairs needs to be examined more directly and regularly before any firm conclusions can be drawn about public sensitivity to constitutional issues.

OBSTRUCTIONS TO HIGHER LEVELS
OF CONSTITUTIONAL CONSCIOUSNESS

Since the Court achieved a recognizing level in the abortion debates, departmentalism seems to be slightly more successful when it is practiced in a context of judicial activism. However, that claim is not warranted because when one looks at the results of each debate taken as a whole, they are more similar than dissimilar. Furthermore, it is not clear that the "role of the Court" is the key contextual factor that determines the success or failure or departmentalism. Of course, it is difficult to generalize after exploring only one case in each con-text. I suspect that departmentalism's success depends more on the level of direct disagreement rather than solely on the role that the judiciary has played in a particular field of adjudication. When Congress directly expressed its disagreement with *Roe* in the human life bill debates, even though that debate occurred in a context of judicial activism, Congress attained as high a level of constitutional consciousness (that is, introducing) as it did in the 1987 Persian Gulf debates, which took place in a context of judicial self-restraint. Furthermore, when Congress indirectly expressed its disagreement with *Roe* in the Abortion Funding Restriction Act hearings, constitutional consciousness fell. Yet those hearings took place in a context of judicial activism. Thus directness of disagreement appears to be a more important factor for successfully broadening constitutional authority than the role of the judiciary.

Each debate also revealed that a successful constitutional discourse will progress through several levels of constitutional consciousness rather than immediately attaining one level, where it remains. At each level, concerns and problems emerge that obstruct movement to the next highest level. These must be addressed in a manner that is satisfactory to the participants before further progress can be made to higher levels of constitutional consciousness.[2]

When Congress challenged judicial supremacy in the abortion debate and executive supremacy in the war powers debates, constitutional consciousness consistently improved to an introducing level. Although there is no denying that constitutional authority deepened significantly, these results also lead one to wonder why it did not continue to deepen to the higher levels of recognizing and engaging. What concerns or problems were not adequately addressed at the introducing level that obstructed the debate from progressing to those higher levels? It is clear that scholars feared that departmentalism would produce chaos, legislative supremacy, or executive supremacy and thus threaten the rule of law by deepening skepticism about constitutional authority. Several participants in the abortion and war powers debates also expressed those fears. Examining the fears in greater detail may provide some insight as to why the debates remained largely fixed at the introducing level.

Legal and Political Chaos

Recall that most scholars who contend that departmentalism would threaten constitutional authority claim that it would produce chaos or anarchy. Because officials are encouraged to express disagreement directly, and because departmentalism tolerates conflicting constitutional interpretations, they claim that departmentalism will encourage public officials and citizens to believe that the Constitution can mean anything and everything and therefore has no meaning at all independent of the will of the current interpreter. Others lessen the stakes by claiming that departmentalism will produce confusion about the meaning of the law. In both cases these critics fear that departmentalism will threaten constitutional authority and deepen skepticism about the nation's commitment to one stable, knowable, predictable rule of law.

The practice of departmentalism in the abortion case did not create anything as drastic as chaos or anarchy. The government continued to function even though the human life bill hearings increased conflict by expressing direct disagreement with *Roe*. Constitutional crisis did not result when Congress challenged judicial supremacy. The rule of law (constitutional authority) clearly did not collapse; in fact it appeared to be strengthened as a result of the conflict.[3] However, a measure of confusion about which standard governed abortion did emerge in the Abortion Funding Restriction Act hearings when Congress expressed disagreement with *Roe* less directly than it did in the human life bill hearings.

Clarity and Skepticism in the Human Life Bill Debates. Two alternative interpretations of the Fourteenth Amendment were presented in the abortion debate. The *Roe* standard favored the woman's right to abortion, and the human life bill standard favored fetal rights, or at least the state's interest in protecting fetal life throughout pregnancy. Most of the human life bill's supporters and opponents clearly understood that the bill's interpretation of the Fourteenth Amendment challenged *Roe*'s interpretation. Accordingly, the human life bill debates reveal little confusion about the meaning of each standard and the challenge that the human life bill posed to *Roe*, the standard that governed abortion policy at that time.

Despite widespread clarity during the human life bill hearings, a few participants in the abortion debate argued that discussing alternative constitutional interpretations would necessarily have a negative impact on the rule of law. They feared that disagreement about the meaning of the Constitution would not broaden constitutional authority but, rather, would threaten the rule of law. For example, although he opposed *Roe* and legal abortion, Senator Orren Hatch (R-Utah) also opposed departmentalism and the human life bill because he believed it would damage the rule of law. He argued that "passage of S. 158 would mean that there would be in existence two conflicting 'laws' derived from the Constitution. . . . Such a situation would be highly detrimental to our constitutional system."⁴ Senator Robert Packwood (R-Ore.) contended that the rule of law demanded one universally applied standard for abortion. Noting that *Roe* "did give us a national uniformity on a constitutional right," he asserted that the rule of law would be abridged and damaged by adopting an alternative yet concurrent abortion standard, such as the human life bill.⁵

In *Akron*, Justice Powell argued that the rule of law required adherence to one clear, knowable, predictable legal standard. He recognized that "arguments continue to be made, in these cases as well [as in other legislation], that [the Court] erred in interpreting the Constitution."⁶ However, he asserted, despite those arguments "the doctrine of *stare decisis*, while perhaps never entirely persuasive on a constitutional question, is a doctrine that demands respect in a society governed by the rule of law. We respect it today, and reaffirm *Roe v. Wade*."⁷ Powell's opinion suggests that disagreement or discussion about alternative constitutional interpretations threatens the rule of law.

In *Thornburgh*, Justices Stevens and White also attempted to indicate the importance of a clearly enunciated legal standard for the rule of law. Like Powell in *Akron*, Stevens argued that challenges to judicial constitutional interpretation threatened order and the rule of law. Stevens contended that "there is a strong public interest in stability, and in the orderly conduct of our affairs, that is served by a consistent course of constitutional adjudication."⁸ Even White, who dissented from *Thornburgh* and thus seemed to favor the fetal rights interpretation of the Fourteenth Amendment, argued that disagreement about constitutional meaning would deepen skepticism about the nation's commitment to the rule of law. More specifically, he contended that challenges to *Roe* would deepen the belief that will, not law, ruled the polity. He argued that "the rule of *stare decisis* is essential if case-by-case judicial decision making is to be reconciled with the principle of the Rule of Law, for when governing legal standards are open to revision in every case, deciding cases becomes a mere exercise of judicial will, with arbitrary and unpredictable results."⁹

To the extent that this fear of confusion deters frivolous or willful challenges to judicial rulings, it may aid in upholding the rule of law. Even though the human life bill does not seem to have generated great confusion, this fear must be addressed more satisfactorily before the debate can heighten constitutional consciousness and broaden constitutional authority.

Legislative Supremacy

Some scholars fear that the practice of departmentalism will lead the legislature to assert its supremacy in defining the scope of individual rights and thus to less vigilant protection of those rights. They fear that instead of nurturing a coequal judicial-legislative dialogue, departmentalism will enable Congress to assert its supremacy, thereby establishing a precedent that Congress rather than the judiciary should ultimately define the scope of individual rights. Additionally, some constitutional democrats fear that the tyranny of the majority will more likely sway the popularly elected branches than the Court, thereby endangering the security of individual rights.[10]

In several places the human life bill states that the Supreme Court would retain the right to review the bill and all state laws and cases that arise under it. Although Section 4 of the bill would restrict the jurisdiction of lower federal courts by prohibiting them from issuing restraining orders, injunctions, or declaratory judgments in cases arising under the human life bill, it also states that "nothing in this section shall deprive the Supreme Court of the United States of the authority to render appropriate relief in any case."[11] Without disturbing the Supreme Court's jurisdiction over abortion cases, the human life bill restricts lower federal court jurisdiction in order to facilitate a full review through state judicial systems. Furthermore, Section 5 also recognizes that the Supreme Court may review the constitutionality of the human life bill, as well as any state legislation that protects fetal rights.[12] Finally, by declaring severability, Section 6 demonstrates that the human life bill assumes and accepts the legitimacy of ongoing judicial review.[13] Severability means that even if the Court uses the power of judicial review to declare a part of the human life bill unconstitutional, that part may be severed, or separated, from the rest of the bill, which will remain in operation unless it is specifically declared unconstitutional as well. In short, the human life bill itself supports coequal constitutional interpretation rather than legislative supremacy.

Supporters of the human life bill maintained that they were not asserting Congress' supremacy to define the scope of individual rights. Rather, they were attempting to create a congressional-judicial dialogue about the constitutional status of the woman's rights and the fetus' rights. During the hearings, supporters of the human life bill steadfastly asserted that they were merely prompting a judicial reconsideration of the abortion issue in light of Congress' findings about when life and personhood begin. For example, Representative Charles Dougherty (R-Penn.) argued that Congress' finding that life begins at conception would not threaten respect for the judiciary but, rather, would initiate a judicial-congressional constitutional dialogue.[14] Claiming that factfinding would not close debate on these matters, Dougherty noted that "any law enacted pursuant to the Human Life Bill would be subject to judicial review."[15]

Arguing that in the long run, despite possible periods of one-branch dominance, a dialogue between coequal branches would be maintained, Senator John East (R-N.C.) also contended that the human life bill did not embrace legislative supremacy. Rather, he argued, shifting back and forth from judicial to legislative interpretation is part of the dialogic process. Thus he conceded that in the end the judiciary will decide what this law means and whether it is constitutional. However, he added: "But then, ultimately, we can come back into the process, too. It's a never ending dialog."[16]

Human life bill supporters also argued that Congress' constitutional interpretation and redefinition of the scope of the right to privacy in this case would not create a general congressional power to define individual rights, nor would it create a precedent that future supporters of such a power could draw upon. The majority report cautiously stated that "the subcommittee does *not* take the position that Congress has a plenary power under the enforcement clause of the Fourteenth Amendment to create new rights or refashion the substantive content of constitutional rights."[17]

A few participants in the abortion debate feared that departmentalism would lead to a tyranny of the majority. Packwood claimed that "passion can obscure judgment and dictatorships and democracies alike are capable of bending to transitory public opinion and popular prejudices which would subjugate individual liberties."[18] Senator Max Baucus (D-Mont.) also argued that the human life bill's interpretation of the Fourteenth Amendment would lead to legislative supremacy in defining the Constitution's scope and meaning.[19] Contending that if Congress passed the human life bill, "the basic terms of the Constitution [would be] left to be determined by the shifting majorities in Congress," Baucus argued that the bill would create a precedent for legislatures to draw on to restrict individual rights and liberties in cases beyond abortion.[20] Thus Baucus concluded that there would be "virtually no constitutional protection that Congress couldn't dilute or eliminate by simple majority vote."[21]

Congress failed to pass the Abortion Funding Restriction Act, in part because several members of Congress thought that the act would create a precedent for Congress to redefine civil rights. Representative Mickey Leland (D-Tex.) of the Black Caucus contended that legislators interested in narrowing the protection of the Civil Rights Act would cite the Abortion Funding Restriction Act as a precedent that established Congress' power to define the status and scope of individual rights.[22] Leland pointed out that the Civil Rights Act had recently been threatened by the Supreme Court's *Grove City College v. Bell* decision and by congressional and executive support for restricting public protection against private discrimination.[23] Thus the fear of legislative supremacy or "tyranny of the majority" in defining the scope of constitutional rights remained strong.

To the extent that this fear of legislative supremacy translates into a watchful check on Congress, it may aid in upholding the rule of law and the supremacy of the Constitution, as well as in securely protecting individual constitutional rights. If the legislative branch established finality, Congress rather than the Constitution or the rule of law would be sovereign. Congress' challenge to judicial supremacy would simply have led to its own willful assertion of power, not to strengthening the rule of law. However, Congress did not assert its supremacy in defining the scope of individual rights in the human life bill (much less in the Abortion Funding Restriction Act). Each bill acknowledged the continuing legitimacy of judicial review. Nevertheless, since this fear may obstruct movement to higher levels of constitutional consciousness, it must be dealt with before constitutional authority can be broadened any further.

Executive Supremacy

Scholars such as Robert Scigliano and Christopher Wolfe argue that although in theory departmentalism does not favor one branch, in practice it favors the executive. They fear that departmentalism would reveal that executive supremacy is inevitable. They argue that since the executive branch implements policy and commands the armed forces it can act unilaterally, force compliance with its decisions, and thus dominate. At best, the other branches can challenge the executive's actions and decisions after they have been implemented. They therefore conclude that departmentalism threatens the rule of law by revealing that the executive has unlimited power.

Yet, during the Persian Gulf period the perception that the executive should or could act unilaterally was not as broadly accepted as it was during the Tonkin Gulf period. If anything, the "inevitability" of executive supremacy was less accepted during the Persian Gulf period than it had been during the Tonkin Gulf period. Congress attempted to limit executive power during the Persian Gulf crisis, and the executive complied—albeit grudgingly—with those limitations. This suggests that both Congress and the executive were beginning to distinguish constitutional authority from executive authority and to limit the "absolute" power of the executive. Even though Congress seemed to accept as given and final the executive's initial decision to commit greater forces to the Persian Gulf, Congress and the public did embrace fuller congressional participation and thus did more effectively challenge executive preeminence in subsequent decisions about troop commitments.

For example, H.R. 2533 obligated Secretary of Defense Caspar Weinberger to issue a report to Congress about security arrangements for American forces sent to the Persian Gulf.[24] Rather than reviewing the executive's decision to reflag and commit armed forces to the Persian Gulf, the bill focused on how best to implement that decision. Following passage of the bill on June 15, 1987, Weinberger issued a brief formal report to Congress to comply with its demand for greater consultation.[25] Consequently it was given grudgingly and in a largely pro forma manner. The report did not offer new information or substantive insight beyond that which various executive officials had already provided during the bill's hearings. Weinberger's report reiterated the administration's goals in the Persian Gulf: to end intimidation of American shipping, to support American friends in the region, to help contain and end the Iran-Iraq war through diplomatic channels, to maintain an undisrupted world oil market, and to preserve economic freedom. The report also argued that since the oil-rich Soviet Union would not be adversely affected by a disruption in the world oil market, the United States aimed to deny the Soviet Union access and influence in the Persian Gulf and thereby prevent Soviet-directed sabotage.

The report reasserted the executive's claim that the risks to American naval forces in the Persian Gulf were "low" and that the risks involved in protecting the reflagged vessels were "moderate." Weinberger conceded that "some risks particularly from unconventional threats, such as Iranian terrorism or sabotage," did exist. However, he insisted that "careful military planning and preparation, adequate cooperation from the allies and the Gulf Cooperation Council states, and full consultation with the Congress" lessened these risks. Furthermore, he stated, the rules of engagement and international law allowed American naval vessels to defend themselves and the reflagged vessels in the region. Weinberger concluded that "there is no risk-free way to safeguard our longstanding vital interests in the Persian Gulf. . . . We can only do our best to minimize and manage the risks, chart a steady course aimed at our strategic goal of ending the war, and reassure our friends—and our adversaries—of our resolve as we move ahead."[26] However, Weinberger's report failed to specify how the administration would minimize the risks in the Persian Gulf.

In short, Weinberger's report did not introduce new information or actively attempt to integrate Congress more fully into the foreign policy decision-making process. Nevertheless, Congress' demand for a formal legal report on the Persian Gulf crisis and the executive's compliance with that demand represent a vast improvement over the Tonkin Gulf period. Congress had finally taken responsibility for reviewing the executive branch's actions and the executive had complied, thereby suggesting a reduction in executive dominance.

Even though Congress relinquished several opportunities to review the executive's initial decision to commit American forces to the Persian Gulf, throughout that period President Reagan continued to behave in a manner that seemed to signal compliance with the reporting requirements of the War Powers Act. However, as was the case for all presidents since Congress passed the act over Nixon's veto, Reagan claimed that he reported to Congress on the basis of his constitutional authority as commander in chief and chief executive, thus implying that he was not reporting to fulfill the statutory obligation of the act. For example, when a U.S. helicopter attacked an Iranian ship laying mines in the Persian Gulf, Reagan reported the attack to Congress in a manner that seemed congruent with the obligations of the War Powers Act. He stated: "In accordance with my desire that Congress continue to be fully informed . . . I am providing this report consistent with the War Powers Resolution."[27] Yet Reagan also reported that he had ordered the "limited defensive action . . . pursuant to [his] constitutional authority with respect to the conduct of foreign relations and Commander in Chief."[28]

Despite this assertion of executive authority, Reagan's report suggests that he was willing to accept a larger role for Congress in decisions about military commitments. For the first time since Congress passed the War Powers Act, a formal presidential report discussed Congress' role in terms that were not wholly adversarial or exclusionary. Reagan stated: "While being mindful of the historical differences between the legislative and executive branches of government and the positions taken by all my predecessors in office, with respect to the interpretation and constitutionality of certain provisions of the War Powers Resolution, I nonetheless am providing this report *in a spirit of mutual cooperation toward a common goal.*"[29]

Although Reagan may have reported simply to placate Congress, any presidential reporting—regardless of motive—signals the executive's inability, or at least reluctance, to act unilaterally or to defy Congress' demands for fuller participation in decisions about troop commitments. Weinberger's and Reagan's reports represent important advances toward broadening Congress' role in foreign policy decision making and thus some limitations on the power of the executive to act unilaterally.

A skeptic might argue that the executive could still unilaterally decide whether to commit troops to foreign lands. And the skeptic might be correct, although until Congress reviews and rejects such a decision, it is virtually impossible to reach firm conclusions about the true extent of executive power. In the meantime, even a skeptic could not deny that Congress clearly has been progressing toward a directly expressed challenge to the executive's unilateral decision to commit forces and military support to foreign lands.

In any case, Congress considered but failed to pass legislation that would have rejected the executive's decision to reflag Kuwaiti ships and commit American naval forces to the Persian Gulf. Congressional supporters of the defeated bill noted that it intended to challenge the president's unilateral decision. They claimed that "the principal purpose of this bill is to avoid greater United States involvement in the Persian Gulf hostilities by prohibiting the implementation of any agreement under which vessels owned by a Persian Gulf nation would be registered under the United States flag."[30] Even though the executive's decision had not yet been implemented, the executive raised the specter of the withdrawal dilemma to discourage Congress from reviewing and questioning the commitment of troops to the Gulf. This suggests that the administration believed that Congress had the ability to limit the president's power to act unilaterally. For example, Weinberger, regarding Congress' power to withdraw troops as a very real limitation on executive power, argued against withdrawal on the grounds that "a retreat by the United States now would have a profoundly negative effect, raising basic questions in the minds of the GCC [Gulf Cooperation Council] states about the character of our commitments and sending a signal to the Iranians and Soviets that our interests in the gulf must no longer be vital."[31]

Attempting to silence those who would consider withdrawal a viable alternative, Reagan also argued vehemently that Congress should not consider that action. Commenting on a proposal for legislation that would have enabled Congress to authorize or reject his reflagging decision, Reagan conceded that Congress had the power to affect Persian Gulf policy. He stated: "I want to make it clear that, despite the damage this legislation could do just by its consideration, we will not abandon our strategic interests or our friends in the Persian Gulf."[32] Under Secretary of State Murphy also attempted to silence any suggestion to consider the president's original decision to increase American naval presence in the Persian Gulf. He stated: "We have no intention—I am sure that is not your suggestion, Congress[men]—to vacate the Gulf."[33]

Support for the bill was diminished by a congressional majority that, in a manner reminiscent of Congress' actions during the Tonkin Gulf period, accepted and reiterated the administration's arguments about the danger of withdrawal and the legitimacy of executive dominance in decisions about troop commitments. For example, congressional opponents of the bill argued that "undercut[ting] the President's foreign policy in such a manner [would] seriously disadvantage our ability to influence events in the Persian Gulf."[34] They argued that withdrawal would cause moderate Arab states to "question the value of American commitment and friendship" and would "look like cut and run in the face of Iranian threats."[35] Thus, they concluded, if Congress defied the president's decision the world would perceive the United States as weak, and Soviet influence, as well as hostile actions, would increase in the Persian Gulf.

Since a fear of executive supremacy may prompt Congress and the public to accept responsibility for reviewing executive decisions, it may aid in upholding the rule of law. However, if one becomes convinced that executive supremacy is inevitable, responsible action will probably not be forthcoming, and executive supremacy will be reinforced. The fear of executive supremacy may obstruct movement to higher levels of constitutional consciousness, particularly since it prompts congressional passivity or silence. This fear must be directly confronted in a more sustained manner in the war powers discourse before constitutional authority can be broadened.

CONFLICT AND CONSTITUTIONAL CONSCIOUSNESS

Scholars and public officials who fear that departmentalism will produce chaos, legislative supremacy, and executive supremacy are skeptical about departmentalism's ability to broaden the scope of constitutional authority. They focus their attention on the transition point between supplanting judicial authority and broadening constitutional authority, fearing that departmentalism will succeed in narrowing the scope of judicial authority but fail to fill that gap with heightened constitutional consciousness. And in some cases these fears may be realized: Departmentalism does run the risk of decreasing the scope of judicial authority without increasing the scope of constitutional authority, thereby weakening the rule of law.

Although the practice of departmentalism poses some risk to the rule of law, it also presents an opportunity to broaden the polity's understanding of and attachment to the Constitution and the rule of law. In the abortion and war powers cases, departmentalism broadened constitutional authority and successfully avoided the risks of chaos, legislative supremacy, and executive supremacy. Whether departmental practice will damage the rule of law in other situations remains to be seen. Nevertheless, although chaos, legislative supremacy, and executive supremacy did not materialize in the abortion and war powers cases, the fact that scholars and public officials feared that they would suggests the concerns and problems that must be addressed before the polity can reach higher levels of constitutional consciousness.

A fear of legislative and executive supremacy on the one hand and chaos on the other suggests the belief that congressional challenges to judicial supremacy (and executive supremacy) will expose either the polity's lack of constitutional consciousness or the Constitution's lack of meaning. These fears further suggest that in the absence of absolute authority, political and legal discourse and action will either result in a chaotic, unlimited, sovereignless free-for-all or ensure dominance by one branch (other than the Court), even though such willful rule threatens the rule of law. Several scholars imply that one institution with final authority must be sovereign to maintain attachment (or, rather, the illusion of attachment) to the rule of law, and given a choice, they favor the Court in domestic affairs and the executive in foreign affairs.

To move to higher levels of constitutional consciousness, conflict must be understood, at least in part, as an opportunity to broaden the polity's shared understanding of what the Constitution means when it is applied to difficult and controversial political problems. If conflict is viewed as an opportunity to foster a common constitutional discussion, then constitutional consciousness will continue to heighten and constitutional authority will continue to deepen. This requires a consciousness that can at least consider the possibility that the Constitution has meaning independent of any one interpreter alongside the alternative, postmodern assumption that meaning is entirely relative to the interpreter. It may be most difficult to maintain this possibility under conditions of intense disagreement about constitutional meaning. This view of conflict requires a consciousness that can at least consider it possible for individuals in the community to speak with one another in a common conversation despite severe differences. In short, it requires a consciousness that considers it possible to discuss commonalities as well as differences in a shared constitutional language. However, if conflict is viewed solely as a willful, forceful assertion and reassertion of narrow self-interest, then constitutional consciousness will diminish and constitutional authority will be rendered meaningless at worst or much less central to the maintenance of the rule of law at best.

These concerns hark back to a much older debate that Thomas Jefferson and Publius had at the time of the founding.[36] Because of the "defect of better motives" in individuals, Publius was extremely skeptical about counting on high levels of civic virtue or constitutional consciousness to maintain the polity and preserve the rule of law.[37] In *Federalist* 51, Publius outlines a plan to maintain limited government and secure individual rights. Publius chooses to rely on individual ambition or self-interestedness to counteract the ambition of other self-interested individuals.[38] In this manner, Publius hoped that the fundamentally self-interested nature of man could be used for a good purpose.[39] Thus "inventions of prudence"—such as checks and balances, federalism, and multiplying the number of competing interests in a commercially diversified republic—assume self-interested behavior and attempt to rechannel it toward the public good.[40]

Jefferson, echoing sentiments of many Antifederalists, insisted that high levels of civic virtue or constitutional consciousness were necessary to maintain and develop a limited government based on the rule of law. In his view, solely self-interested or adversarial relations would not suffice. Commonalities, not just differences, would need to be located and fostered. Jefferson advocated departmentalism and suggested that the people, through constitutional conventions, should resolve any constitutional disputes that might arise between the branches as a result of departmental practice. According to Jefferson and the Antifederalists, Publius's inventions of prudence would afford little protection for individual rights if the polity lacked a common bond or constitutional consciousness.

Jefferson's plan is summarized and rejected by Publius in *Federalist*

49. According to Publius since the people are often guided by passion rather than reason, frequent conflict about fundamental constitutional principles would destroy public "veneration" of the government and law, "disturb the public tranquility," and threaten the security of individual rights.[41] To put it in contemporary language, conflict would foster skepticism about the rule of law and constitutional meaning.

In any case, in a republic based solely on the principle of ambition versus ambition, conflict will be perceived as a product of a willful clash of unrestrained and self-interested individuals. In such a republic, it would not be in a person's self-interest to respect the strengths or admit the validity of an opposing argument. Individuals could not openly consider opposing arguments without risking the defeat of their own position. Indeed, this adversarial consciousness seems to foster a culture in which it is almost as if individuals cannot have broad common interests since nothing tangible seems to exist beyond the self. In such a republic, individuals seem to be solely concerned with advancing their own position and winning the argument at any cost. However, respecting the strengths and admitting the validity of the opposing argument is precisely what the higher levels of constitutional consciousness require. Consequently, it will be extremely difficult, if not impossible, to reach higher levels of constitutional consciousness in a republic that fosters a culture of ambition versus ambition.

Constitutional consciousness will be fostered only if conflict is perceived, at least in part, as an opportunity to broaden the community's discussion about its shared life. In this kind of republic, conflict will be viewed as more than another opportunity to assert and reassert one's own position. Although winning would still probably entail gaining acceptance of one's favored position, it would also entail deepening the polity's understanding of complex constitutional problems, not the least of which is the problem of political commitment and constitutional meaning itself. Unlike Publius and the Federalists, Jefferson and the Antifederalists had confidence in developing this kind of republic—or at any rate, more confidence than they had in maintaining a republic based on ambition and narrow self-interest.

Like the authors of the *Federalist Papers*, many contemporary scholars fear that the people do not have the constitutional consciousness necessary to maintain a decent or just government.[42] Furthermore, in the context of postmodern skepticism, these scholars seem to fear that the Constitution is devoid of meaning and therefore does not provide a solid referent for the nation's discussion about decent and just government. But they have not clearly shown beyond assertion that the people and the people's representatives do not have the requisite constitutional consciousness to engage in thoughtful, sustained constitutional discourse.

Even though many contemporary scholars often assume that the people are more Federalist than Antifederalist, the abortion and war powers debates belie that assumption to some degree and thus offer grounds to hope that the polity will continue to foster deeper levels of constitutional consciousness, particularly if departmentalism is practiced on a much broader basis.[43] Any departmental challenge to judicial supremacy necessarily draws on some preexisting level of constitutional consciousness. The fact that Congress and the people sometimes challenge judicial supremacy and executive supremacy indicates that the polity has retained at least a measure of constitutional consciousness. Departmentalism does not promise to create constitutional consciousness, because the initial departmental challenge to judicial supremacy itself indicates that a certain level of constitutional consciousness already exists. Rather, departmentalism promises to deepen and foster constitutional consciousness. This suggests that asking whether we are, or should be, Federalist or Antifederalist is to ask the wrong question. Perhaps, in terms of constitutional consciousness—if I may paraphrase Jefferson—we are all Federalists and we are all Antifederalists. In this light, the challenge would be to find the proper combination of federalism and antifederalism, or self- and community interestedness.

In his first inaugural address, Jefferson specifically recognized both the commonalities and the differences between the outgoing Federalists and the incoming Republicans following the election of 1800. He stated: "Every difference of opinion is not a difference of principle. We have called by different names brethren of the same principle. We are all Republicans, we are all Federalists. If there be any among us who would wish to dissolve this union, or to change its republican form, let them stand undisturbed as monuments of the safety where reason is left free to combat error."[44] Jefferson gave this speech knowing very well that his Republicans were victorious. Victors in contemporary constitutional conflicts could learn a great deal from Jefferson about processing conflict in a manner that is productive for the polity as a whole—"winners" and "losers" alike.

Scholars who overlook the constitutional consciousness that currently exists may also be prone to deny that departmentalism fosters constitutional consciousness. These scholars highlight and reinforce our tendencies toward narrow self-interest. Yet the facts are that constitutional consciousness exists and that departmentalism is superior to judicial and executive supremacy in terms of fostering constitutional consciousness and broadening constitutional authority. Rather than wrongly asserting that community interestedness is impossible at this late date, scholars would do well to admit that at least a modicum of constitutional consciousness does exist and to imagine alternative institutional structures and political practices, such as departmentalism, that foster a balance between the individual and the community.

Whether the Constitution ultimately has meaning is an enduring question that a healthy polity will continue to ponder on various dimensions and issues. Departmentalism as an alternative to judicial and executive supremacy should continue to be explored because it keeps that question, and the promise of self-government, alive.

APPENDIX ONE

Proposed
Abortion Legislation

S. 158—THE HUMAN LIFE BILL
A Bill to provide that human life shall be deemed to exist from conception.

Be it enacted by the Senate and House of Representatives of the United States of America in Congress assembled, That title 42 of the United States Code shall be amended at the end thereof by adding the following new chapter:

CHAPTER 101
Section 1(a)   The Congress finds that the life of each human being begins at conception.
        (b)   The Congress further finds that the fourteenth amendment to the Constitution of the United States protects all human beings.
Section 2   Upon the basis of these findings, and in the exercise of the powers of Congress, including its power under section 5 of the fourteenth amendment to the Constitution of the United States, the Congress hereby recognizes that for the purpose of enforcing the obligation of the States under the fourteenth amendment not to deprive persons of life without due process of law, each human life exists from conception, without regard to race, sex, age, health, defect, or condition of dependency, and for this purpose "person" includes all human beings.
Section 3   Congress further recognizes that each State has a compelling interest, independent of the status of unborn children under the fourteenth amendment, in protecting the lives of those within the State's jurisdiction whom the State rationally regards as human beings.
Section 4   Notwithstanding any other provision of law, no inferior Federal court ordained and established by Congress under article III of the Constitution of the United States shall have jurisdiction to issue any restraining order, temporary or permanent injunction, or declaratory judgment in any case involving or arising from any State law or municipal ordinance that (1) protects the rights of human persons between conception and birth, or (2) prohibits, limits, or regulates (a) the performance of abortions or (b) the provision at public expense of funds, facilities, personnel, or other assistance for the perfor-

mance of abortions: Provided that nothing in this section shall deprive the Supreme Court of the United States of the authority to render appropriate relief in any case.

Section 5   Any party may appeal to the Supreme Court of the United States from an interlocutory or final judgment, decree, or order of any court of the United States regarding the enforcement of this Act, or of any State law or municipal ordinance that protects the rights of human beings between conception and birth, or which adjudicates the constitutionality of this Act, or any such law or ordinance. The Supreme Court shall advance on its docket and expedite the disposition of any such appeal.

Section 6   If any provision of this Act or the application thereof to any person or circumstance is judicially determined to be invalid, the validity of the remainder of the Act and the application of such provision to other persons and circumstances shall not be affected by such determination.

S. 522—THE ABORTION FUNDING RESTRICTION ACT

A Bill to amend the Civil Rights Act of 1964 to protect the rights of the unborn.

Be it enacted by the Senate and House of Representatives of the United States of America in Congress assembled, That title VI of the Civil Rights Act of 1964 (42 U.S.C. 2000d) is amended by adding at the end thereof the following:

Section 606 Nothing contained in the Civil Rights Act of 1964 shall be construed to authorize the use of Federal financial assistance for abortions and no such assistance shall be used to perform abortions except where the life of the mother would be endangered if the fetus were carried to term.

Selected Congressional Resolutions Relating to the War Powers

THE TONKIN GULF RESOLUTION

Whereas naval units of the Communist regime in Vietnam, in violation of the principles of the Charter of the United Nations and of international law, have deliberately and repeatedly attacked United States naval vessels lawfully present in international waters, and have thereby created a serious threat to international peace; and

Whereas these attacks are part of a deliberate and systematic campaign of aggression that the Communist regime in North Vietnam has been waging against its neighbors and the nations joined with them in the collective defense of their freedom; and

Whereas the United States is assisting the peoples of Southeast Asia to protect their freedom and has no territorial, military or political ambitions in that area, but desires only that these peoples should be left in peace to work out their own destinies in their own way: Now, therefore, be it

Resolved by the Senate and House of Representatives of the United States of America in Congress assembled, That the Congress approves and supports the determination of the President, as Commander in Chief, to take all necessary measures to repel any armed attack against the forces of the United States and to prevent further aggression.

Sec. 2. The United States regards as vital to its national interest and to world peace the maintenance of international peace and security in Southeast Asia. Consonant with the Constitution of the United States and the charter of the United Nations and in accordance with its obligations under the Southeast Asia Collective Defense Treaty, the United States is, therefore, prepared, as the President determines, to take all necessary steps, including the use of armed force, to assist any member or protocol state of the Southeast Asia Collective Defense Treaty requesting assistance in defense of its freedom.

Sec. 3. This resolution shall expire when the President shall determine that the peace and security of the area is reasonably assured by international conditions created by action of the United Nations or otherwise, except that it may be terminated earlier by concurrent resolution of the Congress.

THE WAR POWERS RESOLUTION

Resolved by the Senate and House of Representatives of the United States of America in Congress assembled, That:

Sec. 1. This joint resolution may be cited as the "War Powers Resolution."

Sec. 2. (a) It is the purpose of this joint resolution to fulfill the intent of the framers of the Constitution of the United States and insure that the collective judgment of both the Congress and the President will apply to the introduction of United States Armed Forces into hostilities, or into situations where imminent involvement in hostilities is clearly indicated by the circumstances, and to the continued use of such forces in hostilities or in such situations.

(b) Under article I, section 8, of the Constitution, it is specifically provided that the Congress shall have the power to make all laws necessary and proper for carrying into execution, not only its own powers but also all other powers vested by the Constitution in the Government of the United States, or in any department or officer thereof.

(c) The constitutional powers of the President as Commander in Chief to introduce United States Armed Forces into hostilities, or into situations where imminent involvement in hostilities is clearly indicated by the circumstances, are exercised only pursuant to (1) a declaration of war, (2) specific statutory authorization, or (3) a national emergency created by attack upon the United States, its territories or possessions, or its armed forces.

Sec. 3. The President in every possible instance shall consult with Congress before introducing United States Armed Forces into hostilities or into situations where imminent involvement in hostilities is clearly indicated by the circumstances, and after every such introduction shall consult regularly with the Congress until United States Armed Forces are no longer engaged in hostilities or have been removed from such situations.

Sec. 4. (a) In the absence of a declaration of war, in any case in which United States Armed Forces are introduced—

(1) into hostilities or into situations where imminent involvement in hostilities is clearly indicated by the circumstances;

(2) into the territory, airspace, or waters of a foreign nation, while equipped for combat, except for deployments which relate solely to supply, replacement, repair, or training of such forces; or

(3) in numbers which substantially enlarge United States Armed Forces equipped for combat already located in a foreign nation;

(a) the President shall submit within 48 hours to the Speaker of the House of Representatives and to the President *pro tempore* of the Senate a report, in writing, setting forth—

(A) the circumstances necessitating the introduction of United States Armed Forces;

(B) the constitutional and legislative authority under which such introduction took place; and

(C) the estimated scope and duration of the hostilities or involvement.

(b) The President shall provide such other information as the Congress may request in the fulfillment of its constitutional responsibilities with respect to committing the Nation to war and to the use of United States Armed Forces abroad.

(c) Whenever United States Armed Forces are introduced into hostilities or into any situation described in subsection (a) of this section, the President shall, so long as such armed forces continue to be engaged in such hostilities or situation, report to the Congress periodically on the status of such hostilities or situation as well as on the scope and duration of such hostilities or situation, but in no event shall he report to the Congress less often than once every six months.

Sec. 5. (a) Each report submitted pursuant to section 4 (a) (1) shall be transmitted to the Speaker of the House of Representatives and to the President *pro tempore* of the Senate on the same calendar day. Each report so transmitted shall be referred to the Committee on Foreign Affairs of the House of Representatives and to the Committee on Foreign Relations of the Senate for appropriate action. If, when the report is transmitted, the Congress has adjourned *sine die* or has adjourned for any period in excess of three calendar days, the Speaker of the House of Representatives and the president *pro tempore* of the Senate, if they deem it advisable (or if petitioned by at least 30 percent of the membership of their respective Houses) shall jointly request the President to convene Congress in order that it may consider the report and take appropriate action pursuant to this section.

(b) Within sixty calendar days after a report is submitted or is required to be submitted pursuant to section 4 (a) (1), whichever is earlier, the President shall terminate any use of United States Armed Forces with respect to which such report was submitted (or required to be submitted), unless the Congress (1) has declared war or has enacted a specific authorization for such use of United States Armed Forces, (2) has extended by law such sixty-day period, or (3) is physically unable to meet as a result of an armed attack upon the United States. Such sixty-day period shall be extended for not more than an additional thirty days if the President determined and certifies to the Congress in writing that unavoidable military necessity respecting the safety of United States Armed Forces requires the continued use of such armed forces in the course of bringing about a prompt removal of such forces.

(c) Notwithstanding subsection (b), at any time that United States Armed Forces are engaged in hostilities outside the territory of the United States, its possessions and territories without a declaration of war or specific statutory authorization, such forces shall be removed by the President if the Congress so directs by concurrent resolution.

Sec. 6. (a) Any joint resolution or bill introduced pursuant to section 5(b) at least thirty calendar days before the expiration of the sixty-day period specified in such section shall be referred to the Committee on Foreign Affairs of the House of Representatives or the Committee on Foreign Relations of the Senate, as the case may be, and such committee shall report one such joint resolution or bill, together with its recommendations, not later than twenty-four calendar days before the expiration of the sixty-day period specified in such section, unless such House shall otherwise determine by the yeas and nays.

(b) Any joint resolution or bill so reported shall become the pending business of the House in question (in the case of the Senate the time for debate shall be equally divided between the proponents and the opponents), and shall be voted on within three calendar days thereafter, unless such House shall otherwise determine by yeas and nays.

(c) Such a joint resolution or bill passed by one House shall be referred to the committee of the other House named in subsection (a) and shall be reported out not later than fourteen calendar days before the expiration of the sixty-day period specified in section 5(b). The joint resolution or bill so reported shall become the pending business of the House in question and shall be voted on within three calendar days after it has been reported, unless such House shall otherwise determine by yeas and nays.

(d) In the case of any disagreement between the two Houses of Congress with respect to a joint resolution or bill passed by both Houses, conferees shall be promptly appointed and the committee of conference shall make and file a report with respect to such resolution or bill not later than four calendar days before the expiration of the sixty-day period specified in section 5(b). In the event the conferees are unable to agree within 48 hours, they shall report back to their respective Houses in disagreement. Notwithstanding any rule in either House concerning the printing of conference reports in the Record or concerning any delay in the consideration of such reports, such report shall be acted on by both Houses not later than the expiration of such sixty-day period.

Sec. 7. (a) Any concurrent resolution introduced pursuant to section 5(c) shall be referred to the Committee on Foreign Affairs of the House of Representatives or the Committee on Foreign Relations of the Senate, as the case may be, and one such concurrent resolution shall be reported out by such committee together with its recommendations within fifteen calendar days, unless such House shall otherwise determine by the yeas and nays.

(b) Any concurrent resolution so reported shall become the pending business of the House in question (in the case of the Senate the time for debate shall be equally divided between the proponents and the opponents) and shall be voted on within three calendar days thereafter, unless such House shall otherwise determine by yeas and nays.

(c) Such a concurrent resolution passed by one House shall be referred to the committee of the other House named in subsection (a) and shall be reported out by such committee together with its recommendations within fifteen calendar days and shall thereupon become the pending business of such House and shall be voted upon within three calendar days, unless such House shall otherwise determine by yeas and nays.

(d) In the case of any disagreement between the two Houses of Congress with respect to a concurrent resolution passed by both Houses, conferees shall be promptly appointed and the committee of conference shall make and file a report with respect to such concurrent resolution within six calendar days after the legislation is referred to the committee of conference. Notwithstanding any rule in either House concerning the printing of conference reports in the Record or concerning any delay in the consideration of such reports, such report shall be acted on by both Houses not later than six calendar days after the conference report is filed. In the event the conferees are unable to agree within 48 hours, they shall report back to their respective Houses in disagreement.

Sec. 8. (a) Authority to introduce United States Armed Forces into hostilities or into situations wherein involvement in hostilities is clearly indicated by the circumstances shall not be inferred—

(1) from any provision of law (whether or not in effect before the date of the enactment of this joint resolution), including any provision contained in any appropriation Act, unless such provision specifically authorizes the introduction of United States Armed Forces into hostilities or into such situations and

states that it is intended to constitute specific statutory authorization within the meaning of this joint resolution; or

(2) from any treaty heretofore or hereafter ratified unless such treaty is implemented by legislation specifically authorizing the introduction of United States Armed Forces into hostilities or into such situations and stating that it is intended to constitute specific statutory authorization within the meaning of this joint resolution.

(b) Nothing in this joint resolution shall be construed to require any further specific statutory authorization to permit members of United States Armed Forces to participate jointly with members of the armed forces of one or more foreign countries in the headquarters operations of high-level military commands which were established prior to the date of enactment of this joint resolution and pursuant to the United Nations Charter or any treaty ratified by the United States prior to such date.

(c) For purposes of this joint resolution, the term "introduction of United States Armed Forces" includes the assignment of members of such armed forces to command, coordinate, participate in the movement of, or accompany the regular or irregular military forces of any foreign country or government when such military forces are engaged, or there exists· an imminent threat that such forces will become engaged, in hostilities.

(d) Nothing in this joint resolution—

(1) is intended to alter the constitutional authority of the Congress or of the President, or the provisions of existing treaties; or

(2) shall be construed as granting any authority to the President with respect to the introduction of United States Armed Forces into hostilities or into situations wherein involvement in hostilities is clearly indicated by the circumstances which authority he would not have had in the absence of this joint resolution.

Sec. 9. If any provision of this joint resolution or the application thereof to any person or circumstance is held invalid, the remainder of the joint resolution and the application of such provision to any other person or circumstance shall not be affected thereby.

Sec. 10. This joint resolution shall take effect on the date of its enactment.

PREFACE

1. Walter Murphy has recently revived the term "departmentalism." See "Who Shall Interpret? The Quest for the Ultimate Constitutional Interpreter," *Review of Politics* 48 (1986): 401–423, and Walter F. Murphy, James E. Fleming, and William F. Harris, *American Constitutional Interpretation* (Mineola, N.Y.: Foundation Press, 1986), esp. 184–284.

2. Cass Sunstein has recently called for "more empirical work to be done on the real-world effects of constitutional decisions." He claims that "those who study and discuss constitutional law almost never bother with such empirical questions; but what they say almost always assumes answers to them. We need to know whether those answers are correct. Although they will not compel any particular approach to the Constitution—to say that *Brown* was ineffective is not to say that it was wrong—they might well help show when Supreme Court involvement is most likely to accomplish its purposes." See Sunstein, "The Spirit of the Laws," *New Republic*, March 11, 1991, 32–37.

CHAPTER ONE. WHO SHALL INTERPRET THE CONSTITUTION? JUDICIAL SUPREMACY OR DEPARTMENTALISM

1. Walter F. Murphy, "Who Shall Interpret? The Quest for the Ultimate Constitutional Interpreter," *Review of Politics* 48 (1986): 406–407.

2. *Cooper v. Aaron*, 358 U.S. 1 (1958).

3. *Brown v. Board of Education*, 347 U.S. 483 (1954).

4. 358 U.S. 1, 17. Emphasis added.

5. Generally speaking, a question is said to be political rather than legal when "judicially discoverable and manageable standards for resolving" a question are lacking, or when the Court cannot decide "without an initial policy determination" first being made by the political branches, Congress and the executive. In such instances the decision is said to be fundamentally polit-

ical, and the Court defers to the wisdom of the political branches. See *Baker v. Carr*, 369 U.S. 186, 217 (1962).

6. Ibid., 208. Emphasis added.

7. *Powell v. McCormack*, 395 U.S. 486 (1969).

8. Ibid., 549. The Court implied that challenging judicial supremacy would result in confusion, whereas judicial supremacy would maintain order and clarity. It asserted that "a judicial resolution of petitioners' claim will not result in 'multifarious pronouncements by various departments on one question.'"

9. *U.S. v. Nixon*, 418 U.S. 683, 704 (1974).

10. 1 Cranch 137 (1803).

11. Some scholars claim that federal courts practiced judicial review before *Marbury v. Madison* was decided in 1803. See, for example, P. Allan Dionoso-poulos and Paul Peterson, "Rediscovering the American Origins of Judicial Review: A Rebuttal to the Views Stated by Currie and Other Scholars," *John Marshall Law Review* 18 (1984): 49–76.

12. See, for example, Ronald Dworkin, *Law's Empire* (Cambridge, Mass.: Belknap Press, 1986), 356; Robert K. Faulkner, *The Jurisprudence of John Marshall* (Westport, Conn.: Greenwood Press, 1968), 200 and 222–223; and C. Herman Pritchett, "Judicial Supremacy from Marshall to Burger," in M. Judd Harmon, ed., *Essays on the Constitution of the United States* (Port Washington, N.Y.: Kennikat Press, 1978), 99–112, esp. 100: "The American doctrine of judicial supremacy is generally regarded as founded in John Marshall's decision in the case of *Marbury v. Madison*." But also see 111: "It is not true to say that the Court has the 'last word' on constitutional issues. . . . However, it is final so long as the other branches of government and the political process permit its last word to stand."

13. 1 Cranch 137.

14. See notes 4, 5, 7, and 9 above.

15. On this point, see John Brigham, *Cult of the Court* (Philadelphia: Temple University Press, 1987), 16, 35, 221; Sylvia Snowiss, *Judicial Review and the Law of the Constitution* (New Haven, Conn.: Yale University Press, 1990), viii, 176, 195; and Murphy, "Who Shall Interpret?" 406–407. More generally, see Robert L. Clinton, Marbury v. Madison *and Judicial Review* (Lawrence: University Press of Kansas, 1989).

16. *Dred Scott v. Sandford*, 19 Howard 393 (1856).

17. *U.S. v. Butler*, 297 U.S. 1 (1936).

18. 19 Howard 432.

19. 297 U.S. 1, 18.

20. In an earlier case, *Brown v. Allen* (344 U.S. 450 [1953], concurring opinion), Justice Jackson made his famous comment about the Court: "We are not final because we are infallible, we are infallible because we are final." However, since Jackson made this statement in a concurrence, it does not have the same force as a majority opinion.

21. The act made it a crime to "write, print, utter or publish . . . any false, scandalous and malicious writing or writings against the government . . . with intent to defame said government, or to bring [it] into contempt or disrepute; or to excite against [it] the hatred of the good people of the U.S., or to stir up sedition." As cited in Louis Fisher, *American Constitutional Law* (New York: McGraw-Hill, 1990), 638.

22. Ibid., 642.

23. As cited in ibid., 643. Of course, the states of Virginia and Kentucky also challenged the constitutionality of the Sedition Act in 1798 through a series of resolutions penned by Thomas Jefferson and James Madison. See Walter F. Murphy, James E. Fleming and William F. Harris, *American Constitutional Interpretation* (Mineola, N.Y.: Foundation Press, 1986), 260–264.

24. *New York Times Company v. Sullivan*, 376 U.S. 254, 276 (1964).

25. *McColloch v. Maryland*, 4 Wheaton 315 (1819).

26. This quotation and the next are in James D. Richardson, ed., *A Compilation of Messages and Papers of the Presidents*, vol. 2 (Washington, D.C.: Government Printing Office, 1900), 581–582.

27. Ibid., 2:582.

28. As cited in Fisher, *American Constitutional Law*, 82.

29. Abraham Lincoln, *Selected Writings and Speeches of Abraham Lincoln*, ed. T. Harry Williams (New York: Hendricks House, 1980), 120–121.

30. As cited in Fisher, *American Constitutional Law*, 977.

31. *Roe v. Wade*, 410 U.S. 113 (1973).

32. *Weekly Compilation of Presidential Documents* (Washington, D.C.: Government Printing Office, 1982), 885. Emphasis added.

33. Edwin Meese, "The Law of the Constitution," *Tulane Law Journal* 61 (1987): 981.

34. Ibid., 986.

35. Ibid.

36. Robert Nagel, *Constitutional Cultures: The Mentality and Consequences of Judicial Review* (Berkeley: University of California Press, 1989), 2.

37. Raoul Berger, *Government by Judiciary: The Transformation of the Fourteenth Amendment* (Cambridge, Mass.: Harvard University Press, 1977), 320–321. He reiterates this point throughout his book. See, for example, 413–414: "The only way to overturn judicial decisions is through constitutional amendment."

38. Ibid., 296.

39. Robert H. Bork, *The Tempting of America: The Political Seduction of the Law* (New York: Free Press, 1990), 3 (emphasis added). See also his "Neutral Principles and Some First Amendment Problems," *Indiana Law Review* 47, no. 1 (1971): 1–47, esp. 11.

40. John Hart Ely, *Democracy and Distrust: A Theory of Judicial Review* (Cambridge, Mass.: Harvard University Press, 1980), 4.

41. Dworkin, *Law's Empire*, 356.

42. Ibid., 357.

43. Ibid., 356.

44. See also Ronald Dworkin, *Taking Rights Seriously* (Cambridge, Mass.: Harvard University Press, 1977), esp. Chapter 4; and Dworkin, "The Forum of Principle," *New York University Law Review* 56, nos. 2–3 (1981): 469–518.

45. See Dworkin, *Taking Rights Seriously*, Chapter 8.

46. David A. J. Richards, *Toleration and the Constitution* (New York: Oxford University Press, 1986), 291.

47. Ibid.

48. Ibid., 292.

49. Michael Perry, *The Constitution, the Courts, and Human Rights* (New Haven, Conn.: Yale University Press, 1982), esp. 135–136.

50. Notable exceptions to this generalization include Murphy, "Who Shall Interpret?"; John Agresto, *The Supreme Court and Constitutional Democracy*

(Ithaca, N.Y.: Cornell University Press, 1984), and "The Limits of Judicial Supremacy: A Proposal for 'Checked Activism,'" *Georgia Law Review* 14 (1980): 471–495; Sotirios A. Barber, *On What the Constitution Means* (Baltimore: Johns Hopkins University Press, 1984), and "Epistemological Skepticism, Hobbesian Natural Right, and Judicial Self-Restraint," *Review of Politics* 48, no. 3 (1986): 374–400, esp. 386–387; Brigham, *Cult of the Court*; Paul Dimond, *The Supreme Court and Judicial Choice* (Ann Arbor: University of Michigan Press, 1989); Louis Fisher, *Constitutional Dialogues: Interpretation as a Political Process* (Princeton, N.J.: Princeton University Press, 1988), and *American Constitutional Law*, esp. 1344–1348; Gary J. Jacobsohn, *The Supreme Court and the Decline of Constitutional Aspiration* (Totowa, N.J.: Rowman and Littlefield, 1986); Donald P. Kommers, "The Supreme Court and the Constitution: The Continuing Debate on Judicial Review," *Review of Politics* 47, no. 1 (1985): 113–128; Sanford Levinson, "Could Meese Be Right This Time?" *Nation* 243 (1986): 689–707, and *Constitutional Faith* (Princeton, N.J.: Princeton University Press, 1988); Stephen Macedo, *The New Right v. the Constitution* (Washington, D.C.: Cato Institute, 1986), and "Liberal Virtues, Constitutional Community," *Review of Politics* 50, no. 2 (Spring 1988): 215–240; Albert P. Melone, "Legalism, Constitutional Interpretation, and the Role for Non-Jurists in Responsible Government," in Manuel J. Pelaez, ed., *Papers in Comparative Political Science* (Barcelona: Catedra de Historia del Derecho y de las Instituciones, Facultad de Derecho de la Universidad de Malga, 1990), 4683–4695; and Nagel, *Constitutional Cultures*.

51. The quotation is from Chief Justice Charles Evans Hughes.

52. Ely, *Democracy and Distrust*, 5.

53. See note 20 above.

54. See, for example, Benjamin N. Cardozo, *The Nature of the Judicial Process* (New Haven, Conn.: Yale University Press, 1921); Ronald Dworkin, *Taking Rights Seriously*, *Law's Empire*, and "Forum of Principle"; Perry, *Constitution, Courts, and Human Rights*; Laurence Tribe, *Constitutional Choices* (Cambridge, Mass.: Harvard University Press, 1985); and Ely, *Democracy and Distrust*.

55. See, for example, William H. Rehnquist, *The Supreme Court: How It Was, How It Is* (New York: William Morrow, 1987) and "The Notion of a Living Constitution," *Texas Law Review* 54 (1976): 693–706; Bork, *Tempting of America* and "Neutral Principles and Some First Amendment Problems"; Berger, *Government by Judiciary*; and Christopher Wolfe, *The Rise of Modern Judicial Review* (New York: Basic Books, 1986).

56. For an introduction to these debates, see, respectively, the following seminal articles: Thomas C. Grey, "Do We Have an Unwritten Constitution?" *Stanford Law Review* 27 (1975): 703–718, and Paul Brest, "The Misconceived Quest for the Original Understanding," *Boston University Law Review* 60 (1980): 204–260.

57. For a typology that is broader based than those mentioned in the preceding note but that also, unfortunately, centers on judicial constitutional interpretation, see William J. Harris II, "Bonding Word and Polity: The Logic of American Constitutionalism," *American Political Science Review* 76, no. 1 (1982): 34–46. For a useful introduction to some of the terms and categories used in the current debates, see Philip Bobbitt, *Constitutional Fate: Theory of the Constitution* (New York: Oxford University Press, 1982).

58. Paul Brest, "The Fundamental Rights Controversy: The Essential Con-

tradictions of Normative Constitutional Scholarship," *Yale Law Journal* 90 (1981): 1105. See also Mark Tushnet, "The Dilemmas of Liberal Constitutionalism," *Ohio State Law Journal* 42 (1981): 411–426. More generally, see Roberto M. Unger, *Knowledge and Politics* (New York: Free Press, 1975), *Law and Modern Society* (New York: Free Press, 1976), and *The Critical Legal Studies Movement* (Cambridge, Mass.: Harvard University Press, 1986).

59. Brest, "Fundamental Rights Controversy," 1109.

60. See, for example, Leif H. Carter, *Contemporary Constitutional Lawmaking: The Supreme Court and the Art of Politics* (New York: Pergamon Press, 1985) and " 'Die Meistersinger von Nurnberg' and the United States Supreme Court: Aesthetic Theory in Constitutional Jurisprudence," *Polity* 18 (1985): 272–294.

61. See, for example, Tushnet, "Dilemmas of Liberal Constitutionalism," 424.

62. Walter Berns argues that Congress ought to define the scope of substantive individual rights. See, for example, Berns's "Judicial Review and the Rights and Laws of Nature," in Philip Kurland, ed., *Supreme Court Review* (Chicago: University of Chicago Press, 1982), 49–83, and "The Constitution as Bill of Rights," in Robert A. Goldwin and William A. Schambra, eds., *How Does the Constitution Secure These Rights?* (Washington, D.C.: American Enterprise Institute, 1985): 50–73, esp. 73. Berns argues that "not all wants can be satisfied" and that not all "wants" are rights. Thus, he concludes, the best that can be hoped for is that "rights can be secured, by which I mean the natural right to be governed with one's consent. Under the Constitution's system of representative government, this becomes the right to be part of a governing majority." For support on this point, Berns cites Michael P. Zuckert and Marshall McDonald, "The Original Meaning of the Fourteenth Amendment—Once Again," and Michael P. Zuckert, "Congressional Power under the Fourteenth Amendment: The Original Understanding of Section Five," both unpublished.

63. These arguments are reminiscent of Socrates's exchange with Thrasymachus on justice, where Thrasymachus asserts: "I say that the just is nothing other than the advantage of the stronger." See Plato's *Republic*, trans. Allan Bloom (New York: Basic Books, 1968), 338c. See also Thomas Hobbes, *Leviathan* (New York: Penguin Books, 1985), Part 1, Chapters 14 and 15, and Part 2, Chapter 18.

64. Compare the *Federalist*'s rejection of Jefferson's plan to call periodic constitutional conventions to resolve constitutional conflicts with its argument for judicial review, in *The Federalist* (New York: New American Library, 1960), Nos. 49 and 78. For a more recent version of this debate, compare Abner J. Mikva, "How Well Does Congress Support and Defend the Constitution?" *North Carolina Law Review* 61 (1983): 587–611, with Louis Fisher, "Constitutional Interpretation by Members of Congress," *North Carolina Law Review* 63 (1985): 707–747.

65. Recently, a few scholars have noted that the widespread acceptance of judicial supremacy may impede congressional, executive, and popular interpretation of the Constitution. See note 50 above.

66. See Murphy, "Who Shall Interpret?" 411. See also Christopher Wolfe, *Judicial Activism: Bulwark of Freedom or Precarious Security?* (Pacific Grove, Calif.: Brooks Cole, 1991), 13.

67. Some scholars exclude state interpretation (also called nullification, in-

terposition, or state sovereignty). See, for example, Murphy, "Who Shall Interpret?" 401, and Barber, *On What the Constitution Means*, 5–70.

68. See, for example, Murphy, "Who Shall Interpret?" 417; and Agresto, *Supreme Court and Constitutional Democracy*, 32, 152, and "Limits of Judicial Supremacy: 'Checked Activism,'" 493–496.

69. Departmentalists would also not accept legislative or executive finality. However, since most public law scholars adhere tenaciously to judicial finality and seem much less enamored of other manifestations of finality, I emphasize departmentalism's challenge to judicial supremacy.

70. Murphy characterizes this change as a movement from *who* should interpret the Constitution to *what* the Constitution means.

71. See, for example, Agresto, *Supreme Court and Constitutional Democracy*, 131–137, 152, and "Limits of Judicial Review: 'Checked Activism,'" 487, 493–496; and Murphy, "Who Shall Interpret?" 417.

72. See, for example, Murphy, "Who Shall Interpret?" 417; Macedo, *New Right*, 58; and Agresto, *Supreme Court and Constitutional Democracy*, 143, 144, 147.

73. See J. B. Thayer, "The Origin and Scope of the American Doctrine of Constitutional Law," in his *Legal Essays* (Boston: Chipman, 1907), 1–41; Agresto, *Supreme Court and Constitutional Democracy*, 29 (where Agresto explicitly follows the lead of Thayer); Jacobsohn, *Supreme Court and Decline of Constitutional Aspiration*, 110–111; Macedo, *New Right*, 59; and Levinson, "Could Meese Be Right This Time?" 707.

74. Murphy, "Who Shall Interpret?" 417. Note that Murphy does not promise the same reduction of conflict between the elected branches. See also Agresto, *Supreme Court and Constitutional Democracy*, 37, 152, and "Limits of Judicial Supremacy: 'Checked Activism,'" 493–496.

75. Jacobsohn, *Supreme Court and Decline of Constitutional Aspiration*, 110.

76. Macedo, *New Right*, 59.

77. Macedo, "Liberal Virtues, Constitutional Community," 227.

78. Thayer, "Origin and Scope of American Doctrine," 40.

79. Ibid., 38–39.

80. Agresto, *Supreme Court and Constitutional Democracy*, 166, quoting from Alexander Bickel, *The Least Dangerous Branch* (Indianapolis: Bobbs-Merrill, 1962), 240.

81. Agresto, *Supreme Court and Constitutional Democracy*, 113, 165.

82. See ibid., 131, and "Limits of Judicial Supremacy: 'Checked Activism,'" 487.

83. Jacobsohn, *Supreme Court and Decline of Constitutional Aspiration*, 98 (emphasis added). See also 97–100.

84. Paul Brest, "Meese, the Lawman, Calls for Anarchy," *New York Times*, November 2, 1986, sec. 4, E25. For similar statements, see Perry, *Constitution, Courts, and Human Rights*, 135, and Thomas I. Emerson, "The Power of Congress to Change Constitutional Decisions of the Supreme Court: The Human Life Bill," *Northwestern University Law Review* 77 (1982): 133–142.

85. Murphy, "Who Shall Interpret?" 417. See also Agresto, *Supreme Court and Constitutional Democracy*, 43, 144, 147; and Macedo, *New Right*, 58.

86. See also Macedo, "Liberal Virtues, Constitutional Community," 220: "Actual political conflicts spawn the search for public justification through liberal political institutions."

87. See Jacobsohn, *Supreme Court and Decline of Constitutional Aspiration*, 110.

88. Ibid.

89. Ibid., 100.

90. Macedo, *New Right*, 59.

91. Thayer, "Origin and Scope of American Doctrine," 40, 38–39, respectively. For a similar argument, see Agresto, *Supreme Court and Constitutional Democracy*, 29.

92. Thayer claims he is not calling for an abdication of judicial review: "There will still remain to the judiciary an ample field for determinations." Thayer, "Origin and Scope of American Doctrine," 41.

93. Nagel, *Constitutional Cultures*, 1.

94. Ibid., 3.

95. Levinson, "Could Meese Be Right This Time?" 707.

96. Levinson, *Constitutional Faith*, esp. 5–8, 191–194. See also Leif H. Carter, *An Introduction to Constitutional Interpretation* (White Plains, N.Y.: Longman, 1991), esp. xii–xiii.

97. See, for example, Brest, "Meese, the Lawman, Calls for Anarchy," sec. 4, E25; Burt Neuborne, "The Binding Quality of Supreme Court Precedent," *Tulane Law Review* 61 (1987): 995, 1000; Rex E. Lee, "The Provinces of Constitutional Interpretation," *Tulane Law Review* 61 (1987): 1011, 1014–1015; Ramsey Clark, "Enduring Constitutional Issues," *Tulane Law Review* 61 (1987): 1094. See also Anthony Lewis, "Law or Power," *New York Times*, October 27, 1986, A23, col. 1.

98. See, for example, Murphy, "Who Shall Interpret?" 411; Dawn E. Johnsen, "The Creation of Fetal Rights: Conflicts with Women's Constitutional Rights to Liberty, Privacy, and Equal Protection," *Yale Law Journal* 95 (1986): 612; and Emerson, "Power of Congress to Change Constitutional Decisions of Supreme Court," 142.

99. See, for example, Robert Scigliano, *The Supreme Court and the Presidency* (New York: Free Press, 1971), 16–17; Agresto, *Supreme Court and Constitutional Democracy*, 83; and Wolfe, *Rise of Modern Judicial Review*, 98–101. See also Lewis, "Law or Power," A23, col. 1.

100. Tribe interview in the *New York Times*, October 24, 1986, A17, col. 1 (emphasis added). This statement seems to contradict his textbook, *American Constitutional Law* (Mineola, N.Y.: Foundation Press, 1978), 33. There he appears to support some form of departmentalism when he says, "Despite the growth of federal judicial power, the Constitution remains a fundamentally democratic document, open to competing interpretations limited only by the values which inform the Constitution's provisions themselves, and by the complex political process that the Constitution creates—a process which on various occasions gives the Supreme Court, Congress, the President, or the states, the last word in constitutional debate."

101. Lee, "Provinces of Constitutional Interpretation," 1011.

102. Ibid., 1014 (emphasis added). For various journalistic responses along these lines, see the references cited in Mark Tushnet, "The Supreme Court, the Supreme Law of the Land, and Attorney General Meese: A Comment," *Tulane Law Review* 61 (1987): 1017, note 1.

103. Brest, "Meese, the Lawman, Calls for Anarchy," sec. 4, E25.

104. Clark, "Enduring Constitutional Issues," 1093. See also Lewis, "Law or Power," A23, col. 1.

105. Neuborne, "Binding Quality of Supreme Court Precedent," 995.

106. Ibid., 995.

107. Paul Brest, "Meese, the Lawman, Calls for Anarchy," sec. 4, E25.

108. Lewis, "Law or Power," A23, col. 1.

109. *New York Times*, October 24, 1986, A17, col. 1.

110. See Murphy, "Who Shall Interpret?" 411. This concern about rights stems from a much older fear of the "tyranny of the majority." For early accounts of the tyranny of the majority, see *The Federalist*, Nos. 10, 49, and 78, and Alexis de Tocqueville, *Democracy in America* (New York: Doubleday, 1975), Book 1, Chapter 7.

111. Emerson, "Power of Congress to Change Constitutional Decisions of Supreme Court," 142.

112. Ibid.

113. See Agresto, *Supreme Court and Constitutional Democracy*, 139–141.

114. Ibid., 24–31.

115. Although Scigliano's contention appears to be an accurate description of the current constitutional order, it remains to be seen whether departmentalism would support that order.

116. Scigliano, *Supreme Court and Presidency*, 16.

117. Ibid., 17. Apparently, then, the constitutional plan accepts absolute authority rather than limiting it. See also Agresto, *Supreme Court and Constitutional Democracy*, 83.

118. Of course, the legislature could attempt to force compliance through means other than persuasion, including withdrawing the funds necessary for the enforcement or continued exercise of the executive's decisions.

119. Wolfe, *Rise of Modern Judicial Review*, 98. See also 99–101.

120. I am aware that "cost-benefit" is the established term in the literature, but it reveals the overemphasis of costs and the deemphasis of benefits. Since I want to call attention to that problem, and since I believe the benefits should be taken seriously, I have presented the benefits first and consistently refer to the framework as "benefit-cost" rather than "cost-benefit."

121. In "Constitutional Theory and the Dilemma of Judicial Finality," Gary Jacobsohn briefly discusses parts of the human life bill debate and their import for judicial supremacy (see his *Supreme Court and Decline of Constitutional Aspiration*, 113–137, esp. 129–135). To my knowledge this is the most sustained undertaking of its kind to date. In a slightly different framework, Donald A. Downs also explores whether the theoretical claims made in the public law literature that deals with freedom of expression theory are borne out in practice. See his *Nazis in Skokie: Freedom, Community, and the First Amendment* (Notre Dame, Ind.: University of Notre Dame Press, 1985) and *The New Politics of Pornography* (Chicago: University of Chicago Press, 1989).

Other treatments of the human life bill in the literature analyze the proposed bill without exploring what members of Congress actually discussed in the debates or the significance of their discussion toward improving constitutional authority. See, for example, Emerson, "Power of Congress to Change Constitutional Decisions of Supreme Court," and Robert Nagel, "A Comment on Democratic Constitutionalism," *Tulane Law Review* 77 (1987): 1027–1040. See also, Edward Keynes, *The Court, Congress, Prayer, Busing, and Abortion* (Durham, N.C.: Duke University Press, 1989), esp. 292, 296–297.

122. See Brigham, *Cult of the Court*.

123. Mark Tushnet seems to dispute the claim that the researcher can

avoid arbitrariness in making judgments about the construction of categories and which behaviors fit those categories. He states: "Distinguishing between mere petulance and principled disagreement is likely to prove difficult; people will tend to find petulant an effort to overturn a decision that they like and principled an effort to send a message about a decision they don't like" (Tushnet, "Supreme Court, Supreme Law of Land, and Attorney General Meese," 1017). I contend that the specific behaviors that my levels identify for each category narrow the wide scope of discretion that Tushnet sees.

CHAPTER TWO. DEPARTMENTALISM AND JUDICIAL ACTIVISM:
THE ABORTION DEBATE

1. *Roe v. Wade*, 410 U.S. 113 (1973).
2. Ibid., 153.
3. Ibid., 159.
4. Ibid., 222.
5. Ibid., 158. Scholars on both sides of the debate agree that the Court's arguments about personhood are key to the abortion decision. Donald P. Kommers contends that "the Court's regulatory scheme hinges on its declaration that the fetus is not a person within the meaning of the fourteenth amendment." See Kommers, "Liberty and Community in Constitutional Law: The Abortion Cases in Comparative Perspective," *Brigham Young University Law Review* (1985): 382. Kristin Luker also argues that "the debate about abortion is a debate about personhood." See Luker, *Abortion and the Politics of Motherhood* (Berkeley: University of California Press, 1984), 5.
6. 410 U.S. 157.
7. Ibid.
8. Ibid., 162. Luker argues more broadly: "For the last two thousand years, the embryo, like a child or a woman, was not considered a *legal* person." However, she also casts some doubt on the breadth of the Court's claim. She notes: "In Anglo-American common law it is certainly true that embryos have certain legal rights—the right to inherit property, for example. But, it is equally true that the embryo must generally *be born alive* in order to benefit from them." See Luker, *Abortion and the Politics of Motherhood*, 3. However, Dawn E. Johnsen notes that the "live birth" stipulation, once a hard and fast prerequisite for fetal rights and privileges, has recently begun to be eroded in both civil and criminal cases. See Johnsen, "The Creation of Fetal Rights: Conflicts with Women's Constitutional Rights to Liberty, Privacy, and Equal Protection," *Yale Law Journal* 95 (1986): 599–625, esp. 602–604.
9. 410 U.S. 140.
10. Ibid., 162.
11. Some contend that the *Roe* Court did not recognize the woman's right to choose but only the woman's liberty interest in choice. See, for example, Kommers, "Liberty and Community in Constitutional Law," and Justice White's dissenting opinion in *Thornburgh v. American College of Gynecologists and Obstetricians*, 476 U.S. 747 (1986). Although the latter claim is plausible, several passages from *Roe* cast considerable doubt upon that interpretation. In several places, the Court expressly discusses the woman's right. For example, in 410 U.S. 150 the Court expressly distinguishes the woman's right to choose from the state's interest in protecting potential life. See also 410 U.S. 140.

12. 410 U.S. 155. That is, the Court will not uphold a statute affecting a fundamental right on the basis of mere rationality, or because it is merely related to a legitimate state interest. This is a relatively forgiving standard that the Court applies when it is balancing an individual's interest in freedom against the state's interest in order. Under this relatively loose standard, the Court presumes that statutes are constitutional unless they clearly abridge an express constitutional provision. In short, the rationality test leaves a much wider latitude of action for state regulation or for proscription of an individual's behavior than the compelling state interest standard.

When legislation affects a fundamental individual right, such as the woman's right to privacy (as characterized by *Roe*), the Court applies the much stricter compelling state interest standard, because an individual right is being balanced against a state interest. The state's interest must be compelling rather than simply legitimate, and the relation between the state's interest and the legislation to further it must be more than just a rational one. Thus, the Court views with skepticism state legislation that restricts fundamental rights and therefore presumes that statutes are unconstitutional until the compelling interest standard has clearly been met. In short, the compelling state interest standard leaves much less latitude for state legislation than the rationality test. The Court has adhered to this differentiation between right and interest at least since the Court adopted the so-called double standard for constitutional adjudication. Under this standard, the looser rational relation standard is reserved primarily for economic matters, whereas the stricter compelling state interest standard is reserved for legislation that directly affects fundamental rights, suspect classifications, or discrete and insular minorities who would not have effective recourse for their grievances in majoritarian political processes. See *West Coast Hotel v. Parrish*, 300 U.S. 379 (1937), and *U.S. v. Carolene Products*, 304 U.S. 144 (1938).

13. 410 U.S. 163.

14. Ibid., 150.

15. Following the precedent of *U.S. v. Vuitch*, 402 U.S. 62 (1971), the Court construed maternal health broadly in *Roe*, arguing that health included circumstances beyond those that might directly threaten the woman's life. In *Vuitch*, the Court held that "health" means psychological as well as physical well-being. According to the Court, psychological and physical harm include medical harm, creation of a distressful life, mental and physical strain due to child care and/or an unwanted pregnancy, familial strain and incapacity to care for the child, and stigma caused by unwanted pregnancy. In *Doe v. Bolton*, 410 U.S. 190–192 (1973), *Roe*'s companion case, the Court accepted *Vuitch* as precedent and said that "health" referred to "all factors—physical, emotional, psychological, familial, and the woman's age—relevant to the well-being of the patient."

16. Of course, opponents of *Roe* also have proposed a number of constitutional amendments since 1973. In the first congressional session after the Court decided *Roe*, members of Congress introduced over fifty constitutional amendments. Most amendments attempted to recognize the fetus' right to life, or the states' right to decide the abortion question. The Senate Judiciary Committee never reported most of the proposed amendments to the Senate floor. In 1976 Senator Jesse Helms used a parliamentary maneuver to bypass the Senate Judiciary Committee and obtain discussion of his amendment on the Sen-

ate floor. In 1983 Orren Hatch's amendment became the first anti-abortion amendment reported out of committee. However, it was defeated on the Senate floor. For a comprehensive discussion of the various proposed amendments, see Eva R. Rubin, *Abortion, Politics, and the Courts: Roe v. Wade and Its After-math,* rev. ed. (New York: Greenwood Press, 1987), esp. 151–159.

17. U.S. Congress, Senate, *Human Life Bill: A Bill to Provide That Human Life Shall Be Deemed to Exist from Conception,* 97th Cong., 1st sess., 1981, S. 158, Section 1(a). Hereafter cited as *Human Life Bill.*

18. Ibid., Section 1(b).

19. Ibid., Section 2. Emphasis added.

20. Ibid.

21. Senator Jesse Helms (D-S.C.) and Representative Henry Hyde (R-Ill.) introduced the bill in the Senate and House, respectively. Senator John East (R-N.C.) shepherded this bill through the Committee on the Judiciary's Sub-committee on the Separation of Powers, and Senator Max Baucus (D-Mont.) led the opposition.

22. U.S. Congress, Senate, Committee on the Judiciary, *Hearings before the Subcommittee on the Separation of Powers of the Senate Committee on the Judiciary on S. 158, the "Human Life Bill,"* 97th Cong., 2d sess., 1982, 615. Hereafter cited as HLB, with page number.

23. Ibid., 156.

24. Ibid., 155.

25. Ibid., 65.

26. Ibid., 156.

27. Ibid., 158 (emphasis added). Daniel Moynihan made this claim despite arguing two years earlier that legislators who disagree with a Supreme Court decision should express their disagreement by reenacting the very legislation that the Court struck down. See his "Private Schools and the First Amend-ment," *National Review* 31 (1979): 962.

28. Ibid. Moynihan assumed that *Marbury v. Madison* (1 Cranch 137 [1803]), *Cooper v. Aaron* (358 U.S. 1 [1958]), and *U.S. v. Nixon* (418 U.S. 683 [1974]) established judicial supremacy over congressional, state, and executive laws and actions, respectively.

29. Moynihan, "Private Schools and First Amendment," 962. Moynihan limited judicial finality to constitutional decisions. He claimed that Congress could challenge the Supreme Court's statutory interpretations. He stated: "Congress may, and often does, overturn Supreme Court decisions by chang-ing the law. But these decisions are interpretations of statutes, not the words of the Constitution." See HLB, 160.

30. HLB, 160.

31. Ibid., 183.

32. Ibid., 180.

33. Ibid., 183.

34. Ibid.

35. Ibid.

36. Ibid., 159.

37. Ibid., 167.

38. Ibid., 186.

39. Ibid., 1028.

40. Ibid., 190.

41. Moynihan included Robert Bork and Archibald Cox in this list.

42. HLB, 156.

43. See Chapter 1, note 50.

44. HLB, 761.

45. Ibid., 615.

46. See John Hart Ely, *Democracy and Distrust: A Theory of Judicial Review* (Cambridge, Mass.: Harvard University Press, 1977).

47. HLB, 615.

48. Ibid., 6.

49. Ibid., 5. Emphasis added.

50. Ibid., 6.

51. Ibid., 917.

52. Ibid. Emphasis added.

53. Ibid., 916. See Douglas's dissenting opinion in *Sierra Club v. Morton*, 405 U.S. 727 (1972).

54. HLB, 423. Emphasis added.

55. Ibid., 164.

56. Ibid., 22, 24.

57. Ibid., 6–7.

58. Ibid., 423.

59. Ibid.

60. Ibid., 164.

61. Ibid., 513.

62. Ibid. Emphasis added.

63. Ibid., 189.

64. *Baker v. Carr*, 369 U.S. 186 (1962).

65. See Chapter 1, note 5.

66. HLB, 5.

67. Ibid., 21.

68. Ibid., 20.

69. Ibid., 423.

70. Ibid., 42.

71. Ibid., 181.

72. Ibid., 788. See 410 U.S. 157–158.

73. U.S. Constitution, Fourteenth Amendment, Section 5.

74. For an expanded version of this argument, see Stuart Galebach, "A Human Life Statute," *Human Life Review* (1981): 5ff; and Walter F. Murphy, "Who Shall Interpret? The Quest for the Ultimate Constitutional Interpreter," *Review of Politics* 48 (1986): 415–417.

75. HLB, 174.

76. Dawn E. Johnsen takes an even stronger stance and contends that the decision about the status of the fetus " is a social one, not *dictated* by biology" (see Johnsen, "The Creation of Fetal Rights: Conflicts with Women's Constitutional Rights to Liberty, Privacy, and Equal Protection," *Yale Law Journal* 95 [1986]: 599). For a broader discussion about the role of individual and societal values in scientific research, see Thomas Kuhn, *The Structure of Scientific Revolutions* (Chicago: University of Chicago Press, 1970), esp. 111–135.

77. See Appendix 1 of this volume.

78. Section 1 of the Fourteenth Amendment states: "All persons born or naturalized in the United States, and subject to the jurisdiction thereof, are citizens of the United States and of the State wherein they reside. No State

shall make or enforce any law which shall abridge the privileges or immunities of citizens of the United States; nor shall any State deprive any person of life, liberty, or property, without due process of law; nor deny to any person within its jurisdiction the equal protection of the laws."

79. HLB, 920.
80. Ibid.
81. Ibid., 172.
82. Ibid.
83. Ibid., 2.
84. Ibid., 3.
85. Thomas I. Emerson, "The Power of Congress to Change Constitutional Decisions of the Supreme Court: The Human Life Bill," *Northwestern University Law Review* 77 (1982): 131.
86. Emerson takes an extremely strong stand and contends that the finding of personhood "does not rest upon any judgment subject to objective evaluation. All that empirical judgment teaches us is that 'life' exists in numerous forms, including each individual cell, and that some of these have the genetic potential for becoming human beings under some circumstances. The precise point at which this biological form of life actually becomes a 'human being,' however, is a theological or philosophical conclusion." Thus Emerson concludes that the human life bill's attempt to make a finding of "fact" about when life begins, much less about when personhood begins, is misguided and errant. Ibid., 131.
87. HLB, 8.
88. Ibid., 13.
89. Ibid., 22.
90. Ibid., 84, 73, 49, respectively.
91. Ibid., 25.
92. Ibid., 22.
93. Ibid.
94. Ibid., 58.
95. Ibid., 81.
96. *Human Life Bill*, Section 1.
97. HLB, 18.
98. Ibid., 173.
99. Ibid., 80.
100. Ibid., 157, 158. Cotton Mather was a prominent seventeenth-century Puritan minister who "instructed women to be submissive to their husbands, watchful of their children, and attentive to religious duty" (see M. B. Norton, D. M. Katzman, P. D. Escott, H. P. Chudacoff, T. G. Paterson, and W. M. Tuttle, *A People and a Nation: A History of the United States* [Boston: Houghton Mifflin, 1982], 40).
101. HLB, 921.
102. Ibid., 915.
103. Ibid., 512. Emphasis added.
104. See, for example, ibid., 1034.
105. Laws that allow abortion in "hard circumstances," such as pregnancies due to rape or incestuous rape or pregnancies that would endanger the mother's life, seem to recognize that a tragic element is present in the abortion decision. In those situations the law seems to recognize a practical conflict between two abstract goods. Simply because the conflict is exceedingly

clear in so-called hard cases does not mean that the conflict is any less present in so-called soft cases—even though that conflict may sometimes be more difficult to see. For a discussion of how the laws of other advanced Western democracies have recognized and attempted to address this conflict by being aware of both the woman's and the fetus' perspectives, see Mary Ann Glendon, *Abortion and Divorce in Western Law* (Cambridge, Mass.: Harvard University Press, 1987), 1–142. On the more general problem of society addressing the practical conflict between two abstract goods, see Guido Calabresi and Philip Bobbitt, *Tragic Choices* (New York: W. W. Norton, 1978), esp. 17–28.

106. HLB, 1028.
107. Ibid.
108. Ibid., 178.
109. Ibid.
110. Ibid., 190.
111. Ibid., 499.
112. Although these subtleties may make it more difficult to explore whether judicial constitutional interpretation improved, these distinctions are extremely important since the Court often, if not always, uses the logic of precedent while adjudicating cases. The use of precedent helps to maintain principles basic to the rule of law, such as continuity, stability, and predictability.
113. Although the Court reviewed a local ordinance rather than a federal statute in *Akron v. Akron Center for Reproductive Health* (462 U.S. 421 [1983]), the Court's judicial constitutional interpretation should still improve since the constitutionality of *Roe* and the scope of the right to choose abortion were at issue in the *Akron* decision.
114. As cited in 462 U.S. 416, 421.
115. Ibid., 422.
116. Ibid.
117. Ibid., 421.
118. Ibid., 443.
119. Ibid., 444. It is, of course, arguably correct, and perhaps even probable, that Akron designed the ordinance with the intent of obstructing women. However, from the perspective of improving the debate, the important point is that *any* argument made from the fetal perspective would not be engaged under the Court's reading of *Roe*. The Court here uses *Roe* to resist a broader discussion of abortion that would include the fetal perspective.
120. 462 U.S. 444 (citing *Roe* at 159–162).
121. The Court struck down as inconsistent with the *Roe* framework several of Akron's regulations including requirements that physicians perform abortions in hospitals, that women wait twenty-four hours after deciding to have an abortion, and that minors obtain parental consent. For example, following *Roe*'s trimester framework, the Court said that the state could not require physicians to perform abortions in hospitals since that requirement would not further the state's interest in maternal health. The Court added that the hospital regulation placed a "significant [primarily economic] obstacle" in the path of pregnant women seeking abortions and the "vast majority" of second and third trimester abortions, which went against *Roe* and the constitutional right to abortion (462 U.S. 435). See also 462 U.S. 435, 439.
122. 462 U.S. 455.
123. Ibid., 454.

124. Ibid., 458.
125. Ibid., 461.
126. Ibid.
127. Ibid.
128. Ibid., 466. Citing *Harris v. McRae*, 448 U.S. 297 (1980). See also note 12 above.
129. See 462 U.S. 429, 434.
130. Congressional Record (hereafter cited as CR), 99th Cong., 1st sess., February 27, 1985, S2262–2264. See Appendix 1 (p. 127) for the full text of the Abortion Funding Restriction Act.
131. U.S. Congress, Senate, Committee on the Judiciary, *Hearings before the Subcommittee on the Separation of Powers of the Senate Committee on the Judiciary on S. 522, the "Abortion Funding Restriction Act,"* 99th Cong., 1st sess., 1985, 1 (hereafter cited as AFRA, with page number). In his 1985 State of the Union address, Reagan stated: "Abortion is either the taking of a human life or it isn't. And if it is—and medical technology is increasingly showing that it is—it must be stopped" (see *Weekly Compilation of Presidential Documents* [Washington, D.C.: Government Printing Office, 1985], 144).
132. AFRA, 1.
133. Ibid., 7.
134. Of course, this decision was made through Congress' funding power. However, the funding power was being used as a means to further the end of circumscribing the legality of abortion and, arguably, to challenge the constitutional status of the abortion right. These points were widely recognized in congressional debates about the initial Medicaid restrictions, the Hyde Amendment. For example, Hyde himself argued: "I think in the final analysis you must determine whether or not the unborn person is human. . . . And if you believe that human life is deserving of due process of law—of equal protection of the law, then you cannot in logic and conscience help fund the execution of the innocent defenseless human lives." As cited in Louis Fisher, *American Constitutional Law* (New York: McGraw-Hill, 1990), 1181. Hyde also said that he "would like to prevent, if [he] could legally, anybody having an abortion, a rich woman, a middle class woman, or a poor woman. Unfortunately, the only vehicle available is the HEW Medicaid Bill. A life is a life" (CR, 99th Cong., 1st sess., June 17, 1977, H6083).
135. The Supreme Court upheld the Hyde Amendment in *Harris v. McRae*.
136. AFRA, 101.
137. Ibid., 85.
138. Ibid., 86.
139. Ibid., 84.
140. Ibid.
141. Ibid., 90.
142. Ibid., 87.
143. Ibid.
144. Ibid., 6.
145. 476 U.S. 747.
146. Ibid., 757 (emphasis added). Blackmun added: "Again today we reaffirm the general principles laid down in *Roe* and in *Akron*."
147. 476 U.S. 759. The Court also invalidated Pennsylvania's standard of care provision on the basis of *Colautti v. Franklin* (439 U.S. 378 [1979]) and *Roe. Colautti* reaffirmed *Roe*'s argument that states are prohibited from re-

solving the conflict between the woman's health and fetal life in favor of the fetus. Since the standard of care provision increased the risk to the woman's health, the Court struck it down (see 476 U.S. 469). Adhering to the trimester/ compelling interest framework of *Roe*, the Court also struck down a reporting requirement on the grounds that it did not serve a legitimate state interest but rather served to discourage women from pursuing abortion for fear of identification (see 476 U.S. 766). In a similar adherence to *Roe*, the Court upheld an informed consent provision because it furthered the state's legitimate interest in the woman's health and did not covertly or overtly obstruct the right to abortion (see 476 U.S. 762.)

148. 476 U.S. 762.
149. 358 U.S. 1.
150. 476 U.S. 771.
151. Ibid., 786.
152. Ibid., 787.
153. Ibid., 784.
154. Ibid., 792.
155. Ibid., 795.
156. Ibid., 791. In a concurring opinion, Justice Stevens contended that White did not show that the fundamental premises in *Roe* were mistaken or that liberty and privacy in marriage and childbirth (which White approvingly cited as fundamental) do not include abortion (see 476 U.S. 481). For an argument similar to Stevens's, see David A. J. Richards, *Toleration and the Constitution* (New York: Oxford University Press, 1986), 261–269. Richards contends that the Constitution presupposes that citizens are free moral agents who therefore have the right, obligation, and ability to make responsible moral choices about intimate relationships and reproduction. Thus, Richards concludes, a free and egalitarian democratic society should recognize the fundamental character of the right to choose abortion.

157. Ibid., 777.
158. Ibid.
159. Ibid.
160. Ibid.
161. HLB, 59.
162. Ibid.
163. Ibid., 123.
164. Ibid., 59.
165. Ibid., 64–65.
166. Gallup did break this general rule by asking citizens for their reactions to and feelings about the human life bill. It found 42 percent in favor, 51 percent opposed, and 7 percent without an opinion. The poll also found that to the question "At what point do you believe human life begins?" only 7 percent did not have an opinion and only 5 percent answered "don't know." This suggests that most citizens were able to articulate their own positions on a central issue in the abortion debate. (See *Gallup Opinion Index*, Report 190 [July 1981], published monthly by Gallup Poll, Princeton, N.J.). This poll is unique because it takes seriously the import that congressional constitutional interpretation may have for citizens. Yet, even this poll focuses solely on a decisional outcome and therefore fails to examine citizen awareness and understanding of the public debate about abortion.

For an excellent analysis of the antidemocratic assumptions that underlie survey research, as well as the consequences that such research has had on judicial authority, democratic authority, and constitutional authority, see John Brigham, "Bad Attitudes: Survey Research, Civil Liberties, and Constitutional Practice," paper presented to the Midwest Political Science Association, April 13–15, 1989, Chicago.

167. *Cumulative Codebook for the General Social Survey, 1972–1981*, conducted by the National Opinion Research Center, made available by the Inter-University Consortium for Political and Social Research, 235–237, question 208.

168. See, for example, Samuel Stouffer, *Communism, Conformity, and Civil Liberties* (New York: Doubleday, 1955), and Herbert McCloskey, "Consensus and Ideology in American Politics," *American Political Science Review* 58 (1964): 361–382.

CHAPTER THREE. DEPARTMENTALISM AND JUDICIAL
SELF-RESTRAINT: THE WAR POWERS DEBATE

1. See Chapter 1, note 5, of this volume.

2. See, for example, *Foster v. Neilson*, 27 U.S. 253 (1829).

3. David Gray Adler discusses "the unmistakable trend toward executive dominance of U.S. foreign affairs in the past fifty years" (see Adler, "Foreign Policy and the Separation of Powers: The Influence of the Judiciary," in Michael W. McCann and Gerald L. Houseman, eds., *Judging the Constitution: Critical Essays on Judicial Lawmaking* [Glenview, Ill.: Scott Foresman, 1989], 154). Adler's otherwise very incisive work suffers from an overemphasis on the role of the Court in limiting executive dominance at the cost of overlooking Congress' obligation to do so. In this light, see Michael J. Glennon, *Constitutional Diplomacy* (Princeton, N.J.: Princeton University Press, 1990). Glennon emphasizes the role that Congress and the judiciary must play if executive dominance in foreign affairs is to be limited effectively. See also Francis Wormuth and Edwin Firmage, *To Chain the Dog of War: The War Power of Congress in History and Law*, 2d ed. (Urbana: University of Illinois Press, 1989). They contend: "It remains true the President has dominated even the decision to initiate war in recent decades" (ibid., 150). Wormuth and Firmage object to the tradition of executive dominance and call for Congress to shoulder some responsibility for decisions about troop commitments. Finally, see Harold Koh, *The National Security Constitution* (New Haven, Conn.: Yale University Press, 1990).

4. Adler agrees, claiming that "invocation of the political question doctrine has been a major means by which the judiciary has strengthened the role of the President in the conduct of foreign affairs" (Adler, "Foreign Policy," 172).

5. *Goldwater v. Carter*, 444 U.S. 996 (1979).

6. *Crockett v. Reagan*, 558 F.Supp. 893 (1982).

7. *Sanchez-Espinoza v. Reagan*, 568 F.Supp. 596 (1983).

8. *Lowry v. Reagan*, 676 F.Supp. 333 (1987).

9. *U.S. v. Curtiss-Wright*, 299 U.S. 304 (1936).

10. Ibid., 328.

11. *Mora v. McNamara*, 389 U.S. 934 (1967).

12. See also *McArthur v. Clifford*, 393 U.S. 810 (1968), and *Da Costa v. Laird*, 405 U.S. 979 (1972).

13. *Velvel v. Johnson*, 287 F.Supp. 846 (1968).
14. *Berk v. Laird*, 317 F.Supp. 715 (1970).
15. *Orlando v. Laird*, 443 F.2d 1043 (1971).
16. Ibid.
17. Ibid.
18. *Mitchell v. Laird*, 488 F.2d 611 (1973).
19. *Atlee v. Laird*, 347 F.Supp. 689 (1972).
20. P.L. 91-672, 84 Stat. 2053 (1971).
21. P.L. 93-148, 87 Stat. 555 (1973).
22. Ibid., Section 8(a).
23. Ibid., Section 3.
24. Ibid., Section 4.
25. Ibid., Section 5(b).
26. Ibid.
27. Ibid., Section 5(c). A concurrent resolution, or what has come to be known as a legislative veto, can be obtained without presidential approval. In *Immigration and Naturalization Service v. Chadha* (462 U.S. 919 [1983]), the Court ruled a legislative veto unconstitutional. Even though Congress has continued to use the legislative veto widely, some have argued that the principles upon which *Chadha* was based also serve to invalidate the War Powers Act.
28. Several scholars contend that the War Powers Act restores the original intent of the Constitution and that modern executive supremacy abridges that intent. See, for example, Adler, "Foreign Policy," 157. More generally, see Wormuth and Firmage, *To Chain Dog of War*; Glennon, *Constitutional Diplomacy*; and Koh, *National Security Constitution*.
29. P.L. 93-148, Section 2(a). Some opponents of the War Powers Act argue that the framers intended to create executive supremacy in foreign affairs and that the act is therefore unconstitutional. For example, Robert A. Scigliano claims that the act's constitutional interpretation favors Congress and thus illegitimately counters the president's constitutional authority to act in the national interest (see Scigliano, "The War Powers Resolution and the War Powers," in Joseph Bessette and Jeffrey K. Tulis, eds., *The Presidency in the Constitutional Order* [Baton Rouge: Louisiana State University Press, 1981], 115).
Others have contended that the War Powers Act supports neither executive supremacy nor legislative supremacy but, rather, a departmental sharing of powers. For example, Jean Smith argues: "The passage of the War Powers Resolution . . . reflects the basic tension between the war power of Congress and the Commander in Chief authority of the President" (see Smith, *The Constitution and American Foreign Policy* [St. Paul, Minn.: West Publishing Company, 1989], 236).
30. P.L. 93-148, Section 2(c).
31. Article II, Section 2, of the Constitution states: "The President shall be Commander in Chief of the Army and Navy of the United States."
32. U.S. Congress, House, Committee on Foreign Affairs, *Hearings before the Subcommittee on Arms Control, International Security, and Science and on Europe and the Middle East of the House Committee on Foreign Affairs on H.R. 2533, a Bill to Require a Report on Security Arrangements in the Persian Gulf*, 100th Cong., 1st sess., 1987, 135 (hereafter cited as RSA, with page numbers).

33. See U.S. Congress, House, Committee on Foreign Affairs, *Report by the Subcommittee on Arms Control, International Security, and Science and on Europe and the Middle East of the House Committee on Foreign Affairs on the War Powers Resolution*, 100th Cong., 1st sess., 1987, 42.

34. Ibid., 44.

35. Ibid., 48, 47, respectively.

36. Ibid., 60.

37. Ibid., 62.

38. See *Crockett v. Reagan*, 558 F.Supp. 893 (1982); *Sanchez-Espinoza v. Reagan*, 568 F.Supp. 596 (1983); and *Lowry v. Reagan*, 676 F.Supp. 333 (1987).

39. As cited in Stanley Karnow, *Vietnam: A History* (New York: Viking Press, 1983), 369.

40. *Department of State Bulletin* (hereafter cited as DOS), August 24, 1964, 258. This was the first diplomatic note that the United States sent to Hanoi.

41. Wormuth and Firmage, *To Chain Dog of War*, 42.

42. Larry Berman, *Planning a Tragedy* (New York: W. W. Norton, 1982), 33.

43. Karnow, *Vietnam*, 373. Karnow added that upon interviewing his crew after the incident, Captain Herrick of the *Maddox* found that "not a single sailor on either vessel had seen or heard communist gunfire. Those who claimed to have observed anything at all, such as the lights or shadows of North Vietnamese boats, were not really sure." Although the *Maddox*'s sonar picked up twenty-two blips that the crew interpreted as enemy torpedoes, Karnow contends that weather conditions probably created the blips and that the sonar operator that night may have erred due to inexperience.

44. See U.S. Congress, Senate, Committee on Foreign Relations, *Hearings before the Senate Committee on Foreign Relations on the Gulf of Tonkin: The 1964 Incidents*, 90th Cong., 2d sess., 1968.

45. See Berman, *Planning a Tragedy*, 33.

46. DOS, August 15, 1964, 335.

47. See Karnow, *Vietnam*, 371.

48. See DOS, August 24, 1964, 258.

49. *Public Papers of the President of the United States* (Washington, D.C.: Government Printing Office, 1964) (hereafter cited as PP), August 4, 1964, 928.

50. *Congressional Record* (hereafter cited as CR), 88th Cong., 2d sess., August 5, 1964, 18132.

51. Ibid., 18133.

52. Ibid. Emphasis added.

53. CR, 88th Cong., 2d sess., August 6, 1964.

54. Compare Article II, Section 2, of the Constitution with Article I, Section 10.

55. CR, 88th Cong., 2d sess., August 6, 1964, 18399.

56. Only Senators Ernest Gruening (D-Ark.) and Wayne Morse (D-Ore.) voted against the resolution.

57. P.L. 88-408, 78 Stat. 384 (1964).

58. See note 31 above.

59. DOS, August 24, 1964, 258.

60. PP, August 10, 1964, 946.

61. DOS, August 6, 1964, 267.

62. DOS, August 5, 1964, 269.

63. For example, on August 5, Rusk appeared on "Face the Nation." Although he discussed the Tonkin Gulf Resolution at great length, neither Rusk nor his interviewer, Elie Abel, directly addressed any constitutional questions. They primarily discussed the North Vietnamese attack, the Communist threat from North Vietnam and the Soviet Union, and how the Tonkin Gulf Resolution would further the end of containing communism by showing America's unified support for that goal. DOS, August 5, 1964, 268–270.

64. PP, August 10, 1964, 947.

65. CR, 88th Cong., 2d sess., August 5, 1964, 18132.

66. DOS, August 6, 1964, 268.

67. CR, 88th Cong., 2d sess., August 5, 1964, 18132.

68. Smith, *Constitution and American Foreign Policy*, 235.

69. CR, 88th Cong., 2d sess., August 5, 1964, 18132.

70. PP, August 10, 1964, 938.

71. DOS, August 8, 1964, 267.

72. PP, August 10, 1964, 946.

73. PP, August 7, 1964, 936.

74. PP, August 10, 1964, 507.

75. CR, 88th Cong., 2d sess., August 6, 1964, 18399–18400.

76. Ibid., 18400.

77. Ibid.

78. CR, 88th Cong., 2d sess., August 5, 1964, 18151–18152.

79. CR, 88th Cong., 2d sess., August 7, 1964, 18461–18462.

80. CR, 88th Cong., 2d sess., August 6, 1964, 18420.

81. CR, 88th Cong., 2d sess., August 5, 1964, 18085.

82. Lausche also echoed the corollary of containment, the "domino theory." Thus he suggested that U.S. withdrawal from Southeast Asia would amount to surrendering South Vietnam to the Communists and endangering the Philippines and Australia and so on throughout the world. Lausche added that since Southeast Asia was the first line of defense against Communist aggression, when Communists attacked, it was as if they had "attack[ed] us on our native land" (ibid., 18084).

83. CR, 88th Cong., 2d sess., August 6, 1964, 18420, 18414, respectively. As discussed earlier, the line of precedent is not as direct as Johnson suggested. See note 68 above.

84. CR, 88th Cong., 2d sess., August 6, 1964, 18409.

85. Ibid.

86. Ibid., 18408.

87. Ibid., 18420.

88. CR, 88th Cong., 2d sess., August 7, 1964, 18462.

89. CR, 88th Cong., 2d sess., August 5, 1964, 18256.

90. CR, 88th Cong., 2d sess., August 6, 1964, 18412.

91. Ibid., 18414.

92. Ibid., 18410. Mansfield noted that during the *Maddox* incident, Johnson had "counseled with the congressional leadership, the relevant committee chairman and ranking minority members, and the Republican candidate for President" (ibid., 18399).

93. CR, 88th Cong., 2d sess., August 7, 1964, 18548.

94. Ibid.

95. CR, 88th Cong., 2d sess., August 6, 1964, 18406–18407.

96. As cited in Karnow, *Vietnam*, 376.

97. CR, 88th Cong., 2d sess., August 6, 1964, 18405.

98. Ibid., 18403.

99. Ibid. Emphasis added.

100. Ibid., 18421.

101. Ibid.

102. Ibid., 18412. Emphasis added.

103. Ibid., 18421. Carlson contended that congressional questioning weakened the force behind the policy. He seemed to be referring to military or perhaps political force, not necessarily moral force. Of course, his assertion may or may not be correct even on those more limited grounds.

104. Ibid., 18403.

105. Ibid.

106. Ibid., 18402–18403.

107. Ibid., 18403.

108. Ibid., 18415.

109. Ibid., 18457.

110. CR, 88th Cong., 2d sess., August 5, 1964, 18133.

111. Ibid.

112. Ibid.

113. CR, 88th Cong., 2d sess., August 6, 1964, 18414.

114. Ibid., 18428–18429.

115. CR, 88th Cong., 2d sess., August 7, 1964, 18446.

116. CR, 88th Cong., 2d sess., August 6, 1964, 18412.

117. CR, 88th Cong., 2d sess., August 5, 1964, 18136.

118. Ibid.

119. Ibid., 18139.

120. Ibid.

121. CR, 88th Cong., 2d sess., August 7, 1964, 18133, 18443.

122. Ibid., 18445.

123. CR, 88th Cong., 2d sess., August 5, 1964, 18136.

124. According to Richard W. Murphy, under secretary of state for Near Eastern and South Asian affairs, the president decided to reflag Kuwaiti ships because of the United States' "longstanding commitment to flow oil through the Gulf and because of the importance we attach to the freedom of navigation in international waters, as well as our determination to assist our friends in the Gulf" (DOS, May 19, 1987, 60).

125. Michael H. Armacost, under secretary of state for political affairs, contended that the United States was interested in maintaining freedom of navigation in accordance with its worldwide policy of keeping the sea-lanes open (DOS, June 16, 1987, 78).

126. Under Secretary of State Armacost agreed that an American presence in the region supported the individual and collective self-defense of moderate Arab states and challenged revolutionary Islamic states such as Iran (ibid., 80).

127. Offering a variation on the old containment doctrine, Under Secretary of State Murphy noted that the United States wanted to block increased Soviet influence in the region. He stated: "A constant of United States policy for decades has been United States determination to prevent enhanced Soviet influence and presence in the Gulf" (DOS, May 19, 1987, 61).

128. Under Secretary of State Armacost contended that an American pres-

ence would deter further aggression and thus lead to a negotiated settlement of the Iran-Iraq war.

129. President Reagan claimed that "our overriding aim is peace and stability in the region." *Weekly Compilation of Presidential Documents* (Washington, D.C.: Government Printing Office, 1965–   ) (hereafter cited as WC), September 24, 1987, 1067.

130. See RSA, 10, 155, 170–171, 173–174.

131. DOS, October 21, 1987, 13.

132. RSA, 289–290.

133. See P.L. 100-71, 101 Stat. 391 (1987).

134. RSA, 80.

135. Ibid., 108.

136. Ibid., 83.

137. Ibid., 69–70.

138. Ibid., 143.

139. Ibid., 331.

140. Ibid., 157.

141. Ibid., 151. Leach added that trading arms for hostages to Iran also contributed to destroying American neutrality in the Iran-Iraq war.

142. Ibid., 161–162.

143. Ibid., 91–92.

144. Ibid., 5–6.

145. DOS, May 19, 1987, 60.

146. However, in both cases, members of Congress had challenged the executive's contention that hostilities were not imminent and that the War Powers Resolution did not apply. See, for example, *Crockett v. Reagan*, 558 F.Supp. 893 (1982). Twenty-nine legislators alleged that President Reagan, Secretary of Defense Weinberger, and Secretary of State Haig had sent American forces into imminent hostilities in El Salvador without consulting or reporting to Congress, contrary to the War Powers Act.

147. P.L. 93-148, Section 4(a) (1).

148. RSA, 170.

149. Ibid., 171.

150. Ibid., 98.

151. DOS, May 19, 1987, 60.

152. WC, September 9, 1987, 1066.

153. RSA, 129.

154. Ibid., 135.

155. Ibid., 213.

156. Ibid., 214.

157. Ibid., 88.

158. Ibid., 89.

159. Ibid., 167.

160. Ibid., 135.

161. Ibid., 30.

162. Ibid., 9.

163. Ibid., 82.

164. Ibid.

165. Ibid., 142.

166. Ibid., 54.

167. Ibid.

168. Ibid.

169. Weinberger also would not discuss the circumstances that would constitute imminent hostilities. Ibid., 142.

170. Ibid., 199.

171. Ibid., 142.

172. Ibid., 199. Under Secretary of State Armacost replied that since the reaction time for Silkworms differed from that for Exocets, the situation was difficult to judge. He noted, however, that since Iran had never attacked an American vessel or an American-flagged ship, hostilities might continue not to be imminent even if Iran deployed Silkworms.

173. Ibid., 332.

174. Ibid., 266.

175. Ibid.

176. Ibid., 69.

177. Ibid., 70.

178. Ibid., 72.

179. Ibid., 78.

180. Ibid., 68.

181. Ibid.

182. Ibid., 73.

183. Ibid., 1.

184. Ibid., 250.

185. Ibid., 85.

186. Had the War Powers Resolution been explicitly triggered, Congress would at least have been obliged to review and then authorize or reject the president's decision to commit forces to the Persian Gulf sixty to ninety days after forces had been committed.

187. U.S. Congress, Senate, Committee on Foreign Relations, *Report by the Senate Foreign Relations Committee on a Bill to Require the Use of American Armed Forces to Escort, Protect, or Defend Certain Registered Vessels in the Persian Gulf to Comply with the War Powers Resolution*, 100th Cong., 1st sess., 1987, 5.

188. See ibid., 11.

189. Ibid., 5.

190. RSA, 85.

191. Ibid.

192. Ibid., 88.

193. Ibid.

194. Ibid., 327. The quotation within the citation is from *Congressional Quarterly* 45, no. 25 (June 20, 1987).

195. RSA, 327–328.

196. Ibid., 328.

197. Ibid., 327.

198. Ibid., 86.

199. Fascell, a leading supporter of H.R. 2533, contended that the resolution did not imply congressional approval for the administration's Persian Gulf policy.

200. RSA, 77. Fascell claimed that Roth was reading approval into the bill.

201. Ibid., 72.

202. Ibid., 75.

203. Ibid.

204. Ibid., 264.

205. Ibid.

206. Note that departmentalists claim that an improved constitutional debate would heighten the public's sensitivity. However, the causation could, of course, also work the other way. Heightened public sensitivity could very well have served to improve the institutional debate in this case.

207. Karnow, *Vietnam*, 374. Karnow does not indicate the source of his information.

208. CR, 88th Cong., 2d sess., August 7, 1964, 18400–18402.

209. Ibid.

210. George C. Herring, *America's Longest War* (New York: John Wiley and Sons, 1979), 107.

211. Sidney Verba, Richard A. Brody, Edwin B. Parker, Norman H. Nie, Nelson W. Polsby, Paul Ekman, and Gordon S. Black, "Public Opinion and the War in Vietnam," *American Political Science Review* 51, no. 2 (June 1967): 317–333.

212. Ibid., 318.

213. Ibid.

214. See *The Gallup Poll: Public Opinion, 1935–1971*, vol. 3 (New York: Random House, 1972), 195, June 24, 1965. Question 3b: "Why do you disapprove of the Administration's handling of the Vietnam situation?"

215. This was indicated by a search of public opinion indexes and the data base at the Roper Center, conducted at the Roper Center, University of Connecticut, Storrs, July 1989.

216. *The Gallup Poll*, June 14, 1987. Question 33: "Do you approve or disapprove of the Reagan administration's plan to allow Kuwaiti oil tankers to fly the American flag and for U.S. Navy ships to escort these vessels through the Persian Gulf?"

Two later polls conducted by the ABC-television network suggest that support for the policy grew over time. On August 12, 1987, 57 percent of the sample supported Reagan's Persian Gulf policy, while 39 percent opposed it and 4 percent were unsure. On October 19, 1987, 63 percent supported Reagan's Persian Gulf policy, 34 percent opposed it, and 3 percent were unsure. (Data provided by the Roper Center, University of Connecticut, Storrs.)

217. *Los Angeles Times Poll*, June 24, 1987. The question read: "Is it your impression that the Congress has become too involved in foreign policy decisions, or do you think Congress should be consulted in situations that may lead to war?" Eighteen percent answered "too involved," 75 percent said "Congress should be consulted," 6 percent were "not sure," and 1 percent "refused" to respond. (Polling material obtained from the Roper Center, University of Connecticut, Storrs).

218. *CBS News/New York Times Polling*, September 23, 1987. The question read: "Do you think the President should get the approval of Congress in order to keep the ships in the Persian Gulf, or should he be able to make that decision himself?" The results showed that 63 percent answered "should get approval," 33 percent answered "should make decision himself," and 4 percent said they "don't know." (Polling material obtained from the Roper Center, University of Connecticut, Storrs).

CHAPTER FOUR. DEPARTMENTALISM, CONSTITUTIONAL
CONSCIOUSNESS, AND THE RULE OF LAW

1. One might say that Congress was more quiescent during the Tonkin Gulf period because the president and the congressional majority were both Democratic, whereas during the Persian Gulf debates the president was a Republican and the congressional majority was Democratic. There is no reason such "political" interpretations cannot coexist with the interpretation that Congress' constitutional consciousness heightened—unless one insists upon maintaining a rigid distinction between law and politics or "political" and "legal" interpretations. Of course, the very practice of departmentalism belies a rigid distinction between law and politics.

2. This confirms Gary J. Jacobsohn's suspicion that departmentalism necessarily entails—at least for a time—an attack on judicial power. See Chapter 1, note 84, of this volume.

3. For a more general critique of the fear that chaos will ensue if the Court is challenged, see John Brigham, *Cult of the Court* (Philadelphia: Temple University Press, 1987), 60–62.

4. U.S. Congress, Senate, Committee on the Judiciary, *Report by the Subcommittee on the Separation of Powers of the Senate Committee on the Judiciary on S. 158, the "Human Life Bill,"* 97th Cong., 2d sess., 1982, 37. (Hereafter cited as HLB Report, with page numbers.)

5. U.S. Congress, Senate, Committee on the Judiciary, *Hearings before the Subcommittee on the Separation of Powers of the Senate Committee on the Judiciary on S. 158, the "Human Life Bill,"* 97th Cong., 2d Sess., 1982, 85. (Hereafter cited as HLB, with page numbers.)

6. Ibid., 419. Powell added, "Legislative response to [*Roe*] required us on several occasions, and again today, to define the limits of a state's authority to regulate the performance of abortions."

7. Ibid., 419–420.

8. *Thornburgh v. American College of Gynecologists and Obstetricians*, 476 U.S. 747 (1986).

9. Ibid., 786. Of course, White disagreed with the majority about what constituted legitimate precedent in Fourteenth Amendment due process clause cases. Where the majority saw *Roe* as settled precedent, White saw it as a derelict.

10. See, for example, Walter F. Murphy, "Who Shall Interpret? The Quest for the Ultimate Constitutional Interpreter," *Review of Politics* 48 (1986): 411. Interestingly, Murphy cites a judicial opinion, *Eakin v. Raub* (12 S. & R. 330 [1825]), as an example of legislative supremacy.

11. See Appendix One of this volume.

12. Ibid.

13. Ibid.

14. HLB, 171.

15. Ibid., 170.

16. Ibid., 502. East stated: "My whole quarrel with *Roe v. Wade* is we never ever had a public debate on this issue" (HLB, 175).

17. HLB Majority Report, 28.

18. HLB, 156.

19. Ibid., 65.

20. HLB Minority Report, 43.

21. Ibid.

22. U.S. Congress, Senate, Committee on the Judiciary, *Hearings before the Subcommittee on the Separation of Powers of the Senate Committee on the Judiciary on S. 522, the "Abortion Funding Restriction Act,"* 99th Cong., 1st sess., 1985, 87. (Hereafter cited as AFRA, with page numbers.)

23. *Grove City College v. Bell,* 465 U.S. 555 (1984).

24. H.R. 2533 became P.L. 100-71, 101 Stat. 391 (1987).

25. U.S. Congress, House, Committee on Foreign Affairs, *Hearings before the Subcommittee on Arms Control, International Security, and Science and on Europe and the Middle East of the House Committee on Foreign Affairs on H.R. 2533, a Bill to Require a Report on Security Arrangements in the Persian Gulf,* 100th Cong., 1st sess., 1987, Appendix 14, 312–315. (Hereafter cited as RSA Appendix, with page numbers.)

26. Ibid., 312–315.

27. WC, September 22, 1987, 601.

28. Ibid.

29. Ibid. (Emphasis added). After each American attack, Reagan followed the same reporting formula. He announced the facts surrounding the attack, noted that he reported on the basis of his constitutional authority as commander in chief, distanced himself from the War Powers Resolution, and pledged to cooperate with Congress toward a common goal. See, for example, his reports on October 8 and 19, 1987, in ibid., 1060, 1206.

30. U.S. Congress, Senate, Foreign Relations Committee, *Report by the Senate Foreign Relations Committee on a Bill to Prevent United States Involvement in Hostilities in the Persian Gulf,* 100th Cong., 1st sess., 1987, 1. Hereafter cited as PH, with page numbers.

31. RSA Appendix, 314.

32. WC, September 25, 1987, 1073.

33. RSA, 147.

34. PH, 9.

35. Ibid.

36. Publius was the collective pseudonym of John Jay, Alexander Hamilton, and James Madison, who wrote a series of newspaper pieces, now collectively known as the *Federalist Papers,* to persuade the state of New York to ratify the Constitution.

37. Publius [Alexander Hamilton, James Madison, and John Jay], *The Federalist,* ed. Clinton Rossiter (New York: Mentor Books, 1961), 324.

38. Ibid., 322.

39. Ibid., 324.

40. Ibid., 322, 79, 80, respectively.

41. Ibid., 315, 317.

42. Robert Nagel argues that "political constraints on the Court nearly always are labeled illegitimate when they might be implemented and . . . this sort of doubt exemplifies *the inadequacy of our language* at the point where politics and the Constitution converge" (Nagel, "A Comment on Democratic Constitutionalism," *Tulane Law Review* 77 [1987]: 1040; emphasis added).

43. The January 1991 Persian Gulf debate and the *Webster* decision, 492 U.S. 490 (1989), seem to confirm this speculation. Although President Bush was initially reluctant to approach Congress without an assurance of overwhelming support, in the end he asked Congress for a resolution to support the use of force in the Persian Gulf stating: "We, frankly, are welcoming the

fact that there will be a debate in Congress" (*New York Times*, January 7, 1991, A1, A9). Over two hundred members of Congress actively took part in the debate; very few encouraged shortening the debate or stifling views that challenged the executive. Senator Strom Thurmond (R-S.C.), for example, asserted that "the time to tend the debate is now." More typically, most members argued that Congress had a responsibility to choose whether to authorize force independent of executive authority. Representative Ted Weiss (D-N.Y.) argued that when members of Congress take the oath of office, "that's not just a formula we're going through. We swear to preserve and protect and defend the Constitution of the United States. . . . When we think that it's O.K. to wage small wars ourselves, without the prior approval of the Congress, it seems to me that we're eroding the Constitution."

Furthermore, some members argued that conflict was not to be feared but, rather, should be welcomed as a means of broadening unity and strengthening policy. Representative Richard Gephardt (D-Mo.) agreed that the expectation and desire was that all representatives would "vote their conscience, what in their mind is the right thing for this country to do." He argued further that "some have expressed concern that when there is a division of opinion even on strategy, that that lends help to the other side. I hope that we'd never mistake disagreement on means as disunity within our country. I can't remember a time when our country has been as unified around a set of goals, as focused on what we're trying to do, in as much agreement and unity as I think we are tonight. . . . In this vote we are not Democrats. We are not Republicans. We are Americans." Summarizing the congressional debate as a whole, the *New York Times* noted that as "the House and the Senate debated whether to authorize the President to go to war in the Persian Gulf, the lawmakers have struggled to step up to what the framers of the Constitution had in mind" (January 11, 1991, A1).

In *Webster*, the Court discussed fetal rights, or at least the states' interest in fetal life, more directly than in any of the previous cases, stating that the *Roe* framework is "unsound in principle and unworkable in practice." According to *Webster*, the *Roe* standard varies with changes in medical technology in a manner that is inconsistent with principled, stable rule of law. Furthermore, a plurality asserted that it did "not see why the State's interest in protecting potential human life should come into existence only at the point of viability."

44. James D. Richardson, ed., *A Compilation of Messages and Papers of the Presidents*, 10 vols. (Washington, D.C.: Government Printing Office, 1897–   ), 1:322.

SELECTED BIBLIOGRAPHY

Adler, David Gray. "Foreign Policy and the Separation of Powers: The Influence of the Judiciary." In Michael W. McCann and Gerald L. Houseman, eds., *Judging the Constitution: Critical Essays on Judicial Lawmaking.* Glenview, Ill.: Scott Foresman, 1989.

Agresto, John. "The Limits of Judicial Supremacy: A Proposal for 'Checked Activism.'" *Georgia Law Review* 14 (1980): 471–495.

———. *The Supreme Court and Constitutional Democracy.* Ithaca, N.Y.: Cornell University Press, 1984.

Barber, Sotirios A. "Epistemological Skepticism, Hobbesian Natural Rights, and Judicial Self-Restraint." *Review of Politics* 48, no. 3 (1986): 374–400.

———. *On What the Constitution Means.* Baltimore: Johns Hopkins University Press, 1984.

Berger, Raoul. *Government by Judiciary: The Transformation of the Fourteenth Amendment.* Cambridge, Mass.: Harvard University Press, 1977.

Berman, Larry. *Planning a Tragedy.* New York: W. W. Norton, 1982.

Berns, Walter. "The Constitution as Bill of Rights." In Robert A. Goldwin and William A. Schambra, eds., *How Does the Constitution Secure These Rights?* Washington, D.C.: American Enterprise Institute, 1985.

———. "Judicial Review and the Rights and Laws of Nature." In Philip Kurland, ed., *Supreme Court Review.* Chicago: University of Chicago Press, 1982.

Bobbitt, Philip. *Constitutional Fate: Theory of the Constitution.* New York: Oxford University Press, 1982.

Bork, Robert H. "Neutral Principles and Some First Amendment Problems." *Indiana Law Journal* 47, no. 1 (1971): 1–47.

———. *The Tempting of America: The Political Seduction of the Law.* New York: Free Press, 1990.

Brest, Paul. "The Fundamental Rights Controversy: The Essential Contradictions of Normative Constitutional Scholarship." *Yale Law Journal* 90 (1981): 1063–1109.

———. "Meese, the Lawman, Calls for Anarchy," *New York Times,* November 2, 1986, sec. 4, E25.

_____. "The Misconceived Quest for the Original Understanding." *Boston University Law Review* 60 (1980): 204–260.

_____. "Who Decides?" *Southern California Law Review* 58 (1985): 505–515.

Brigham, John. "Bad Attitudes: Survey Research, Civil Liberties, and Constitutional Practice." Paper presented to the Midwest Political Science Association, April 13–15, 1989, Chicago.

_____. *Cult of the Court.* Philadelphia: Temple University Press, 1987.

Calabresi, Guido, and Bobbitt, Philip. *Tragic Choices.* New York: W. W. Norton, 1978.

Cardozo, Benjamin N. *The Nature of the Judicial Process.* New Haven, Conn.: Yale University Press, 1921.

Carter, Leif H. *Contemporary Constitutional Lawmaking: The Supreme Court and the Art of Politics.* New York: Pergamon Press, 1985.

_____. "'Die Meistersinger von Nurnberg' and the United States Supreme Court: Aesthetic Theory in Constitutional Jurisprudence." *Polity* 18 (1985): 272–294.

Choper, Jesse H. *Judicial Review and the National Political Process: A Functional Reconsideration of the Role of the Supreme Court.* Chicago: University of Chicago Press, 1980.

Clark, Ramsey. "Enduring Constitutional Issues." *Tulane Law Review* 61 (1987).

Clinton, Robert L. Marbury v. Madison *and Judicial Review.* Lawrence: University Press of Kansas, 1989.

Cox, Archibald. *The Role of the Supreme Court in American Government.* New York: Oxford University Press, 1976.

Dimond, Paul. *The Supreme Court and Judicial Choice.* Ann Arbor: University of Michigan Press, 1989.

Dionosopoulos, P. Allan, and Peterson, Paul. "Rediscovering the American Origins of Judicial Review: A Rebuttal to the Views Stated by Currie and Other Scholars." *John Marshall Law Review* 18 (1984): 49–76.

Downs, Donald A. *Nazis in Skokie: Freedom, Community, and the First Amendment.* Notre Dame, Ind.: University of Notre Dame Press, 1985.

_____. *The New Politics of Pornography.* Chicago: University of Chicago Press, 1989.

Dworkin, Ronald. "The Forum of Principle." *New York University Law Review* 56, nos. 2–3 (1981): 469–518.

_____. *Law's Empire.* Cambridge, Mass.: Belknap Press, 1986.

_____. *A Matter of Principle.* Cambridge, Mass.: Harvard University Press, 1984.

_____. *Taking Rights Seriously.* Cambridge, Mass.: Harvard University Press, 1977.

Elshtain, Jean. "Reflections on Abortion, Values, and the Family." In Sidney Callahan and Daniel Callahan, eds., *Abortion: Understanding Differences.* New York: Plenum, 1984.

Ely, John Hart. *Democracy and Distrust: A Theory of Judicial Review.* Cambridge, Mass.: Harvard University Press, 1980.

Emerson, Thomas I. "The Power of Congres to Change Constitutional Decisions of the Supreme Court: The Human Life Bill." *Northwestern University Law Review* 77 (1982): 133–142.

Faulkner, Robert K. *The Jurisprudence of John Marshall.* Westport, Conn.: Greenwood Press, 1968.

Fisher, Louis. *American Constitutional Law.* New York: McGraw-Hill, 1990.

———. *Constitutional Conflicts between Congress and the President.* Princeton, N.J.: Princeton University Press, 1986.

———. *Constitutional Dialogues: Interpretation as a Political Process.* Princeton, N.J.: Princeton University Press, 1988.

Galebach, Stuart. "A Human Life Statute." *Human Life Review* (1981): 5ff.

Glendon, Mary Ann. *Abortion and Divorce in Western Law.* Cambridge, Mass.: Harvard University Press, 1987.

Glennon, Michael J. *Constitutional Diplomacy.* Princeton, N.J.: Princeton University Press, 1990.

Grant, George Parkin. *English-Speaking Justice.* Notre Dame, Ind.: Notre Dame University Press, 1985.

Grey, Thomas. "Do We Have an Unwritten Constitution?" *Stanford Law Review* 27 (1975): 703–718.

———. "Origins of the Unwritten Constitution: Fundamental Law in American Revolutionary Thought." *Stanford Law Review* 30 (1978): 843–893.

Harris, William J., II. "Bonding Word and Polity: The Logic of American Constitutionalism." *American Political Science Review* 76, no. 1 (1982): 34–46.

Herring, George C. *America's Longest War.* New York: John Wiley and Sons, 1979.

Hobbes, Thomas. *Leviathan.* New York: Penguin Books, 1985.

Hughes, Charles Evans. *The Supreme Court of the United States: Its Foundations, Methods, and Achievements.* Garden City, N.Y.: Garden City Publishing Company, 1936.

Jacobsohn, Gary J. *The Supreme Court and the Decline of Constitutional Aspiration.* Totowa, N.J.: Rowman and Littlefield, 1986.

Johnsen, Dawn E. "The Creation of Fetal Rights: Conflicts with Women's Constitutional Rights to Liberty, Privacy, and Equal Protection." *Yale Law Journal* 95 (1986).

Karnow, Stanley. *Vietnam: A History.* New York: Viking Press, 1983.

Keynes, Edward. *The Court, Congress, Prayer, Busing, and Abortion.* Durham, N.C.: Duke University Press, 1989.

Koh, Harold. *The National Security Constitution.* New Haven, Conn.: Yale University Press, 1990.

Kommers, Donald P. "Liberty and Community in Constitutional Law: The Abortion Cases in Comparative Perspective." *Brigham Young University Law Review* (1985): 371–409.

———. "The Supreme Court and the Constitution: The Continuing Debate on Judicial Review." *Review of Politics* 47, no. 1 (1985): 113–128.

Kuhn, Thomas. *The Structure of Scientific Revolutions.* Chicago: University of Chicago Press, 1970.

Lee, Rex E. "The Provinces of Constitutional Interpretation." *Tulane Law Review* 61 (1987).

Levinson, Sanford. *Constitutional Faith.* Princeton, N.J.: Princeton University Press, 1988.

———. "Could Meese Be Right This Time?" *Nation* 243 (1986): 689–707.

Lewis, Anthony, "Law or Power." *New York Times*, October 27, 1986, A23, col. 1.

Lincoln, Abraham. *Selected Writings and Speeches of Abraham Lincoln.* T. Harry Williams, ed. New York: Hendricks House, 1980.

Luker, Kristin. *Abortion and the Politics of Motherhood*. Berkeley: University of California Press, 1984.

McCloskey, Herbert. "Consensus and Ideology in American Politics." *American Political Science Review* 58 (1964): 361–382.

Macedo, Stephen. "Liberal Virtues, Constitutional Community." *Review of Politics* 50, no. 2 (Spring 1988): 215–240.

_____. *The New Right v. the Constitution*. Washington, D.C.: Cato Institute, 1986.

Meese, Edwin. "The Law of the Constitution." *Tulane Law Review* 61 (1987): 979–990.

Melone, Albert P. "Legalism, Constitutional Interpretation, and the Role for Non-Jurists in Responsible Government." In Manuel J. Pelaez, ed., *Papers in Comparative Political Science*, 4683–4695. Barcelona: Catedra de Historia del Derecho y de las Instituciones, Facultad de Derecho de la Universidad de Malga, 1990.

Mikva, Abner J. "How Well Does Congress Support and Defend the Constitution?" *North Carolina Law Review* 61 (1983): 587–611.

Moynihan, Daniel. "Private Schools and the First Amendment." *National Review* 31 (1979).

Murphy, Walter F. *Congress and the Court*. Chicago: University of Chicago Press, 1962.

_____. "Who Shall Interpret? The Quest for the Ultimate Constitutional Interpreter." *Review of Politics* 48 (1986): 401–423.

Murphy, Walter F., James E. Fleming, and William F. Harris. *American Constitutional Interpretation*. Mineola, N.Y.: Foundation Press, 1986.

Nagel, Robert. "A Comment on Democratic Constitutionalism." *Tulane Law Review* 77 (1987): 1027–1040.

_____. *Constitutional Cultures: The Mentality and Consequences of Judicial Review*. Berkeley: University of California Press, 1989.

Neuborne, Burt. "The Binding Quality of Supreme Court Precedent." *Tulane Law Review* 61 (1987): 991–1002.

Perry, Michael. *The Constitution, the Courts, and Human Rights*. New Haven, Conn.: Yale University Press, 1982.

Pritchett, C. Herman. "Judicial Supremacy from Marshall to Burger." In M. Judd Harmon, ed., *Essays on the Constitution of the United States*. Port Washington, N.Y.: Kennikat Press, 1978.

Rehnquist, William H. "The Notion of a Living Constitution." *Texas Law Review* 54 (1976): 693–706.

_____. *The Supreme Court: How It Was, How It Is*. New York: William Morrow, 1987.

Richards, David A. J. *Toleration and the Constitution*. New York: Oxford University Press, 1986.

Richardson, James D., ed. *A Compilation of Messages and Papers of the Presidents*. 10 vols. Washington, D.C.: Government Printing Office, 1897- .

Rossiter, Clinton, ed. *The Federalist*. New York: New American Library, 1960.

Rubin, Eva R. *Abortion, Politics, and the Courts: Roe v. Wade and Its Aftermath*. Rev. ed. New York: Greenwood Press, 1987.

Scigliano, Robert A. *The Supreme Court and the Presidency*. New York: Free Press, 1971.

_____. "The War Powers Resolution and the War Powers." In Joseph Bessette and Jeffrey K. Tulis, eds., *The Presidency in the Constitutional Order*. Baton Rouge: Louisiana State University Press, 1981.

Skowornek, Stephen. "The Presidency in Political Time." In Michael Nelson, ed., *The Presidency and the Political System*. Washington, D.C.: Congressional Quarterly Press, 1984.

Smith, Jean. *The Constitution and American Foreign Policy*. St. Paul, Minn.: West Publishing Company, 1989.

Snowiss, Sylvia. *Judicial Review and the Law of the Constitution*. New Haven, Conn.: Yale University Press, 1990.

Stouffer, Samuel. *Communism, Conformity, and Civil Liberties*. New York: Doubleday, 1955.

Sunstein, Cass. "The Spirit of the Laws." *The New Republic*, March 11, 1991, 32–37.

Thayer, J. B. "The Origin and the Scope of the American Doctrine of Constitutional Law." In *Legal Essays*. Boston: Chipman, 1907.

Tocqueville, Alexis de. *Democracy in America*. New York: Doubleday, 1975.

Tribe, Laurence H. "The Abortion Funding Conundrum: Inalienable Rights, Affirmative Duties, and the Dilemma of Independence." *Harvard Law Review* 99 (1985).

———. *American Constitutional Law*. Mineola, N.Y.: Foundation Press, 1978.

———. *Constitutional Choices*. Cambridge, Mass.: Harvard University Press, 1985.

Tushnet, Mark. "The Dilemmas of Liberal Constitutionalism." *Ohio State Law Journal* 42 (1981): 411–426.

———. "The Supreme Court, the Supreme Law of the Land, and Attorney General Meese: A Comment." *Tulane Law Review* 61 (1987).

Unger, Roberto M. *The Critical Legal Studies Movement*. Cambridge, Mass.: Harvard University Press, 1986.

———. *Knowledge and Politics*. New York: Free Press, 1975.

———. *Law and Modern Society*. New York: Free Press, 1976.

United States Congress. House. Committee on Foreign Affairs. *Hearings before the Subcommittee on Arms Control, International Security, and Science and on Europe and the Middle East of the House Committee on Foreign Affairs on H.R. 2533, a Bill to Require a Report on Security Arrangements in the Persian Gulf*. 100th Cong., 1st Sess., 1987.

———. *Report by the Subcommittee on Arms Control, International Security, and Science and on Europe and the Middle East of the House Committee on Foreign Affairs on the War Powers Resolution*. 100th Cong., 1st Sess., 1987.

———. Senate. Committee on Foreign Relations. *Hearings before the Senate Committee on Foreign Relations on the Gulf of Tonkin: The 1964 Incidents*. 90th Cong., 2d Sess., 1968.

———. Committee on the Judiciary. *Hearings before the Subcommittee on Separation of Powers of the Senate Committee on the Judiciary on S. 158, the "Human Life Bill."* 97th Cong., 2d Sess., 1982.

———. *Hearings before the Subcommittee on the Separation of Powers of the Senate Committee on the Judiciary on S. 522, the "Abortion Funding Restriction Act."* 99th Cong., 1st Sess., 1985.

———. *Report by the Subcommittee on the Separation of Powers of the Senate Committee on the Judiciary on S. 158, the "Human Life Bill."* 97th Cong., 2d Sess., 1982.

———. Foreign Relations Committee. *Report by the Senate Foreign Relations*

Committee on a Bill to Prevent United States Involvement in Hostilities in the Persian Gulf. 100th Cong., 1st Sess., 1987.

_____. *Report by the Senate Foreign Relations Committee on a Bill to Require the Use of American Armed Forces to Escort, Protect, or Defend Certain Registered Vessels in the Persian Gulf to Comply with the War Powers Resolution.* 100th Cong., 1st Sess., 1987.

_____. Department of State. *Department of State Bulletin.* Washington, D.C.: Government Printing Office, 1964.

Verba, Sidney, Richard A. Brody, Edwin B. Parker, Norman H. Nie, Nelson W. Polsby, Paul Ekman, and Gordon S. Black. "Public Opinion and the War in Vietnam." *American Political Science Review* 51, no. 2 (June 1967): 317–333.

Weekly Compilation of Presidential Documents. Washington, D.C.: Government Printing Office, 1965– .

Weinberger, Caspar. *Report to the Congress on Security Arrangements in the Persian Gulf.* Washington, D.C.: Government Printing Office, 1987.

Wellington, Harry. "The Nature of Judicial Review." *Yale Law Journal* 91 (1982): 486–520.

Wolfe, Christopher. *Judicial Activism: Bulwark of Freedom or Precarious Security?* Pacific Grove, Calif.: Brooks Cole, 1991.

_____. *The Rise of Modern Judicial Reivew.* New York: Basic Books, 1986.

Wormuth, Francis, and Edwin Firmage. *To Chain the Dog of War: The War Power of Congress in History and Law.* 2d ed. Urbana: University of Illinois Press, 1989.

INDEX

Abortion Funding Restriction Act, x, xi, 52–54, 64
  and constitutional authority, 110
  and legislative supremacy, 112–117
  and personhood, 53
Adler, David Gray, 152n.28
Agresto, John, 13, 15, 21, 137n.50
Aiken, George, 83
Akron v. Akron Center for Reproductive Health, x, 49–52, 55
  on interest in potential life, 109
  and rule of law, 114
Anarchy, and departmentalism, 20, 113
Armacost, Michael H., 94, 155nn.124, 125,128, 157n.172
Atlee v. Laird, 67
Attacking level, 16, 24–25
  and abortion debates, 35–36
  and Persian Gulf debates, 90–92

Baker v. Carr, 1, 38
Barber, Sotirios A., 137n.50, 139n.67
Baucus, Max, 39, 145n.21
  and engaging level, 46–47
  and judicial supremacy, 31–33, 34
  and legislative supremacy, 116
Benefit-cost framework, critique of, xi, 22–27. *See also* Attacking level; Deferring level; Engaging level; Introducing level; Nonparticipating level; Recognizing level
Bennett, Charles, 102–103
Berger, Raoul, 7, 10
Berk v. Laird, 67
Berman, Howard, 96–97

Berman, Larry, 71
Bobbitt, Philip, 138n.57, 147n.105
Bonker, Daniel, 95–97
Bork, Robert, 7, 10, 146n.41
Brest, Paul, 10, 16, 20
Brewster, Daniel, 80–81
Brigham, John, 136n.15, 137n.50, 150n.166, 159n.3
Broomfield, William, 98–99
Brown v. Allen, 136n.20
Brown v. Board of Education, 1, 21, 38

Cardozo, Benjamin, 9
Carlson, Frank, 81–82
Carter, Jimmy, and War Powers Act, 70
Carter, Leif, 139n.59, 141n.96
Chaos, and departmentalism, 20, 112–114
Church, Frank, 81
Civic virtue, 17, 19, 24. *See also* Constitutional authority; Constitutional consciousness; Constitutional language
Clark, Ramsey, 20
Colautti v. Franklin, 149n.147
Commander in chief clause, 69–70, 72, 73, 87, 119
Conflict, 13, 29, 40
  and departmentalism, 20, 113
  directness of, 110, 112–113
  perceptions of, xii, 121–125
Confusion, 19–20, 113, 114
Congressional-executive unity, 76, 79
Constitutional aspiration. *See* Constitutional authority; Constitutional consciousness; Constitutional language
Constitutional authority, 12

Constitutional authority *(continued)*
  broadening of, 44, 64, 103, 107–108,
    109, 121, 122
  and executive authority, 88, 126
  and judicial authority, 3–6, 126
  resistance to, 31–36, 110
  skepticism about, ix, 11, 19
Constitutional consciousness, xii, 14, 19
  and individual rights, 123–124
  levels of, xi, 22–27
  obstructions to, 111–121
Constitutional language, 23, 26, 40, 64,
    123, 124–125
Constitutional meaning, 3, 10, 12, 17, 19,
    26, 27, 34, 38, 48, 122–123, 124, 126
Containment, 68, 75, 76, 83, 84, 89, 104
Cooper, John, 80–81
Cooper v. Aaron, 1–3, 32, 55
Cost-benefit framework. *See* Benefit-cost
    framework
Cox, Archibald, 146n.41
Critical Legal Studies Movement, 10
Crockett v. Reagan, 66, 156n.146

DaCosta v. Laird, 67
Declaration of Independence, 44
DeConcini, Dennis, 52
DeFazio, Peter, 91, 94, 97
Deferring level
  in abortion debate, 31–35, 52–54, 54–57
  defined, 24–25
  in Persian Gulf debate, 90
  in Tonkin Gulf debate, 76–84
Denton, Jeremiah, 38, 39, 45–46
Departmentalism
  claims about, xi, 13–22
  defined, ix, 12
  and judicial supremacy, xii, 22, 126
  See also Chaos; Confusion; Rule of law
Dimond, Paul, 137n.50
Dirksen, Everett, 78
Disagreement. *See* Conflict
Djerejian, Edward, 95
Dodd, Thomas, 76–77
Doe v. Bolton, 144n.15
Dougherty, Charles, 38, 39, 42, 47–48,
    116
Douglas, Stephen, 6, 16
Downey, Thomas, 91–92
Downs, Donald, 142n.121
Dred Scott v. Sandford, 2–3, 16, 43
Dworkin, Ronald, 7, 10, 136n.12

Eakin v. Raub, 159n.10

East, John, 30, 35, 36, 39, 43, 44–47,
    57–58
Ellender, Allen, 80, 82
El Salvador, 66
Ely, John Hart, 7–10, 35
Emerson, Thomas, 21, 42
Engaging level
  in abortion debate, 44, 45–47
  defined, 24–26, 44
Error, judicial, 3, 12
Executive supremacy, x, 19, 21–22, 85,
    97, 107, 112, 117–121

Fascell, Dante, 95
Faulkner, Robert, 136n.12
Federalist, 123–124, 139n.64
Feighan, Edward, 95–96
Fenwick, Millicent, 31–33, 39, 46–47
Fetal rights, 21, 45, 110, 143n.8, 160n.43
Final authority, 20. *See also* Executive
    supremacy; Judicial supremacy;
    Legislative supremacy
Fisher, Louis, 136n.21, 137n.50, 139n.64
Ford, Gerald, 69–70
Fourteenth Amendment, 28–31, 39–41,
    53, 64, 108, 113, 116
Fulbright, J. William, 73, 76, 78–82, 104
Fundamental rights, 29, 56
Furman v. Georgia, 44

Galebach, Stuart, 34
Gephardt, Richard, 160n.43
Gilman, Benjamin, 98–99
Glendon, Mary Ann, 147n.105
Goldwater v. Carter, 65
Gonzalez, Henry, 98
Grove City College v. Bell, 117
Gruening, Ernest, 84–88, 103

Haig, Alexander, 66, 156n.146
Harris, William, ix, 138n.57
Harris v. McRae, 149nn.128,135
Hatch, Orren, 52–53, 113, 144n.16
Helms, Jesse, 144n.16, 145n.21
Herring, George, 105
Hickenlooper, Bourke, 78–79, 81–82
Hope, xiii, 10
Hughes, Charles Evans, 7, 138n.51
Human life bill, x, xi, 30–49
  and broadening of constitutional
    authority, 44
  and confusion, 113
  and Fourteenth Amendment, 108, 116
  on life, 30

on personhood, 30
and *Roe*, 30–31, 37, 39
Humphrey, Hubert, 78
Hyde, Henry, 35, 36, 41, 42, 45–46, 145n.21
Hyde Amendment, 52–53

Imminent hostilities, 93–100
Infallibility, and the Supreme Court, 9, 136n.20
Informed consent, 49–50, 54–55
Institutional competence, 11–12, 36
Interpretivism, 10
Introducing level
    in abortion debate, 40–48
    defined, 25–26
    in war powers debate, 92–100, 107
Iran-Iraq war, 88–89, 91, 94

Jackson, Andrew, 3–5
Jacobsohn, Gary J., 13–18, 137n.50, 159n.2
Jefferson, Thomas, 3–4, 123–125, 139n.64
Johnsen, Dawn, 141n.98, 143n.8, 146n.76
Johnson, Lyndon Baines, 72–76
Judicial activism, x, xi, 7–9, 13–14, 28–64, 109, 111–112
Judicial authority, 10, 15–17, 126
Judicial constitutional interpretation, quality of, 48–52, 54–57
Judicial finality. *See* Judicial supremacy
Judicial self-restraint, x, xii, 7, 9, 13, 14, 65–108, 109–110
Judicial supremacy, ix, xi, 1–2, 13, 15, 16, 20, 31–33, 37, 54
Jurisdiction restrictions, 115

Karnow, Stanley, 71, 104
Kastenmeier, Robert, 78–79
Koh, Harold, 152n.28
Kommers, Donald, 137n.50, 143n.5
Kostmeyer, Robert, 91–92, 106
Kuchel, 78–79
Kuhn, Thomas, 146n.76

Lantos, Thomas, 99–100
Lausche, Frank, 77–78
Leach, James, 91, 95
Lebanon, 102
Legislative supremacy, 19–21, 112, 115–117
Leland, Mickey, 117
Levine, Mel, 99
Levinson, Sanford, 13, 137n.50

Lewis, Anthony, 20
Life, beginning of, 30, 36–37, 39–, 51, 116
Lincoln, Abraham, 3, 5–6, 16, 37, 4,
Lowry, Michael, 101–102
Lowry v. Reagan, 66
Luker, Kristin, 143nn.5,8

McArthur v. Clifford, 151n.12
McCloskey, Herbert, 151n.168
McCulloch v. Maryland, 4
Macedo, Stephen, 13–15, 17–18, 137n.50
McGovern, George, 80
McNamara, Robert, 71, 73
Maddox, USS, 70–72, 75, 77, 105, 154n.92
Madison, James, 137n.23
Mansfield, Mike, 79–80
Marbury v. Madison, 2, 32, 37
Matheson, Michael, 42–43, 93
Meese, Edwin, 6
Melone, Albert, 137n.50
Metzenbaum, Howard, 54
Mica, Daniel, 95
Mikva, Abner, 139n.64
Mitchell v. Laird, 67
Mora v. McNamara, 66
Morse, Wayne, 84–88, 103
Moynihan, Patrick, 31–34, 39
Murphy, Richard, 89, 93, 96–98, 121
Murphy, Walter, ix, 1, 13, 21, 139nn.66,67, 159n.10

Nagel, Robert, 7, 13, 19, 160n.42
Nelson, Gaylord, 80
Neuborne, Burt, 20
Nicaragua, 66
Nixon, Richard, 2, 32, 68
Nonparticipating level, 24–25
Noonan, John, 34

Originalism, 10
Orlando v. Laird, 67

Packwood, Robert, 31, 34, 45–46, 114, 116
Perry, Michael, 7, 8–9, 10
Persian Gulf debates, x, xi, 88–108
    historical background of, 88–89
    of 1991, 160n.43
Personhood, beginning of, 28–30, 36, 37, 39, 41–44, 53, 116
Political question, 65–67, 70, 135n.5
Powell v. McCormack, 2
Precedent, 17, 48–50, 55–56, 74, 85, 109–110, 114

Pritchett, C. Herman, 136n.12
Public opinion
  on abortion, 60–62, 110–111
  and war powers, 104–108, 111
Public sensitivity to constitutional issues, 9, 11, 14, 17–19, 57–64. *See also* Public opinion
Publius. *See Federalist*

Rationality test, 51, 144n.12
Reagan, Ronald, 3, 6, 52, 66, 70, 94, 102, 119–121, 156n.129
Recognizing level
  in abortion debate, 110, 111
  defined, 25–26, 44
  in Persian Gulf debate, 101–105
  in Tonkin Gulf debate, 84–88
Reflagging, of Kuwaiti ships, 89, 91, 94, 96, 98, 120
Responsibility, congressional, 86–87, 92–94, 97, 99–100
Richards, David, 7, 8–9, 150n.156
Roe v. Wade, x, 6, 21, 28–31, 39
  constitutionality of, 35–48
  and human life bill, 30–31
Roosevelt, Frankin D., 87
Roth, Toby, 91, 102–103
Rubin, Eva, 144n.16
Rule of law, departmentalism and, ix, 11, 12, 19, 110, 113–114, 117, 121–123
Rule of man, 11, 85–86, 122
Rusk, Dean, 73–74

Sanchez-Espinoza v. Reagan, 66
Scientific arguments, in abortion debate, 41–43, 50–52, 56–57
Scigliano, Robert, 21, 117, 152n.29
Scott, Hugh, 78–79
Self-interest, 18, 121–126
Separation of powers, and departmentalism, 33, 35, 86
Shared value. *See* Constitutional consciousness
Sierra Club v. Morton, 146n.53
Silencing, 91–92, 97, 121
Smathers, George, 76–77
Smith, Jean, 152n.29
Smith, Larry, 90–91, 95–96, 100
Snowiss, Sylvia, 136n.15
Solarz, Stephen, 90–91, 98
Solomon, Gerald, 90, 91
Stare decisis. See Precedent
Stark, USS, 89, 93, 95, 96, 99
Stouffer, Samuel, 151n.168

Studds, Gerry, 91–92, 98–99, 101
Sunstein, Cass, ix
Supreme Court. *See* Judicial activism; Judicial authority; Judicial constitutional interpretation; Judicial self-restraint; Judicial supremacy

Thayer, J. B., 13, 14–15, 18
Thornburgh v. American College of Gynecologists and Obstetricians, x, 54–57, 110, 114
Thurmond, Strom, 76–79, 160n.43
Tonkin Gulf debate, xii, 67, 68, 73–76
  compared with Persian Gulf debate, 87, 90, 97, 103–104, 107–108
Tonkin Gulf period, 70–88
Torricelli, Robert, 91–92, 95–97
Tribe, Laurence, 10, 20
Tushnet, Mark, 138n.58, 142n.123

Ultimate interpreter, 1–3. *See also* Judicial supremacy
Unger, Roberto, 138n.58
U.S. v. Butler, 2–3
U.S. v. Carolene Products, 144n.12
U.S. v. Curtiss-Wright, 66
U.S. v. Nixon, 2, 68
U.S. v. Vuitch, 144n.15

Velvel v. Johnson, 67
Verba, Sidney, 105

War Powers Act
  and executive supremacy, x, 67–70, 88
  and Persian Gulf debate, 66, 89, 92–100, 111
  provisions of, 68, 93
  veto of, 68, 69
War Powers Resolution. *See* War Powers Act
Webster v. Reproductive Health Services, 144n.12
Weinberger, Caspar, 66, 89, 91, 93–95, 98, 101–102, 118–120
Weiss, Theodore, 94, 160n.43
White, Hugh Lawson, 5
Withdrawal dilemma, from Vietnam, 83–84, 120–121
Wolfe, Christopher, 10, 22, 101, 117, 139n.66
Wormuth, Francis, 71, 152n.28